W9-AUI-580

RUPTURE, REPRESENTATION,
AND THE REFASHIONING OF
IDENTITY IN DRAMA FROM THE
NORTH OF IRELAND, 1969–1994

Recent Titles in
Contributions in Drama and Theatre Studies

RUPTURE, REPRESENTATION, AND THE REFASHIONING OF IDENTITY IN DRAMA FROM THE NORTH OF IRELAND, 1969–1994

Bernard McKenna

Contributions in Drama and Theatre Studies, Number 102

Westport, Connecticut
London

Library of Congress Cataloging-in-Publication Data

McKenna, Bernard, 1966–
    Rupture, representation, and the refashioning of identity in drama from the North of
Ireland, 1969–1994 / Bernard McKenna.
       p.   cm.—(Contributions in drama and theatre studies, ISSN 0163–3821 ; no. 102)
    Includes bibliographical references (p.) and index.
    ISBN 0–313–32029–2 (alk. paper)
    1. English drama—Irish authors—History and criticism. 2. Politics and
literature—Northern Ireland—History—20th century. 3. Literature and history—Northern
Ireland—History—20th century. 4. English drama—20th century—History and criticism. 5
Northern Ireland—Intellectual life—20th century. 6. Identity (Psychology) in literature. 7.
Northern Ireland—In literature. 8. Group identity in literature. I. Title. II. Series.
PR8789.M436   2003
822′.914099416—dc21   2003053554

British Library Cataloguing in Publication Data is available.

Library of Congress Catalog Card Number: 2003053554
ISBN: 0–313–32029–2
ISSN: 0163–3821

First published in 2003

Praeger Publishers, 88 Post Road West, Westport, CT 06881
An imprint of Greenwood Publishing Group, Inc.
www.praeger.com

Printed in the United States of America

The paper used in this book complies with the
Permanent Paper Standard issued by the National
Information Standards Organization (Z39.48–1984).

10 9 8 7 6 5 4 3 2 1

Copyright Acknowledgments

The author and publisher gratefully acknowledge permission for use of the following material:

The Gallery Press for permission to quote from W. R. Rodgers ("Home Thought from Abroad"), Gerald Dawe ("Solstice"), Paula Meehan ("The Statue of the Virgin at Granard Speaks"), Stewart Parker (*Catchpenny Twist*), and John Montague ("Heroics").

Wake Forest University Press for permission to quote from John Montague ("Heroics").

The Guilford Press for permission to quote material from *Traumatic Stress: The Effects of Overwhelming Stress on Mind, Body, and Society*.

Vincent Woods for permission to quote from the unpublished version of *At the Black Pig's Dyke*.

Kenneth Branagh for permission to quote from *Public Enemy*.

The Blackstaff Press (Belfast) for permission to quote from Bell, Johnston, and Wilson's *Troubled Times*, from Bardon's *History of Ulster*, and from O'Conor's *In Search of a State*.

The Smithsonian Institution Press for permission to quote from Buckley and Kenney's *Negotiating Identity: Rhetoric, Metaphor, and Social Drama in Northern Ireland*, 1995.

Frank McGuinness for permission to quote from his plays *Observe the Sons of Ulster Marching Towards the Somme* (© Frank McGuinness, 1986; London: Faber and Faber, 1986) and *Carthaginians* (© Frank McGuinness, 1988; London: Faber and Faber, 1988).

Methuen Publishing Limited for permission to quote from *Cristina Reid—Reid Plays 1* (*Did You Hear the One about the Irishman?* and *The Belle of Belfast City*).

Christina Reid for permission to quote from her correspondence and from the unpublished version of *My Name? Shall I Tell You My Name?*

The Nobel Foundation for permission to quote from Seamus Heaney's *Crediting Poetry*. © The Nobel Foundation, 1995.

Faber and Faber Ltd. (London) and Farrar, Straus, and Giroux, LLC (United States) for permission to quote from Seamus Heaney's *The Cure at Troy: A Version of Sophocles' Philoctetes* (Copyright © 1990 by Seamus Heaney) and "Tollund Man," and "Casualty" from *Opened Ground: Selected Poems 1966–1996* (Copyright © 1998 by Seamus Heaney).

Faber and Faber (London) for permission to quote from Frank McGuinness's *Carthaginians*, Anne Devlin's *Ourselves Alone* and *After Easter*.

Mairead O'Connor for permission to quote from her poem, "The Troubles."

David Higham Associates for permission to quote from Louis MacNeice's "Autumn Journal."

In each case the authors or their representatives grant permission for use as represented to them in this volume. Any permission to reproduce the work of individual authors must be directed to the authors or their representatives.

Dedicated to Robert Hogan

Contents

1

Drama and the "Troubles"

Certain aspects of the dramatic production in the North of Ireland from 1969 to 1994 detail the effect of sectarian conflict on individuals' conceptions and formulations of social, historical, and mythic identity. Specifically, drama, in part, reflects the rupture in the factors that inform identity, the attempted yet failed efforts to reconstruct identity, and the more successful attempts to refashion a conception of self in relation to community, continuity, and communion with the mythic. Also helpful in coming to terms with the issues associated with Northern drama is "trauma theory." Specifically, it can be used as a means of examining the formal theatrical expression of the staged aftermath of a violent event or series of events on individuals and communities in the North of Ireland. Clinical research indicates that traumatized individuals come to terms with violence in three general ways. (1) Rupture occurs after initial exposure to violence; the main factors that inform identity are destroyed. (2) Masks come into play when individuals exposed to trauma make an effort to shield themselves from trauma. Victims will construct insular identities drawn from societal cues, but those identities do not fully integrate the traumatic structures into an individual's psychological character. (3) Ultimately, some individuals create a fully integrated identity. These individuals are able to integrate traumatic structures into their identity and to come to terms with subsequent contingencies.

Within the discussion of individual works of drama that emphasize one of these particular areas, I focus not simply on the literary and psychological structure of the plays but also on their theatrical components. I have seen productions of most of the plays in either the North of Ireland or in the Republic. Without exception, I consider works of drama that were written and staged between 1969 and 1994, and all the works in question either directly or indirectly confront issues of sectarian conflict. In the first chapter I lay out the historical and theoretical components of my argument, taking care to provide a sociological and cultural context for my analysis of drama. Specifically, I place my study within the context of critical examinations of the connection between theatre and violence, and art and violence in general, referencing a variety of theoretical disciplines including cultural theory, gender studies, colonialism, postcolonialism, Marxist theory, performance theory, and racial and ethnic studies. I also trace out the factors and conditions that inform individual and community identity in the North with reference to historical and sociological works. In addition, I map out the application of "trauma theory" to my analysis, structuring my exposition as the chapters themselves will be structured (i.e. examining the relationship between trauma and the various components of identity).

The third chapter explores dramatic works that focus specifically on violent acts that rupture a sense of individuality and community. Within the chapter, I emphasize the theatrical representation of the traumatic event, placing particular emphasis on six common symptoms of traumatic rupture: "distancing," a psychic construction of a fantasy life designed to protect an individual from further damage; "anxiety," an exaggerated fear of death and attack; "guilt" regarding survivability; "loneliness and vulnerability," which arises as a consequence of the disruption in normal social relationships and a reluctance, as a consequence of trauma, to expose oneself to further relationships; "loss of self-control," which results in an individual yielding control to external, seemingly more powerful forces, including mythic and historical forces; and "disorientation," which involves a debilitated capacity for reasoning and making individual associations. I will examine Stewart Parker's *Catchpenny Twist* (1977), his *Northern Star* (1984), and John Wilson Haire's *Within Two Shadows* (1972) because of the implications they raise regarding the formation of cross-community relationships and their breakdown in the face of sectarian violence. Brian Friel's *Freedom of the City* (1973) and Martin Lynch's *The Interrogation of Ambrose Fogarty* (1982) explore a specific violent act or acts perpetrated by the British army against the Catholic population. The plays provide insights into the disruption of identity in the face of external threat. Conversely, Graham Reid's plays, *The Death of Humpty Dumpty* (1979) and *The Closed Door* (1980), focus more on internal conflicts and on threats to identity to the Protestant population. In addition, the characters in each play are threatened by external factors associated with the Troubles.

The fourth chapter explores the failed attempt to reconstruct identity. Within the plays I examine in this context, the protagonists attempt to reestablish an integrated identity. However, they fail to do so because they take the structures of that identity from external sources and do not fully incorporate the external structures of identity into their personalities, resulting in cycles of violence and traumatic response that manifest themselves in six ways: intrusions of traumatic recollections, compulsive exposure to trauma, numbed responsiveness, inability to control responses to stress, difficulty in stimulus discrimination, and altered identities. Within this chapter I will consider Kenneth Branagh's *Public Enemy* (1987), which explores the ways in which Protestant young people look to the myths of Hollywood gangsters to reinforce shattered conceptions of self. Brian Friel's *Volunteers* (1975), Patrick Galvin's *We Do It for Love* (1975), and Frank McGuinness' *Observe the Sons of Ulster Marching towards the Somme* (1985) examine how received roles and images from history can disrupt and disunify a culture. Christina Reid's *Did You*

Hear the One about the Irishman? (1985) and Anne Devlin's *Ourselves Alone* (1985) detail social relationships within the context of the Troubles and how the backdrop of sectarian violence undermines the ability of the characters to develop meaningful contacts.

Chapter 5 explores more successful attempts to reconstruct a fully integrated identity by synthesizing and unifying the trauma experience into the individual's personality. The chapter explores the methods for successful integration, including the rejection of external identities in favor of more fully realized conceptions of self. The process involves six components: education, identification of feelings, deconditioning of traumatic memories and responses, restructuring of traumatic personal schemes, reestablishment of secure social connections and interpersonal efficacy, and the accumulation of restitutive emotional experiences. Without exception, the plays considered in this chapter present a view of Northern Irish society in which sectarian divisions are reconciled in the personal and artistic imagination. Seamus Heaney's *The Cure at Troy* (1990) and Vincent Woods's *At the Black Pig's Dyke* (1992) explore the implications associated with a spiritual and mythic reconstruction of individual and community identity. Anne Devlin's *After Easter* (1994) and Stewart Parker's *Pentecost* (1987) focuses on the factors that inform positive social relationships within the context of sectarian violence. Christina Reid's *My Name? Shall I Tell You My Name?* (1987) and Frank McGuinness' *Carthaginians* (1988) examine ways in which individuals can escape the violent archetypes of history that label both Catholic and Protestant traditions.

My concluding chapter explores the parallel representations of violence in poetry, short stories, novels, painting, and sculpture, placing emphasis on how current Northern drama functions within the thematic context of and contributes to what some critics call a second renaissance in Irish writing.

I also rely heavily on previous research, focussing directly on the theatre in the North of Ireland, including reference sources, histories, and critical articles that explore particular aspects of theatre in relation to the Troubles. *The Dictionary of Irish Literature* contains a comprehensive record of primary and secondary sources in regard to individual authors and theatre companies; other reference sources include *The Oxford Companion to Irish Literature* and *Irish Playwrights, 1880 to 1995*. In addition, several histories of twentieth-century Irish theatre survey a number of Northern writers; these works include D.E.S. Maxwell's *A Critical History of Modern Irish Drama, 1891-1980*, Anthony Roche's *Contemporary Irish Drama: From Beckett to McGuinness*, and Michael Etherton's *Contemporary Irish Dramatists*. Of the histories and references devoted specifically to the study of Northern theatre, Ophelia Byrne's *The Stage in Ulster from the Eighteenth Century* contains entries on theatre and the Troubles, which draw on the Linen Hall's extensive holdings. Finally, David Grant's *Playing the Wild Card* details the work of community and more established theatres in Northern Ireland, offering valuable insights into the work being done to foster an appreciation of drama within neighborhoods. Other critical studies tend to fall into two categories. One area examines individual theatre companies. The other area studies individual authors. Most notably, Maria Di Cenzo's "Charabanc Theatre Company: Placing Women Center-Stage in Northern Ireland" explores the connection between issues associated with gender and feminism and sectarian violence. Other notable critical studies include Lionel Pilkington's "Violence and Identity in Northern Ireland: Graham Reid's *The Death of Humpty Dumpty*," in which Pilkington explores Reid's play within the larger context of violence in the North; Marilyn Richtarik's *Acting between the Lines: The Field Day Theatre Company and Irish Cultural Politics 1980-1984*, in which the author explores the Field Day Company within a social and political context; and Frances Gray's "Radio Drama and the Politics of Northern Ireland," in which Gray and Janet Bray explore the larger issues associated with the representation of violence. Further, two notable Ph.D. dissertations have focused on issues associated with theatre and the North. The two are Lionel Pilkington's *Representation of the Northern Ireland Crisis in Contemporary Drama: 1968 to 1980* and Claudia Harris's *At the End of the Day: Theatre as Politics and Politics as Theatre in Northern Ireland*.

The most important critical analyses of theatrical representations of the Troubles are D.E.S. Maxwell's "Northern Ireland's Political Drama," Ian Hill's "Staging the Troubles," and the sections on contemporary theatre in Christopher Murray's *Twentieth-Century Irish Drama*. Murray's work, taken in conjunction with the themes discerned by Maxwell, provides a critical basis for three motifs this study also explores: community and social discourse, the continuity of history, and the relationship of sectarian conflict to myth and ritual.

Within the context of contemporary political and cultural developments in the North, this study's conclusions regarding the impact of conflict on identity and the attempted reconstruction of a nonsectarian, cross-community identity find a resonance with the struggle to build a new Northern community through democratic means. All but the most extreme elements of Catholic and Protestant paramilitary organizations have renounced violence and accept that the ultimate fate of the multifarious Northern communities relies on creating a new self-conception comprised not of the ascendency of one view at the expense of others but in the recognition of the right of all communities in the North to find a means of living together. The process will not be easy, as violence in Belfast, Omagh, and on the Garvaghy Road indicates. However, as recent Northern drama suggests, the new conceptions of identity do have a growing currency in the North, and, as recent universal condemnations of sectarian bombings and killings demonstrate, the peace process also has strong and growing support. However, as clinical examinations of trauma indicate, recovery from violence must not vest itself in forgetting traumatic rupture but rather in integrating traumatic structures into a newly fashioned identity that can then grow beyond violent conceptions and reactions.

Finally, like many studies of the "Troubles," my work draws much on personal experience and on personal and familial recollections. Inevitably, because my name suggests an Irish Catholic heritage, some may come to this work expecting to find a Nationalist or even a Republican political agenda. Indeed, there are times when my choice of words or images or metaphors might betray Nationalist tendencies. However, in reading over my work I can discern, in retrospect, a much clearer familial inheritance. These pages explore a lament for the conditions of war in the North of Ireland and the ruptured and damaged lives contained within many of the communities of the North. Moreover, in the end the study advances the view that the future of the North of Ireland lies in an embrace of a community identity that exists beyond sectarianism and beyond violence, and it is this view that represents my most immediate familial inheritance. My father and mother, through their personal example and in their words, rejected sectarianism, prejudice, and violence as a means of coming to terms with the world. Consequently, as I finished this study I came, quite unexpectedly, to a point quite close to their political views. I am grateful to them for opening my mind to such possibilities.

I also owe a tremendous debt to the late Robert Hogan, who helped to frame the direction and scope of my research from its inception to its conclusion. I feel a great deal of satisfaction knowing that he read an nearly complete draft of this work before he succumbed to the effects of cancer. We spent many an hour in his office in Newark, Delaware, discussing the writers and plays that should be included in such a study. Later, his frequent letters from his home in Bray, Co Wicklow, gently guided me through the project, often urging me on despite my occasional bouts of discouragement. Of the professors and teachers that guided my work, none deserve more credit than Zack Bowen and Pat McCarthy. Their help and cheerful assistance proved invaluable. John Paul Russo, Robert Casillo, and Sam McCready also deserve special thanks. The late David Payne-Carter of the University of Delaware guided me through the intricacies of ancient Greek theatre and its use of violence and ritual. Jamie Hovey suggested the incorporation of performance theory, and Margaret McPeake introduced me to trauma theory. Thanks also to Linda Pelzer of Wesley College. I am also grateful to Kenneth Branagh and Frank McGuinness.

Many students and friends assisted me in the production of this work. I would like to thank all of them. However, space only allows mention of a few. Jacquiline Alfonso, Yessina Correa, Monse Rodriguez, and Tanya Martinez deserve special mention. Kathia Martinez also helped me through the work of Antonio Benitez-Rojo. I would also like to thank Lisa Gonzon for her sweet patience. Peter Campbell and Shawn Dorazio-Hull also offered encouragement. Mary Rose Callaghan deserves special thanks, as does my family: my mother and father, Thomas, Shannon, Michael, Grace, Gabriel, Joan, Jean-Gabrielle, and all of you. Finally, a special lady has my eternal gratitude for her charity and kindness.

2

"Fire in the North, Sun in the South": Rupture, Representation, and the Refashioning of Identity

In a series of charcoals and pastels on paper titled "No Fire in the Hearth, No Sun in the South," completed in the early 1980s, the North of Ireland artist Deirdre O'Connell represents three aspects of the Northern conflict: violence, mimicry, and belief. One facet of her work details arched pillars and white walls, which summon memories of police and army barracks, barricades and checkpoints, and their seeming mirrored (mimicked) images in the peace line in Belfast or the borders of "Free Derry." Another facet reveals that the harshness and inflexibility of the structures speak to the dehumanizing aspects of violence and how institutions created from violence and institutionalized violence, not only in the abuses of military and paramilitary groups but also the force or power of the Troubles, can overwhelm and ultimately eliminate the sense of control individuals have over their lives; significantly, there are no images of people in these works. Curiously, though, the structures themselves betray fissures, hint at an almost human vulnerability, a susceptibility to time and the past and the caprices of the present. The pillars have gaps through which can be seen black earth and grass. The wild (and the resonance of belief) returns to the scorched, controlled earth, mocking man's faith in the supposed permanence of created structures. The structures themselves form into circles in a clearing, and the grass, otherwise encroaching on the stone, forms its advance into circular movements. The art commands that all, structures and grass and even the forces of violence, obey the commands of some unspoken but irresistible power. Ultimately, the landscapes of violence find themselves transformed by that power that is constantly in movement, that incorporates and alters a sense of violent rupture, that converts the masks of power into more integrated forms. The work revitalizes a traumatized landscape.

In a structure reminiscent of Deirdre O'Connell's work, much clinical research indicates that traumatized individuals come to terms with violence in three general ways. (1) Rupture: After initial exposure to violence, the main factors that inform identity are destroyed. Specifically, many individuals suffer "an acute dissociative reaction in combination with phenomena of PTSD [post-traumatic stress disorder], which engage[s] at the time of exposure to the [traumatic] event."[1] (2) Masks: In an effort to shield themselves from trauma, victims will construct insular identities drawn from societal cues, but those identities do not fully integrate the traumatic structures into an individual's psychological character. "This results in part from the need to try to construct a meaning network, in order to solve the equation of fear and uncertainty that are provoked"[2] as a consequence of violence. (3) Fully Integrated Identity: Ultimately, some individuals who have been exposed to violence are able to integrate traumatic structures into their identity and to come to terms with subsequent contingencies. Basically,

merely uncovering memories is not enough; they need to be modified and transformed (i.e. placed in their proper context and restructured in a personally meaningful way). Thus, in therapy, memory paradoxically needs to become an act of creation rather than a static recording of events. Because the essence of the trauma is that it once confronted the victim with unacceptable reality, the patient needs to find a way of confronting the hidden secrets that no one, including the patient, wants to face. Like memories of ordinary events, the memory of the trauma needs to become merely a (often distorted) part of the patient's personal past. Exploring the trauma for its own sake has no therapeutic benefits unless it becomes attached to other experiences, such as feeling understood, being safe, feeling physically strong and capable, or being able to empathize with and help fellow sufferers.[3]

This study utilizes "trauma theory" and examines the formal theatrical expression and the staged effects of a violent event or series of events on individuals and communities in the North of Ireland. Specifically, the study explores the theatrical portrayal of the individual's efforts to reconstruct an identity in the aftermath of a traumatic event, as well as the ability of the reconstructed identity to function effectively.

"BRISEADH NA TSEANGHATHAIMH": THE RUPTURE

The colonial dynamics that precipitated the outbreak of violence in the North of Ireland in 1968, and that informed the continuing violence of the subsequent quarter century, have an origin in England's historical relationship with Ireland. Indeed, the experience of rupture of a historical, personal, community, and spiritual identity at the hands of an imperial power has informed the consciousness of the Irish people for centuries. Specifically, the Irish phrase "briseadh na tseangháthaimh" literally means "breaking of the old ways" and can usefully be applied as a description of the general state of England's period of colonial dominance over Ireland. After the Battle of Kinsale, the representatives of the English crown began, in earnest, to implement Edmund Spenser's program for the colonization of Ireland, including the racialization of the Irish, representing them as "barbarous," "savage," and less than human. They were "white chimpanzees."[4] Indeed, they were literally categorized as a different races as the

white/non-white classification did not follow strict epidermal schemas of visibility or skin colour so that, in an important sense, the Irish historically were classified as "non-white," and treated accordingly. The widespread equation of the "mere Irish" with the native Americans in the seventeenth century served as a pretext for wholesale confiscations and plantations, and more ominous expressions of genocidal intent as in Edmund Spenser's advice to Queen Elizabeth that "until Ireland can be famished, it cannot be subdued."[5]

As British occupation solidified, an idea of Ireland began to emerge, functioning "as England's unconscious. Victorian imperialists attributed to the Irish all those emotions and impulses which a harsh mercantile code had led them to suppress in themselves."[6]   In addition, the Irish were represented as "hot headed, rude, and garrulous." They were "the perfect foil to set off British values."[7]   It is in this light of English hegemony and anti-Irish discourse that the phrase "briseadh na tseangháthaimh" could also usefully be applied to the situation in the North of Ireland, a region that highlights the assumed dichotomy of Protestant British rule that saw, and sees, that the "strife in Ireland is the consequence of a battle between English civilisation, based on laws, and Irish barbarism, based on local kinship loyalties and sentiments," and "that the added complication of religion helps to intensify that Irish barbarism by fostering ignorance and sloth, disrespect for English law and respect for papal decrees instead, conspiracy and rebellion by cherishing foreign connections hostile to England."[8]   In order to subdue the Irish, the English must rupture those factors of Irish identity that threaten British values, military occupation, and colonial administration.

Much of the drama that takes as its subject the violence in the North of Ireland tends to "perform" moments of rupture that consciously emphasize the destruction of individual's and communities's identities. The performativity of the loss of a sense of self and of community stresses the contrast between two views of the North. One view represents the North as a collection of communities caught and lost within ancient tribal conflicts that currently organize themselves around religious boundaries; under this schema, the Presbyterians, although Protestant, become Irish like the Catholics. Within this view, the two main tribes find themselves further divided into sects and fragments that fall under the titles of confusing and secret organizations (the Ulster Freedom Fighters, the Ulster Volunteer Force, the Ulster Defence Force, the Irish National Liberation Army, the Irish Republican Army, the Provisional Irish Republican Army, the Continuity Irish Republican Army) or under various subfactions and divisions (Loyalist, Unionist, Nationalist, Republican). This view implies that the Irish, on both sides of the peace line, find themselves trapped within a culture and society that ceased to progress sometime in the tenth or eleventh century. Implicit within this view is the notion that the Irish people, whether Protestant or Catholic, are somehow less evolved than the British. Warren Hoge,[9] London bureau chief of the *New York Times*, gives voice to this view, detailing the violence of both communities as indistinguishable, writing that "you can't tell one side from the other."[10] Atrocities, for Hoge and those who credit the veracity of this view, are "the results of deeds of harsh and purposeful men,"[11] placing the ultimate responsibility of the Northern War within the province. The British military occupation and colonial administration of the troublesome territory then takes on the characteristics of a historic mission to protect the Irish from themselves. If the British did withdraw, according to this view, the Protestants and Catholics would revert to an even more primitive stage and destroy each other.

Another view of the Troubles sees that a group of communities' sense of identity and coherence was shattered by colonial intervention, by the very same presence that the alternative view posits as saving the North from itself. Specifically, as the provisional IRA (PIRA) observes, "all violence in the North" is "the result of British occupation of the area," arguing that "the war could not be ended until its prime cause had been removed."[12] The PIRA argues that the British colonial occupation and administration are, ultimately, responsible for Northern violence and, therefore, must be struggled against and eliminated in order to eliminate the violence. In essence, it is a "subjugated language" and "knowledge" in the sense that "subjugated languages" and "knowledges" are "concerned with a *historical knowledge of struggles*." They are "the memory of hostile encounters which even up to this day have been confined to the margins of knowledge."[13] Like all subjugated knowledges, the PIRA view of the Northern Troubles has "been buried and disguised in a functionalist coherence or formal systemisation"[14] and "located low down on the hierarchy, beneath the required level of cognition or scientificity."[15] Essentially, the PIRA view of Northern violence has been cast aside and dismissed as inferior in the same way the Irish people have been renounced as not equal to their English neighbors, as somehow less than human. However, by staging the two altenative views of the Troubles, North of Ireland dramatists sometimes directly and sometimes indirectly historicize the relationship between these views and posit an identity within the Northern struggle that sanctions the view that colonial control and manipulation are the underlying cause of conflict and trauma.

In clinical terms, violence inflicted on colonized territories, like all "traumatic experiences, can alter people's psychological, biological, and social equilibrium to such a degree that the memory of one particular event comes to taint all other experiences."[16] Particularly, victims of violence experience six common symptoms: "distancing," a psychic construction of a fantasy life designed to protect an individual from further damage; "anxiety," an exaggerated fear of death and attack; "guilt" regarding survivability; "loneliness and vulnerability," which arises as a consequence of the disruption in normal social relationships and a reluctance, as a consequence of trauma, to expose oneself to further relationships; "loss of self-control," which results in an individual yielding control to external, seemingly more powerful forces, including mythic and historical forces; and "disorientation," which involves a debilitated capacity for reasoning and making individual associations. All of these symptoms are themselves a consequence of and contribute to a further sense of loss of self-control.

In performing individual's and communities's varying responses to trauma within the context of colonial domination in the North of Ireland, Irish theatre values an interpretation of the Troubles that sees violence not as an endemic trait to the people of the North but, rather, as a creation of an outside power that imposed on the people traumatic circumstances that inevitably produced "feelings of irretrievable loss, anger, betrayal, and helplessness."[17] Essentially, the staged representation of the Troubles discredits the colonial interpretation of the North of Ireland crisis in favor of the alternative version creating the foundation for a clearer understanding of the circumstances that led to an outbreak of violence in October 1968 and for subsequent attempts, however successful, to reconstitute a shattered conception of self, community, and nation.

UBERTRATUNG: THE MASK OF PROTECTION/PROJECTION

After the initial experiences of "rupture," victims of violence will attempt to construct identities to counter trauma. Significantly, many of these identities tend to be projections of societal identifiers, informed by colonial discourse and hegemony, placed onto individual consciousness. In psychoanalytic terms, Carl Jung used the word "Ubertratung" to designate what he called "projection" and what he defined as "carry[ing] something over from one place to another" or "one form into another."[18] Specifically, for Jung, in "projection , the apparent fact you are confronted with the object is in reality an illusion."[19] Applying Jung's theories to the traumatized focuses attention on the way victims of violence project masks of protection (against dealing with trauma or against possible further trauma) onto their identities. The victims unconsciously associate alien identities with their own and cannot distinguish between them; they assume the identities to be their own. Consequently, many never fully recover from trauma.

Much of the drama that focuses on the twenty-five years of violence in the North of Ireland performs the masking process highlighting the distinction between the mask and the emptiness (the subjectivity) behind the mask. Essentially, trauma victims create what they consider to be an authentic identity from the chaos that was and is their trauma. In reality, that identity is simply a reproduction assembled from cues from their society's history and culture. Certainly, all identities are constructed from such cues. Indeed, the "authenticity of a thing is the essence of all that is transmissible from its beginning, ranging from its substantive duration to its testimony to the history which it has experienced."[20] However, trauma victims take the most superficial of these factors and never fully integrate them into their personality; they simply fuse them onto the surface of their repressed trauma reproducing a mask of identity that cannot be authentic for the individual. Therefore, "since the historical testimony rests on the authenticity, the former, too, is jeopardized by reproduction when substantive duration [integration] ceases to matter. And what is really jeopardized when the historical testimony is affected is the authenticity of the object."[21] The victims of trauma (the objects of violence) never fully come to terms with their experience, never fully integrate it into their identities. Rather, through their masking process they aestheticise their history, their politics, their culture in an effort to fashion a seeming identity. Consequently, it never becomes an authentic identity, never offers comprehensive refuge from trauma. They, as a consequence, experience frustration and project that frustration onto their environment. It is as Walter Benjamin writes about the masking process of history and politics: "all efforts to render politics aesthetic culminate in one thing: war."[22] As complicated and multifactored as is the current political situation in the North, the masking process related to trauma adds a further complication and factor. Violence may continue as a direct result of victims attempting to come to terms with their trauma and producing repeated cycles of violence and further victimization until even the prepackaged cues of identity seem arbitrary but, nonetheless, inescapable. Many plays that focus on the recent Northern Troubles highlight the arbitrariness of the masking process and perform the desperate cycles of violence that inevitably result.

In clinical terms, "it is the persistence of intrusive and distressing recollections, and not the direct experience of the traumatic event itself, that actually drives the biological and psychological dimensions of PTSD."[23] In addition, another "element of these experiences is the way that they cannot be left behind in the past, and the resultant way that they come to haunt the individual's life in the present. This results in part from the need to try to construct a meaning network, in order to solve the equation of fear and uncertainty that are provoked."[24] Essentially, victims fashion or adopt masks to counter the "intrusive and distressing recollections." The masks trauma victims construct include and are related to intrusions of trauma memories, compulsive reexposure to trauma, numbed emotions, loss of physiological ability to adapt to stress, increased distractibility, and the alterations of identity. All the reactions represent "an attempt of the self-regulating psychic system to restore the balance, in no way different from the function of dreams, only rather more forceful and drastic."[25]

In performing the various attempts to structure masks of identity, Irish theatre focuses attention on the disparity between the efforts to repair the rupture caused by violence and the actual rewards of the mask. The former promises comfort and security: "the ego dedicates itself to the specific job of ensuring the security of the organism, and of trying to protect itself against recollection of trauma."[26] The latter grants dissatisfaction and further violence. In essence, "traumatized people employ a variety of methods to regain control over their problems with affect regulation. Often these efforts are self destructive and bizarre; they range from self-mutilation to unusual sexual practices, and from binging and purging to drug and alcohol abuse."[27] In the North, the practices range from repeated exposure to trauma to problems re-forming identity and to difficulty in adopting behavior to non-traumatic or stressful situations. In short, the individuals who substitute masks of identity for identity, suffer an "impairment of basic trust."

After traumatic events, perceptions of relationships tend to become filtered through those experiences. . . . Most traumatized patients were clinging and dependent on the one hand, but socially isolated without mutually rewarding relationships on the other. Many had retreated into social isolation after years of frantic searches for rescuers. . . . When they were in a position of power, they often inspired fear and loathing; when they were in a subordinate position, they often felt helpless, behaved submissively, did not stand up for themselves, and tended to engage in idealization (and/or devaluation) at the expense of being able to experience their own competence.[28]

Significantly, the problems of the traumatized in the North are particularly acute, because when

cultural security and protection fail, the individual's problems are proportional to the cultural disintegration. The avenues of vulnerability resulting from trauma follow the roots vacated by culture: Paranoia substitutes for trust; aggression replaces nurturance and support; identity confusion or a negative identity substitutes for a positive identity. Social bonding becomes a regression to nationalism and tribalism, thereby permitting individuals to deny the experienced losses or to defend themselves against expected additional losses.[29]

However, it must be noted that the disfunction of the mask is really an attempt at self-cure. Ultimately, some individuals are able to reach a point when they can reject the masks of identity and embrace a more comprehensive self fashioning.

CARNIVAL: POST-TRAUMATIC RESTORATIVE NARRATIVES

In order to recover from trauma, an individual must construct new personal and interpersonal structures of identification that incorporate the violent past into the nontraumatic functions of everyday life. The carnival functions as an ideal metaphor for such a process in the sense that "carnivals can be taken as symptoms of social complexity."[30] It involves seeing past the facade of fear and anguish, anger and betrayal and seeing into the true nature of individual suffering and community displacement and potential re-establishment. The

carnival symbolizes a double sacrifice that is paradoxical in itself; through it . . . the groups in power channel the violence of the oppressed groups in order to maintain yesterday's order, while the latter channel the former's violence so that it will not recur tomorrow. Culturally speaking, the complexity of the . . . [post-traumatic restorative carnival] cannot be reduced to binary concepts. It is one thing and the other at the same time . . . since it serves the purpose of unifying through its performance that which cannot be unified (the impossible desire to reach social and cultural unity, sociocultural synthesis, that runs within the system)[31].

It is an embrace of social engagement. Significantly, the carnival functions differently in this context than it does in the definitions of Bakhtin and others. For Benitez-Rojo, carnival functions as a forum to expose the masks of those in power, to reveal their motives for maintaining order. It also functions as a forum for insurgency. In both cases, it functions as a way to come to terms with violence. However, ultimately, its performative aspects are "unifying" and represent a "sociocultural synthesis." Like Homi Bhabha's hybrid, the carnival is "at once a mode of appropriation and of resistance. . . . As the discriminated object, the metonym of presence becomes the support of an authoritarian voyeurism, all the better to exhibit the eye of power. Then, as discrimination turns into the assertion of the hybrid, the insignia of authority becomes a mask, a mockery."[32] As a consequence, the hybrid space becomes "a 'separate' space,"[33] no longer governed by the colonial power. Specifically, it is a "space of *separation* that has been denied by both colonialists and nationalists who have sought authority in the authenticity of 'origins.'"[34] An analogous understanding of Benitez-Rojo's carnival comes in the work of the Earl of Shaftesbury, the late-seventeenth and early eighteenth-century essayist, who saw it as a forum to reveal the masks of society's repressions, writing that if

a native of Ethiopia were on a sudden transported into Europe, and placed either at Paris or Venice at a time of carnival, when the general face of mankind was disguised, and almost every creature wore a mask, 'tis probable he would for some time be at a stand, before he discovered the cheat; not imagining that a whole people could be so fantastical as upon agreement, at an appointed time, to transform themselves by a variety of habits, and make it a solemn practise to impose on one another, by this universal confusion of characters and persons. Though he might at first look on this with a serious eye, it would hardly be possible for him to hold his countenance when he had perceived what was carrying on. The Europeans, on their side, might laugh perhaps at this simplicity. But our Ethiopian would certainly laugh with better reason. 'Tis easy to see which of the two would be ridiculous. For he who laughs and is himself ridiculous, bears a double share of ridicule.[35]

For the Earl of Shaftesbury, the carnival becomes a forum of ridicule for those who think themselves superior but who are, in actuality, ridiculous. The supposedly superior European dons masks at carnival and sees an individual whom they would perceive as inferior, an Ethiopian, as absurd. However, Shaftesbury makes abundantly clear that it is the masks of the Europeans that make them ridiculous. Further, he reveals that, although the Ethiopian initially was fooled by the masks, the outsider ultimately understands their transitory nature. Shaftesbury's carnival, then, finds a resonance with the restorative carnival. In both, the powerful, yet masked, continue to be deceived by their disguises and their ridiculous behavior. Conversely, the outsiders, the oppressed, liberate themselves through the carnival by seeing past the transitory nature of the mask.

The theatre of the Troubles that focuses on the restorative functions in a way that would be familiar to the practitioners of Benitez-Rojo's and Shaftesbury's carnival. Much of contemporary Irish drama "performs" the masks of oppression and the means for liberation from those masks. The theatre, then, becomes a type of carnival in which the oppressive form is portrayed and shown to be cruel, and, subsequently, an alternative manifests itself, an alternative that offers the possibility for liberation. Indeed,

could a performative utterance succeed if its formulation did not repeat a 'coded' or iterable utterance, or in other words, if the formula I pronounce in order to open a meeting, launch a ship or a marriage were not identifiable in some way as a citation? . . . In such a typology, the category of intention will not disappear; it will have its place, but from that place it will no longer be able to govern the entire scene and system of utterance.[36]

Essentially, by citation and then through variation, by demonstrating that the original "intent" of the utterance does not "govern" all manifestations of that utterance, the citational yet varied manifestation usurps the power of the "coded," masked utterance. In addition, the mask of authority can be donned as a means of more deliberate, yet nonetheless covert (to an extent), insurrection; Derrida's concept argues for a subtle usurpation of authority, but he suggests that the process may not always be intentional. In contrast, Declan Kiberd offers an alternative citational utterance, one in which the citation and variation are clearly intentional and clearly aim at insurrection:

In order to get a fair hearing in conservative society, the exponents of revolution had to present their intentions under the guise of a return to the idealized patterns of the past. . . . Claiming to revere the scaffolding of the older forms, the Pearses, Connollys and Joyces were not-so-secret innovators. They understood that one must forget much of the past if anything is to be created in the present: or, at least, one must constantly re-edit that past in the light of current needs.[37]

In much the same way, a portion of contemporary Northern drama stages the "conservative" forces of violence and seemingly intractable confrontation only to subtly or not so subtly reveal alternatives to violence at a time when alternatives are necessary.

Indeed, the North of Ireland, and the entire island, requires restorative narratives in the context of violence:

We have urgent need of stories in Ireland at the moment, as our society comes to terms with painful memories. All at once, it seems, we are trying to cope with the famine of the mid-nineteenth century, when a million people died of fever and starvation and another million emigrated; with twenty-five years of violence in the North of Ireland, followed by the sudden possibility of peace, and then more violence; and with a heartbreaking series of revelations about betrayal of trust, about domestic violence, and about cruelties secretly inflicted on women and children. The old narratives will no longer serve.[38]

The new narratives will certainly "cite" the old narratives, to provide a sense of historical continuity, but they will also subtly, or not so subtly, revise and refashion the old. The new restorative narratives will integrate violence and trauma into their form; they will no longer mask it. However, they will also integrate means for overcoming violence. In addition, the ideal performative utterance will also be open to contrast and reinterpretation, so that it too does not become a calcified mask of trauma.

In terms of a strictly clinical response, restorative narratives, like "rituals, support the individual, repair rents in the social fabric, and reestablish the group."[39] Further, the restorative rituals must be all encompassing. Basically, methods "for reestablishing a personal sense of control . . . can range from engaging in physical challenges to reestablishing a sense of spiritual meaning."[40] In general, in order to reduce traumatic response, "two conditions are required [the citational and the revisionary]. . . . First, memory must be activated. Second, new information must be provided--information including elements that are incompatible with existing pathological elements in the structure, so that a new memory can be formed. Exposure procedures activate the structure . . . and constitute an opportunity for corrective information to be integrated, and thus to modify the fear structure."[41] More specifically, a series of conditions must be met, either individually or as a set, in or to overcome chronic traumatic reactions. They include (1) "stabilization" through "education," (2) "identification of feelings through verbalizing somatic states," (3) "deconditioning of traumatic memories and responses," (4) "restructuring of traumatic personal schemes," (5) "reestablishment of secure social connections and interpersonal efficacy," and (6) "accumulation of restitutive emotional experiences."[42] Together, the clinical criteria offer a means for coming to understand restorative theatrical narratives.

By performing various methods of establishing restorative narratives, Irish drama focuses attention on the dynamics of effectual integration of trauma into all aspects of an individual's life, the emotional, intellectual, ethical, and even spiritual. Indeed,

> the search for meaning is a critical aspect of traumatized people's efforts to master their helplessness and sense of vulnerability. . . . Concepts such as fragmentation of awareness and conditioning do not address the spiritual and philosophical beliefs that are central to individual identity and motivation. These beliefs are also sustained by the cultural context and social fabric, which bind individuals to their social groups. These beliefs can be damaged in many traumas. . . . Religion provides a historical lineage of human suffering and capacity for regeneration. Prayers, music, and icons provide a powerful sense of endurance, despite the repeated onslaughts of disaster and war; prayer and the identification with the suffering of others can also provide a way forward.[43]

Essentially, restorative narratives offer a means for reestablishing a sense of individual identity and continuity with the past, a sense of community, and a communion with something beyond transience, putting individuals in touch with "that *terra incognita* called Beyond Nationalism, Beyond Catholic and Protestant."[44] Other names could be applied to restorative narratives, including "carnivalesque." In addition,

> we might label these theater pieces semiotic realism, for the referent is not expunged but rather rerouted through voices, film, photographs, patterns of light, musical phrases. The presence of historical figures . . . creates a sense of history as an assemblage of patriarchal narratives that are ripe for revision. If there is a referent in these texts it is historical experience, never fully describable, but invoked as nodal points of memory and desire.[45]

The past is cited, incorporated into the present, and the newly refashioned identity projects itself out into the future, "performing" the relation between violence and recovery, oppression and liberation, conformity and insurrection.

FIRE IN THE NORTH/SUN IN THE SOUTH

To an observer who accepts the colonial version of Irish history, all sides in the Northern conflict consider themselves allied with a sacred language, a belief which for the observer explains Northern sectarianism and a notion of a calcified history. Moreover, if an observer accepts the colonizer's view of Ireland, any possibility for movement beyond a society of violent rupture remains impossible, as the Irish appear to such an observer to be lost in an ancient past. After all, the official observers point out, the factionalized communities in the North of Ireland like

> the great classical communities conceived [and conceive] of themselves as cosmically central, through the medium of a sacred language linked to a superterrestrial order of power. . . . Such classical [Northern] communities linked by sacred languages had [have] a character distinct from the imagined communities of modern nations. One crucial difference was the older communities's [Northern communities'] confidence in the unique sacredness of their languages, and thus their ideas about admission to membership.[46]

Ireland, then, from the imperial perspective, becomes an interesting relic or case study, an alternative to Britain and to modern, sophisticated British values. The North, from a colonial perspective, grants insight into the arcane notion of "myth." In the Six Counties, according to the colonial view, individual communities's traditions are

> thought to express the absolute truth because . . . [they] narrate a sacred history; that is, [the belief in] a trans-human revelation which took place in the holy time of the beginning. . . . Myth becomes exemplary and consequently repeatable, thus serving as a model and justification for all human actions. . . . By imitating the exemplary acts of myths deities and heroes, man detaches himself from profane time and magically re-enters the Great Time, the Sacred Time.[47]

For those who accept the colonial view of events in the North, the British military presence is necessary to keep the various factionalized Northern communities from destroying themselves and each other. Certainly, from the colonizer's perspective, Ireland is not a nation capable of modern self-government.

Unfortunately, far too many within the North's communities have accepted the colonial version of the history of their society, mirroring the discourse of imperial conquest through the ideals and customs of sectarianism:

> Sectarianism is characterised by dogmatism and exclusivism. It occurs when a denomination or religious group identifies its expressions of truth with the truth itself and then excludes all others who do not conform to its expressions. It is when interpretations of doctrines or Scripture are proclaimed as absolute and all other interpretations are dismissed as being in error. Sectarianism also views its particular position as superior and all others as inferior.[48]

Indeed, "sectarianism," is akin to the notions of "myth" and "sacred language." In a horrifying example of religious hatred, Seamus Heaney, in his Nobel Prize acceptance speech, relates the story of a Catholic worker on a bus with predominantly Protestant coworkers:

> One of the most harrowing moments in the whole history of the harrowing heart in Northern Ireland came when a minibus full of workers being driven home one January evening in 1976 was held up by armed and masked men and the occupants of the van ordered at gunpoint to line up at the side of the road. Then one of the masked executioners said to them, 'Any Catholics among you, step out here.' As it happened, this particular group, with one exception, were all Protestants, so the presumption must have been that the masked men were Protestant paramilitaries about to carry out a tit-for-tat sectarian killing of the Catholic as the odd man out, the one who would have been presumed to be in sympathy with the IRA and all its actions. It was a terrible moment for him, caught between dread and witness, but he did make a motion to step forward. Then, the story goes, in that split second of decision, and in the relative cover of the winter evening darkness, he felt the hand of the Protestant worker next to him take his hand and squeeze it in a signal that said no, don't move, we'll not betray you, nobody need know what faith or party you belong to. All in vain, however, for the man stepped out of line; but instead of finding a gun at his temple, he was thrown backward and away as the gunman opened fire on those remaining in the line, for these were not Protestant terrorists, but members, presumably, of the Provisional IRA.[49]

Moreover, some individuals, on both sides of the peace line, practice a sectarianism modeled for them in the colonial discourse. For some, in the Nationalist/Republican community, Nationalism has come to view

tradition as something which has come to a conclusion. Its exponents fancy that they are the final point of history and the past a foil to their narcissism. Such a past has in effect lost its future, its power to challenge and disrupt: it exists only as a commodity to be admired, consumed, reducing its adherents to the position of tourists in their own country, whose monuments and heritage centres can be visited or re-entered by an act of will. Its people are lulled by their leaders to 'become drunk on remembrance,' to recover the past as fetish rather than to live in the flow of actual history.[50]

Likewise, for some in the Unionist/Loyalist community history has become a frozen monument, a sacred memory that must be reproduced devotedly and accurately in the present. An ideal metaphor for their view can be found in a mural which stood in a Unionist neighborhood. In the Fountain area of Derry, history spoke in a clear and resounding voice. Like many other murals in Unionist areas, this mural depicted King William crossing the Boyne and the Siege of Derry not as some ancient memory but as a living presence. This particular mural was an exact replica of a mural "originally painted in the 1920s." It was "repainted every year until the wall fell down in 1994."[51] Coincidentally, 1994 also marked the beginning of the recent peace process. It is as if the calcified version of history proved too heavy a burden for the wall to bear, just as sectarian violence proved too heavy a burden for many in both the Republican and Loyalist movements to bear. Certainly, the masks of Nationalism/Republicanism and Unionism/Loyalism adopted by many in the North appear to support the colonial version of the conflict.

However, many others in both communities seek to move beyond the masks of violence and colonial oppression, embracing an identity based in pluralism, a memory not a replica of the past (even the pain of past conflict), and the creation of narratives and works of art that express a different type of sacred language. The new nation, the new sacred myths, must be rooted in cooperation. As Seamus Heaney observes, the "birth of the future we desire is surely in the contraction which that terrified Catholic felt on the roadside when another gripped his hand, not in the gunfire that followed, so absolute and so desolate, if also so much a part of the music of what happens."[52] In addition, the future is not simply an empathetic bond. The "role of intellectual practices is to identify the current crisis of the nation and in identifying it to provide part of the apparatus of recognition for post-national social forms."[53] For the North, according to Richard Kearney,

the notion of an 'Irish mind' can only properly be comprehended in terms of a multiplicity of Irish minds! . . . This tension between unity and difference . . . must be preserved in the face of ideological reductionism. Irish modernist culture is larger than the distinct ideological traditions, nationalist, unionist, or otherwise, from which it derives and which it critically questions or negates or rewrites. The modernist horizon of experimental exploration enables Irish writers to reinterpret their tradition(s), and to do so in such a way that they reinvent their past as a living transmission of meaning rather than revive it as a dogmatic deposit of unchangeable truth.[54]

For Kearney and Heaney, violence and rupture, the separation of Catholic from Protestant on the roadside, or the "tyranny of a single dominant identity," is a product of the colonial discourse of "sectarianism or irreducibly opposed tribes." The alternative is an emotional and intellectual acknowledgment of cooperation and shared identity, in the gesture of unity and in the intellectual acknowledgment of the possibility for unity and plurality.

The new concept of the Irish nation created from such an acknowledgment would mean building new cultural forms not only in the history of cooperation but in an acknowledgment of past sectarian cultural failure, which led and can possibly lead to further hatred and conflict. In a striking resonance with the conflict in the North, a clinical analysis of trauma and its aftermath determines that

when cultural security and protection fail, the individual's problems are proportional to the cultural disintegration. The avenues of vulnerability resulting from trauma follow the roots vacated by culture: Paranoia substitutes for trust; aggression replaces nurturance and support; identity confusion or a negative identity substitutes for a positive identity. Social bonding becomes a regression to nationalism and tribalism, thereby permitting individuals to deny the experienced losses or to defend themselves against expected additional losses.[55]

An acknowledgment and recognition of violence and hatred, conducted jointly, can lead to the basis for a new national understanding rooted in "trust," "nurturance and support," and "positive identity." Indeed, such an understanding, to the contrary of the colonizer's view of Ireland, would form the basis for a people very much capable of self-government, because

a nation exists when a significant number of people in a community consider themselves to form a nation, or behave as if they formed one. It is not necessary that the whole of the population should so feel, or so behave, and it is not possible to lay down dogmatically a minimum percentage of a population which must be so affected. When a significant group holds this belief, it possesses 'national consciousness.'[56]

The people of the North, in a joint exploration and expression of their shared heritage, even a heritage of violence, would, in such an exploration, "behave as if they formed" a nation.

Narrative, drama, and other forms of artistic expression are a major factor in the formation of a new identity despite their seeming impotence in the face of violence. Certainly,

only the very stupid or the very deprived can any longer help knowing that the documents of civilization have been written in blood and tears, blood and tears no less real for being very remote. And when this intellectual predisposition coexists with the actualities of Ulster and Israel and Bosnia and Rwanda and a host of other wounded spots on the face of the earth, the inclination is not only not to credit human nature with much constructive potential but not to credit anything too positive in a work of art.[57]

However,

[even the] form of the poem [or theatre or any form of artistic creativity] . . . is crucial to poetry's power to do the thing which always is and always will be to poetry's credit: the power to persuade that vulnerable part of our consciousness of its rightness in spite of the evidence of wrongness all around it, the power to remind us that we are hunters and gatherers of values, that our very solitudes and distresses are creditable, in so far as they, too, are an earnest of our veritable human being.[58]

Heaney's words and various other forms of artistic expression acknowledge that, rather than being a calcified society, the North "is an evolving community, full of doubts and scepticism." Indeed, "some are willing to work the system, in the hope that it will evolve as they do."[59] The vulnerabilities, the doubts and scepticism, the ruptured consciousness and masks of violence represent only a part of North of Ireland society. From these wounds, artistic creation can help "society . . . organise the processes of suffering, rendering it a meaningful mode of action and identity within a larger social framework,"[60] creating a "unified" and even (within diversity and plurality and shared experience) "ethical" and positive community and national identity. Indeed, a person's or a community's "ethical identity" is "dependent on our ability to tell our story and to learn from the stories of others"[61] The narrative, with all its various components, would speak with a unified voice, an empowering voice. Undoubtedly, a "national poetry must speak with one voice and, . . . must represent the Irish people as the agent of its own history, of a history which has 'the unity and purpose of an epic poem.' This demands a 'translational' aesthetic, in the sense that it must constantly be carried over is the essential spirit rather than the superficial forms of Irish poetry in each language."[62] David Lloyd's "translational aesthetic" would interpret the multifarious forms of the Irish nation into a unified voice that conveys the "essential spirit" of diverse communities, an essential spirit that involves relating tales of conflict and division, hatred and violence, but also involves relating the more cooperative and positive cultural representations that comprise Ireland. Significantly, the "unified" voice cannot and should not become a calcified historical form in itself. It must constantly, like Northern and Southern Irish society, evolve just as its residents do.

Irish drama ultimately "performs" such an evolving and unified society, creating on the stage the same multilayered understanding and representation of Northern society that is contained in Deirdre O'Connell's charcoal and pastels; it is a form that simultaneously represents violent rupture, mirrored masks, and creative potentialities rooted in deep historical and mythical realities.

NOTES

[1] Zahava Solomon, Nathaniel Laror, and Alexander McFarlane, "Acute Posttraumatic Reactions in Soldiers and Civilians," *Traumatic Stress: The Effects of Overwhelming Experience on Mind, Body, and Society*, ed. Bessel Van der Kolk, Alexander McFarlane, and Lars Weisaeth, (London: The Guilford Press, 1996), 103.

[2] Alexander McFarlane and Giovanni de Girolamo, "The Nature of Traumatic Stressors and the Epidemiology of Posttraumatic Reactions," *Traumatic Stress: The Effects of Overwhelming Experience on Mind, Body, and Society,* ed. Bessel Van der Kolk, Alexander Mc Farlane, and Lars Weisaeth. (London: The Guilford Press, 1996), 132.

[3] Bessel Van der Kolk and Alexander Mc Farlane, "The Black Hole of Trauma," *Traumatic Stress: The Effects of Overwhelming Experience on Mind, Body, and Society*. Ed. Bessel Van der Kolk, Alexander McFarlane, and Lars Weisaeth. (London: The Guilford Press, 1996), 19.

[4] Luke Gibbons, *Transformations in Irish Culture*, (Cork: Cork University Press, 1996), 150.

[5] Ibid., 175-76.

[6] Declan Kiberd, *Inventing Ireland*, (London: Jonathan Cape, 1995), 31.

[7] Declan Kiberd, "Anglo-Irish Attitudes," *Ireland's Field Day*, (Derry: Field Day Theatre Company, 1985), 83.

[8] Seamus Deane, "Heroic Styles: The Tradition of an Idea," *Ireland's Field Day*, (Derry: Field Day Theatre Company, 1985), 35.

[9] Warren Hoge, "The Troubles," *New York Times Book Review*, March 15 1998, 18.

[10] Ibid.

[11] Ibid.

[12] Kevin Kelley, *The Longest War: Northern Ireland and the IRA*, (Dingle, Co Kerry, Brandon Press, 1982), 315.

[13] Michel Foucault *Power/Knowledge: Selected Interviews and Other Writings, 1972-1977*, ed. by Colin Gordon,. Trans. by Colin Gordon, Leo Marshall, John Mepham, and Kate Soper, (New York Pantheon Books, 1980), 83.

[14] Ibid., 81.

[15] Ibid., 82.

[16] Van der Kolk, "Black Hole," 4.

[17] Ibid., 9.

[18] Carl Jung, *Analytical Psychology*, (New York: Vintage Books, 1968),153 54.

[19] Ibid., 1.

[20] Walter Benjamin, *Illuminations*, (New York: Schocken Books, 1969), 221.

[21] Ibid.

[22] Ibid., 241.

[23] Van der Kolk, "Black Hole," 6.

[24] McFarlane, 132.

[25] Jung, *Analytical Psychology*, 190.

[26] Abram Kardiner, *The Traumatic Neuroses of War*, (New York: Hoeber, 1941), 184.

[27] Bessel Van der Kolk, "The Complexity of Adaptation to Trauma," *Traumatic Stress:The Effects of Overwhelming Experience on Mind, Body, and Society*, ed. Bessel Van der Kolk, Alexander Mc Farlane, and Lars Weisaeth, (London: The Guilford Press, 1996), 188.

[28] Ibid., 196-97.

[29] Marten de Vries, "Trauma in Cultural Perspective," *Traumatic Stress: The Effects of Overwhelming Experience on Mind, Body, and Society*, ed. Bessel Van der Kolk, Alexander Mc Farlane, and Lars Weisaeth, (London: The Guilford Press, 1996), 408.

[30] Antonio Benítez-Rojo, *The Repeating Island: The Caribbean and the Postmodern Perspective*, trans. by James Maraniss, (Durham: Duke University Press, 1996), 306.

[31] Ibid., 306-307.

[32] Homi Bhabha, *The Location of Culture*, (New York: Routledge, 1994), 120.

[33] Ibid.

[34] Ibid.

[35] Anthony Ashley Cooper, Earl of Shaftesbury, *Characteristics of Men, Manners, Opinions, Times*, ed. by John Robertson, (Indianapolis: Bobbs-Merrill, 1964), 57.

[36] Jacques Derrida, "Signature Event Context," *Margins of Philosophy*, trans. by Alan Bass, (Chicago: University of Chicago Press, 1982), 22.

[37] Kiberd, *Inventing Ireland,* 293-94.

[38] Angela Bourke, "Language, Stories, Healing," *Gender and Sexuality in Modern Ireland*, ed. by Anthony Bradley and Maryann Gialanella Valiulis, (Amherst: University of Massachusetts Press, 1997),305.

[39] de Vries, 402.

[40] Bessel Van der Kolk, Alexander Mc Farlane, and Onto Van der Hart, "A General Approach to the Treatment of Posttraumatic Stress Disorder," *Traumatic Stress: The Effects of Overwhelming Experience on Mind, Body, and Society*, ed. Bessel Van der Kolk, Alexander Mc Farlane, and Lars Weisaeth, (London: The Guilford Press, 1996), 420.

[41] Barbara Olasov-Rothbaum, and Edna Foa, "Cognitive-Behavioral Therepy for Posttraumatic Stress Disorder," *Traumatic Stress: The Effects of Overwhelming Experience on Mind, Body, and Society,* ed. Bessel Van der Kolk, Alexander Mc Farlane, and Lars Weisaeth, (London: The Guilford Press, 1996), 492.

[42] Van der Kolk, "General Approach," 426.

[43] Stuart Turner, Alexander Mc Farlane, and Bessel Van der Kolk, "The Therapeutic Environment and New Explorations in the Treatment of Posttraumatic Stress Disorder," *Traumatic Stress: The Effects of Overwhelming Experience on Mind, Body, and Society*, ed. Bessel Van der Kolk, Alexander Mc Farlane, and Lars Weisaeth, (London: The Guilford Press, 1996), 551.

[44] John Wilson Foster, "Richard Kearney - A Reply," *The Honest Ulsterman,* 82 (Winter 1986), 46.

[45] Elin Diamond, *Unmaking Mimesis: Essays on Feminism and Theater,* (New York:Routledge, 1997), 38-9.

[46] Benedict Anderson, *Imagined Communities: Reflections on the Origins and the Spread of Nationalism,* (London: Verso, 1991), 13.

[47] Micrea Eliade, *Myths, Dreams, and Mysteries*, (London: Fontana, 1968) 68.

[48] Johnstan Mc Master, *The Churches and Cross Community Work with Young People,* (Belfast: Youth Link, 1993), 4.

[49] Seamus Heaney, *Crediting Poetry,* (Loughcrew, Co Meath: Gallery Press, 1995), 17-18.

[50] Kiberd, 294.

[51] Bill Rolston, *Drawing Support 2: Murals of War and Peace,* (Belfast: Beyond the Pale,1995) 53.

[52] Heaney, 19.

[53] Arjun Appadurai, *Modernity at Large*, (Minneapolis: University of Minnesota Press, 1997), 158.

[54] Richard Kearney, "The Transitional Crisis in Irish Culture," *The Honest Ulsterman* 92 (Winter 1986), 41.

[55] de Vries, 408.

[56] Hugh Seton-Watson, *Nations and States. An Inquiry Into the Origins of Nations and the Politics of Nationalism,* (Boulder: Westview Press, 1977), 5.

[57] Heaney, 19.

[58] Ibid., 29.

[59] Fionnuala Ó Connor, *In Search of a State: Catholics in Northern Ireland*, (Belfast: Blackstaff Press, 1993), 378.

[60] De Vries, 402.

[61] Richard Kearney, *Poetics of Modernity*, (Atlantic Highlands: Humanities Press, 1995), xiv.
[62] David Lloyd, *Anomalous States: Irish Writing and the Post-Colonial Moment,* (Durham:Duke University Press, 1993), 97.

3

"Briseadh na tseanghathaimh": The Rupture of Identity

In a figure titled "Vagina Dentata," the Northern Irish artist Catherine Harper creates an image reminiscent of bodies recovered from bogs in the North of Ireland and across Europe. Like Seamus Heaney's poems that focus on the bog people, her work can be taken as a metaphor for the Troubles. In "The Tollund Man," Heaney writes of riding in "Jutland/In the old man-killing parishes/I will feel lost,/Unhappy and at home" (ll.41-44). He summons images of religious divisions and links them to a "lost" feeling, an "unhappy" feeling. However, he also writes that in the place of death and loss and sorrow, he will feel at home. Like Jutland bog, in Heaney's North of Ireland sanctified death and the mummified remains of life haunt those individuals who survive religious violence. Their individual identities are subsumed in ritual violence and habitual loss. Catherine Harper's figure is also an image of ritualized death. Animal and human bones lie in a vaguely human form, but the bones themselves, arraigned in a manner that suggests a ritual purpose, also imply something not at all human. Ram's horns form eye cavities and a brow ridge. Pelvic bones resemble skulls, and the figures of bones rotted in the earth assume an almost animal-like hairy skin. Human identity finds itself subsumed within ritualized death and centuries of burial. Harper's figure reveals some deep truths about the human connection with the animal, even within a sanctified death, but her figure also reveals, like Heaney's poems, the consequences of violence and brutality. Even associated with religious ritual, even sanctified by creed, traumatic death ruptures basic elements of human self-conception and coherent individual identity. Harper's image then stands as a metaphor for an aspect of Irish identity within the context of the Troubles.

Within the dynamics of the North of Ireland conflict, the clinical diagnosis that studies the loss of identity in the face of traumatic rupture and the six symptomatic areas in which rupture manifests itself are present not only in both the Protestant and Catholic communities but also in terms of their relation to one another and in terms of the relation between the North of Ireland and the Irish Republic. However, as a consequence of the Troubles, each community and its relation to other communities, within the North and within the island, tends to more clearly express the loss of identity or coherence, as a consequence of the Troubles, in one or two of the six diagnostic areas more so than the others. Specifically, the Catholic experience of traumatic rupture tends to express itself in terms of "disorientation" and "loss of self-control." Conversely, the Protestant reaction to violence generally finds its clearest voice in relation to feelings of "anxiety" and "vulnerability." The differing emphasis on particular areas of traumatic rupture is, most likely, a result of the different communities's experience of the potential consequences of violence. For the Protestant majority, insurrection threatens their exclusive hold on power, resulting in heightened feelings of anxiety and vulnerability. For the Catholic population, the Troubles result in a heightened police and military presence and in the sectarianization of many of their traditions and beliefs. For relations between communities and between the Irish Republic and the North, isolation from violent conflict by an imaginative withdrawal from conflict and a sense of guilt regarding personal responsibility are the clearest manifestations of traumatic rupture. In each circumstance, the Troubles threaten vital components of self- conception and community or national coherence.

In terms of the Catholic experience in the North, the decades of manifest violence give rise to both external and internal forces that threaten identity. Indeed, any level of self-conception has always been difficult for Catholics in the Six Counties, expressing its confusion on many levels, including what to call themselves and their country:

Once, 'Northern Ireland' was a term many Catholics refused to use. To speak or write the name would have recognised the existence of a state they denied the validity of, even though that was where they lived their lives. Who were they? Not Northern Irish Catholics's , certainly: that would have suggested acceptance of a minority status and smacked of the reservation. . . . They were, they insisted, 'Irish Catholics's , no different from Catholics anywhere else in Ireland --but they preferred the simple description 'Irish.'[1]

Fionnuala Ó Connor's description regarding Catholics confused expression of self identity finds a resonance in the reactions to traumatic violence. The forces that tend to confuse or threaten identity in her description of self-naming find themselves heightened as a consequence of the Troubles. State authority, the object of denial by Catholics, wrests control from the populace through brutal means, including a constant military presence and laws that deprive the people of fundamental rights. Furthermore, the idea of "Irishness," within the context of the Troubles, becomes not simply an intellectual expression but a sectarian gesture, not a force of self recognition but rather a weapon used to destroy another community.

For some in the Northern Protestant community the Troubles threaten a sense of hegemony and a feeling of divinely sanctioned rule. Throughout the decades of violence, and before, many in the Protestant majority saw their enduring and controlling presence in the North as a temporal manifestation of and reward for spiritual fidelity. A striking example of Protestant certainty appeared in the early years of the Troubles:

In August 1971, during the violence which accompanied the introduction of internment in Northern Ireland, a handbill circulated on the Newtownards Road in Belfast proclaiming: 'the enemies of our Faith and Freedom are determined to destroy the state of North of Ireland and thereby enslave the people of God'. The statement was a reflection of all those basic protestant tenets which outsiders find so enigmatic and so repugnant: the incongruous association of liberty with a self-righteous élitism: a crusading fundamentalism with an embattled sense of conspiracy . . . Above all, this appeal to freedom rings false in a religious grouping which is intolerant of others and whose virulent anti-Catholicism reveals itself in a puzzling rejection of all things Irish.[2]

Marianne Elliott's observations stress how a violent revolt against Protestant rule, accompanied by a demonstration of prejudice and racism in the North, threaten Protestant identity, resulting in feelings of vulnerability and anxiety. The civil rights marches of the late 1960s and early 1970s point out the hypocrisy in "a religious grouping which is intolerant of others." Moreover, the very real possibility that the supposedly inferior Catholic population might succeed in threatening if not destroying elite Protestant rule questions the supposedly divine origins of that rule. Basically, the Troubles strike at the heart of Protestant security in the North.

Viewed as a whole, the Troubles threaten not only individual communities in the North but also a sense of nationhood or community beyond sectarian divisions. Importantly, the consequences of violence seem to suggest that "the Catholic group has been growing in stature while the protestant group has come more and more under attack,"[3] indicating the development of more equitable power structures in the North. However, even though in "social identity terms this would mean that the way the Catholic group evaluates its social identity is becoming more and more positive," although with considerable negative elements, it also means that

the Protestant group's identity has become increasingly threatened. . . . The important point is that one group attaining a sense of superiority at the other group's expense will not lead to a peaceful solution of the conflict but rather will ensure its perpetuation.[4]

The sense of rivalry and the consequent violence extends itself across the border into the South, causing the government and people there to attempt to distance themselves from what seems to be an ever-increasingly brutal and intractable situation. In addition, for both communities within the island and within the North, there also exists a desire for fidelity with the past, an almost obligatory sense of duty to history, and sectarianism, which contributes to a further escalation of violence. Essentially, the Troubles puts certain forces in motion that, even while attempting to pay homage to their individual communities and peoples, threaten the essential identity of not only both Protestants and Catholics but also the island and the region as a whole.

NORTHERN CATHOLIC EXPERIENCE

Seamus Deane, in "After Derry, 30 January 1972," writes that "Death is our future" (1.33), capturing the anguish and hopelessness of a Catholic population devastated by the news of the thirteen dead in the Bloody Sunday massacre. Other poets also speak of the victims and of the effects of their deaths. Seamus Heaney, in "Casualty," captures the sense of anger and rage contained in graffiti: "PARAS THIRTEEN, the walls said,/BOGSIDE NIL" (ll.43-44). In Heaney's poem, an inanimate object speaks for the populace, the voice of rage converting pain to an unfeeling need for revenge. Thomas McCarthy, in "Counting the Dead on the Radio, 1972," speaks of the British as "adolescent soldiers" (1.31). However, he also speaks of the images of the event promulgated on Irish radio and television: within the poem, a child tells his mother about a priest seemingly attacked by the British army (ll.35-37). McCarthy accurately represents the popular media image, designed for ultimate melodramatic effect, of the representative of Catholicism standing up to imperial violence. Although the image is an accurate one, and the priest, later bishop of Derry, did administer last rites to one of the victims, the media's fixation on this particular image indicates an appeal to a religious heritage not designed to provoke re-assurance in a time of threat and crisis, but rather, one designed to provoke rage and hatred. The poets, speaking of the events of a specific time and specific place, could also be speaking of the various actions and reactions to the re-emergence of sectarian conflict in the North since 1968. Contained in their reflections are the myriad of Catholic responses to conflict and oppression, including pain, anguish, anger, rage, and even the turning of these emotions onto themselves and the authorities in the North, conjuring legitimate outrage at oppression and violence into self-destructive images of Nationalism and Catholicism.

Since the re-emergence of open and manifest sectarian conflict in the late 1960s, Catholic identity in North of Ireland has suffered from disorientation and a loss of self-control. Essentially, the direct and indirect experience of traumatic circumstance ruptured Catholic structures of self identification and of community. Most notably, violence directed at Catholics, because of their religion and native traditions has secularized indigenous customs and faith. Specifically, "for many Northerners, . . . Irish culture means language, music, literature, sport: a cultural nationalism that can encompass different political affiliations and none, and which has become more evident as Northern Catholics assert their identity."[5] However, like the cultural nationalism of the Revival generation, the pride consequent of Northern cultural nationalism has potentially negative consequences.

The strategy for the revivalists became clear: for bad words substitute good, for superstitious use religious, for backward say traditional, for irrational suggest emotional. The positive aspect of this manoeuvre was that it permitted Irish people to take many images which were rejected by English society, occupy them, reclaim them, and make them their own: but the negative aspect was painfully obvious, in that the process left the English with the power of description and the Irish succumbing to the pictures which they had constructed. The danger was that, under the guise of freedom, a racist slur might be sanitized and worn with pride by its very victims; and that the act of national revival might be taken away from a people even as they performed it. Sometimes in "their progress the revivalists would seem to reinforce precisely those stereotypes which they had set out to dismantle"[6]

For contemporary Northern cultural nationalists, the positive implications of holding up religion and tradition as marks of opposition to British and Protestant rule include a sense of identity invulnerable to colonial manipulation. Conversely, "religious fanaticism, degenerate politics, and fundamental inferiority"[7] are potentially negative consequences of identity structures revived in *opposition* to power. In essence, the sectarianism that prompted a renewed interest in tradition and religion has the potential to give birth to another type of sectarianism that "is imprinted by the fiction and follies of the dominant realm,"[8] becoming the modern counterpart for the more contemporary Northern cultural nationalists to what Declan Kiberd calls the "sanitized racial slur"[9] of the Revival generation. Consequently, the potential benefit of a revival in regards to native religion and tradition becomes confused as to its origins and purposes resulting in a disoriented identity that might actually reinforce the abuses of sectarian authority.

Importantly, there are numerous reports of sectarian abuses perpetrated by both the Protestant authorities in the North and by the British political and military establishment against the Catholic population. In terms of the RUC,

policing in North of Ireland [in the early 1970s] . . . moved from a retroactive form where those suspected of illegal activities are arrested and processed through the courts of evidence obtained after the event, to a pre-emptive form where large sections of those communities which are perceived as being a distinct threat to the existing status quo are regularly and systematically monitored.[10]

Specifically, British and Protestant policies resulted in arrest and internment without trial, most notably as a consequence of the Prevention of Terrorism Act, "which . . . allowed British police to hold those suspected of terrorist activities without charge for forty-eight hours or up to seven days on higher authority."[11] Importantly, rather than used sparingly and only in cases where terrorism was likely, the Act "was an exceptional power that the police used repeatedly, if often to very little effect, seemingly detaining Irish citizens only to annoy."[12] Moreover, legal and legislative abuses found themselves complemented by brutal and horrific violations by the authorities. Particularly, "in Derry's Bogside on 30 January 1972, . . . thirteen people were shot dead by soldiers of the First Parachute Regiment."[13] The official enquiry blamed the deaths on the victims, asserting that the soldiers "heard shots or saw snipers or fired at nail bombers and gunmen."[14] However, "most witnesses . . . had not heard any provocative shots or noted any gunman."[15] Moreover, the "Derry coroner . . . noted that many of the victims were shot in the back," and "one army officer recalled that a section of the Parachute Regiment 'quite frankly, lost control. . . . You could hear their CO bellowing at them to cease firing.'"[16] The effect of such abuses on Catholic identity involves a rupture of

fundamental assumptions of security and safety, having a deleterious effect on
identity and attempts to fashion a self-conception in the face of violence.

Loss of Self-Control

Clinical research concludes that individuals, in "response to the threat of injury
and death,"[17] relinquish command of basic physiological functions, manifesting
excessive "weeping, screaming, and a range of impulsive behaviors, as well as
somatic reactions such as vomiting, wetting, and diarrhea."[18]   The theatrical
representations of the Troubles "perform" the conflict between the colonial
discourse of absolute control, through an occupation force that includes military
and police oppression of the populace, and the alternative discourse of freedom and
independence from control. Drama also "performs" the repeated subjugation of the
alternative discourse resulting in the rupture of individuals's control over their
lives. In other words, because the colonizing force and its agents take electoral
control away from the local populace, deprive them of the freedom of speech and
association without fear of imprisonment, impose on the populace a police force
and a military presence whose members and tactics aim at the disruption of family
and social structures, the community under colonial authority has lost the ability
to define itself, to control its own responses to the environment. All terms of
interaction are dictated by the occupation force with its "preoccupation with the
control, classification, and surveillance of its subjects."[19] Therefore, the populace
cannot free itself from trauma and its realization of the full extent of their colonized
existence can lead not to a sense of self-control but rather continuing trauma and
violence. In the North of Ireland during the twenty-five years of the Troubles,
covered by this study, this effort of control clearly manifests itself in the frequent
army patrols and military observations of Catholic neighborhoods, in electronic
surveillance and road blocks, and in searches and detentions without trial.
Essentially, "the security forces are not in reality subject to the rule of law,
whatever may be claimed to the contrary,"[20] and they abuse their positions of power
to terrorize the local populace. The products of colonial dominance include not
only support for Republican organizations but also a weakened social structure
within neighborhoods; a sense of siege rather than a sense of community
dominates; a fractured sense of unity within the family exists, in which traditional
life is disrupted by dead or imprisoned members, and where abuse, both physical
and emotional, is far too common and a direct result of societal violence; further,
many individuals experience the inability to imaginatively restructure the self,
family, and community.
    In selected plays of Martin Lynch and Brian Friel (considered in this analysis),
humans, as a consequence of the Troubles, lose control over their most basic
psychological characteristics, manifesting, in response to the threat of violence and
death, mechanical attributes, designed to insulate individuals from violence or
designed to demean or negate the humanity of people, and becoming instruments

of torture, denuding the most essential human instincts in favor of methods of interrogation and intimation. Essentially, like the clinical/physiological response to the threat of violence, humans lose control of instinctual and fundamental psychological characteristics, either in an effort to control the populace or as a consequence of the brutality and force of the authorities.

In *The Freedom of the City* and in *The Interrogation of Ambrose Fogarty*, Brian Friel and Martin Lynch portray a relationship between the human and the mechanized in which machines and mechanical language control and overpower the human. Within the plays, Friel and Lynch represent a hybrid of human and machine. Subsequently, the mechanical is given the advantage and overwhelms human elements, and, finally, human self-control cedes itself to the mechanical. This three-part process occurs twice: for the authorities and for the Catholic Irish in the North. The authorities wield the mechanical, speaking in a mechanized code language through radios and receivers. In Friel's play, a British soldier initiates contact with a fellow soldier standing on the opposite side of the stage, saying "Blue Star to Eagle," and the reply comes back, "Eagle receiving. Come in, Blue Star."[21] Within the language of the radios, the human voice of the British soldiers becomes an almost mechanical signal, virtually a part of the radio and receiver. Each speaks his password into a machine, clutching the machine to his cheek and ear, fusing himself with the machine. Within such a matrix, human frailties and vulnerabilities do not exist. Hesitation and conscience void themselves in the efficiency of mechanized communication. Likewise, in *The Interrogation of Ambrose Fogarty*, soldiers and police officers communicate in mechanical terms. Martin Lynch's play begins with voices coming through a radio which says "Echo Tango Eight One. Echo Tango Eight One to Bravo Hotel, over. Echo Tango Eight One. Echo Tango Eight One to Bravo Hotel, over."[22] As in Friel's play, a code language substitutes for human communication. However, Lynch's play, significantly, does not initially show a human form speaking the mechanized code language. Rather, the stage directions call for the "radio" to speak the words. The human element is purged from primacy within the scenario; a human voice does appear on stage, but it is consumed by the mechanical. Similarly, within Friel's play, a British soldier describes the "force" at his disposal, not by numbering the men, but by naming their designations, referring to them as the "8th Infantry Brigade, 1st Battalion Parachute Regiment, 1st Battalion King's Own Border Regiment, two companies of the 3rd Battalion Royal Regiment of Fusiliers."[23] It is as if the soldiers under his command do not possess a human element. Rather, they have become their designation, and a group designation.

The human reduces itself to regimental labels, an organizational term in which, as the Brigadier uses it, compartmentalizes the human element, negates its frailties in the more efficient designation. The Brigadier mentions no individuals. However, his litany does identify the names and numbers of the mechanical force at his disposal: "Twelve Saracens, ten Saladins, two dozen Ferrets and four water-cannons, and a modicum of air cover."[24] The mechanical, not subject to individual expression, is given an individual designation and numbered. Essentially, the

British presence, and by extension, the presence of the local authorities in the North becomes mechanized and invulnerable. Indeed, during the course of the Troubles, the authorities did make an effort, clearly designed to intimidate the populace, to represent themselves within the context of the mechanized. Specifically, "video cameras are mounted outside most, if not all, government buildings, many commercial premises and even in every public bus in Belfast."[25] The video eye sees the "truth" and "efficiently" surveys the populace. Further, helicopters, during the Troubles, were a regular sight and sound over Catholic neighborhoods, providing "the 'eye in the sky' in the shape of binocular observation, photographic techniques, and video cameras."[26] For the authorities, control became mechanized dominance. They ceded, as in Friel's and Lynch's work, individual human nature and identity in order to express themselves through the mechanical. Essentially, they voluntarily lose authority over their human components in order to exercise intimidation and control.

Further, they project their control onto the populace, forcing the mechanical onto the human. Friel's play, like *Ambrose Fogarty*, begins with a mechanized presence. "Suddenly all sounds are drowned by the roar of approaching tanks. Their noise is deafening and fills the whole auditorium. . . Panic. Screaming. Shouting.[27] Friel consumes even the audience into the militarized noise of dominating machines. No individual characters initially appear. Michael, the first recognizable person, "staggers onstage. . . . He has been blinded by CS gas, can scarcely breathe, and is retching."[28] Ultimately, Friel ends his play with the directions, "the entire stage is now black, except for a battery of spotlights beaming on the faces of the three. Pause. The air is filled with a fifteen-second burst of automatic fire. It stops. The three stand as before."[29] Friel carefully and consciously juxtaposes the mechanical and human, producing individual human forms whose identity and individuality becomes consumed by the mechanical. In the initial scene, Michael emerges only after the sounds of war precede him. Theatrically, the mechanized sounds function as a type of musical identifier, his motif. Michael becomes associated with the sounds of tanks and the sights of artificial smoke. Emerging from these elements, he ultimately does take individual form. However, in the play's final scene, his individuality loses itself once again in the mechanical. He stands, frozen into an inanimate form, his individuality consumed by the army's bright lights. Michael, initially and finally, is indistinguishable from the machine. Like the British soldiers who speak in code language, he finds himself part human and part machine. However, unlike the soldiers, he does not voluntarily surrender his identity to the mechanical. Rather, the machine appropriates his identity. Similarly, Friel constructs his play so that, even as the spectators come to terms with the individual characters, their self-control and individual identity become lost within the militarized and mechanized presence. Essentially, the action of Friel's play takes place on two levels. On one level, the characters play out their final hours of life. On another level, the authorities conduct an enquiry into the deaths of the characters, exploring them in terms of the number and type of their wounds: "in the case of Fitzgerald there were eight distinct bullet wounds; in the case of the woman

Doherty-thirteen; and in the case of Hegarty-twelve, thirteen, fourteen; I couldn't be sure. . . . [T]he majority of injuries were in the head and neck and shoulders, and the serious mutilation in such a concentrated area made precise identification almost . . . guesswork."[30]

When the British soldier makes use of the word "identification," he does not do so in reference to the three individuals. Rather, he uses it in reference to the bullet wounds in the individuals, as if the bullets carry more of an identity than do the characters themselves. Indeed, his clearest description of any component in the scene comes in reference to the bullets, explaining that "the 7.62 is a high-velocity bullet which makes a small, clean entry into the body . . . as it passes out of the body -at the point of exit- it makes a gaping wound and as it exits it brings particles of bone and tissue with it which make the wound even bigger."[31]

Certainly the soldier knows more about the bullets than the victims. Rhetorically, he reduces them to terms of identification dictated by the bullets. The victims become cases with a certain number of wounds, losing control of their individuality within the context of mechanized violence and mechanical analysis. The act of the authorities in the North, within Friel's play, details military figures actively engaged in "disregarding, essentializing, [and] denuding the humanity of another culture, [and] people."[32] The mechanized presence of the military power wrests individual control and identification from the populace.

Martin Lynch's play details a similar process. However, rather than mechanized control robbing people of self-control, Lynch focuses on the very human components of physical and psychological torture denuding and negating the humanity of individuals. Within *Ambrose Fogarty*, the authorities become instruments of torture, focusing their energies in an effort to display their power, imposing their brutality onto the objects of their physical and psychological intimidation. Their reasoned calculations intend to fundamentally destroy any sense of control their victims have over their lives. Within Lynch's play, the authorities declare that "it's harder to penetrate a person's mind than their body, but once you do get in, they're yours for the taking," adding that they have "seen guys walk out of here, wrecked, who never had a finger laid on them."[33] The object of intimidation does not appear to focus on gaining information or intelligence but rather on destruction. The officer says that the victim left the police compound. He was not arrested and charged with a crime, the ostensible goal of intimidation. Rather, no crime is mentioned. The focus remains not on punishing those individuals who violate the rules of society but rather on the display of authority and power. Certainly, "it is . . . evident [within the play as well as within Northern society] that the general physical and psychological ordeals of interrogation are designed to have lasting effects on suspects, independent of any criminal prosecution."[34] Another guard, Jackie, tells Fogarty to "just remember that you have three long days and nights ahead of you. . . . Just think about what we can do to you over three days."[35] Jackie then adds that a "good going-over is more than enough for most of them," but Peter suggests that "the fear of a good going-over is even worse."[36] Ultimately, when their methods do not seem to work, the authorities decide to keep Fogarty "in complete isolation. No cellmates, no newspapers, no news, no conversation."[37] They focus their brutality in an effort to drain Fogarty's mind of any individual thoughts and to replace them with fear and intimidation. Indeed, in order to survive, Fogarty begins to purge himself of thoughts of home and family, becoming simply a victim, and losing control of his individuality:

Fuck this! Three frigging days in this kip, Jesus Christ! How am I gonna stick this? Fuck it, fuck it, fuck it. . . . Three days! seventy-two hours! What to hell's it all about? Nobody has said dickie bird up to now, except 'All our evidence collected.' What are they on about, what evidence? What about Gerry? I wonder do they know anything about Gerry? I wonder will I get my bollocks knocked in. They don't bring you in here for nothing. That was wild in the house this morning. Christine. Her eyes. You could actually see the terror in her eyes. Thank Christ the kids didn't waken. . . . I have to stop thinking about her. Or the children, while I'm in here.[38]

Clearly affected by the brutal treatment of his wife and family, Fogarty at first resists by venting his anger, affirming his feelings and bonds with those he loves. Ultimately, in an effort to survive, he relinquishes his emotional ties to his family coming to understand the controlling elements of his current situation: "The not knowing. The uncertainty. The fear. The breaking-point."[39] Fogarty succumbs to what are the "central objectives of these techniques," which is the "personality breakdown"[40] of the victim on every level. Fogarty loses all sense of control over his emotions and circumstance. In creating the details of Ambrose Fogarty's ordeal, Martin Lynch relied heavily on first-hand experience. He "was arrested with monotonous regularity during the 1970s, about thirty times-mostly for four-hour screenings. On five occasions he was taken in for three days, three times to Castlereagh."[41] Lynch succeeds in his "attempt to show intimidation and torture, lies and abuse, as part of ordinary British and Irish society. Indeed, it [the play] goes further and shows that the enforcement of the laws and restrictions of the dominant society specifically requires this behaviour."[42] *Ambrose Fogarty* details the successful destruction of an individual's self-conception by the Northern Irish authorities. Although Fogarty's release from detention without charge leaves him free to return to his former life, his sense of autonomy and individuality remain permanently altered. In a very real sense, he loses control over his life. His prison sentence never really ends.

Indeed, the technique of questioning in this manner serves the purposes of the authorities. It enables them to maintain control over a significant proportion of the population. Essentially, the authorities arbitrarily exercise power through intimidation. The intimidation lasts well after the interrogation. The remainder of the population then witnesses the released prison's trauma, and they too are intimidated. However, the authority is a short-term gain. In the long run, the arbitrary exercise of the rule of law and the inequity of the laws themselves, undermines confidence in the institutions of the government. The people feel that government authority relies not only on force but also rests only in force.

Disorientation

As a consequence of sectarian violence, certain support structures within the Catholic community become disoriented. Essentially, the traumatuic situation confuses the source of cultural identities's original meanings and distorts their potential as sources of strength within a traumatic situation. Clinically, "disorientation" as the consequence of a trauamtic event includes "difficulty in concentrating, focusing thoughts, and making mental associations."[43] In terms of the manifestation of these clinical symptoms within the North of Ireland, disorientation includes a difficulty in making associations between components of community identity and anything but violence.

Theatre that takes its subject from the violence in the Six Counties performs the rupture created by colonial discourse and its effects on the alternative discourse. Essentially, the colonial projection of the colonized territory traumatically and violently shatters the coherent whole of that territory so that even the inhabitants of the colonized space can no longer see themselves as anything but disorganized objects of the colonizing mind; no longer do the colonized have the associations with their former culture and history that characterized and vitalized their coherent identity. Within a colonial context, the colonizing power directed at colonial subjects, can produce symptoms that, on a societal scale, mimic the individual sense of disorientation. In this regard, the colonial enterprise begins with a process that involves "the systematic accumulation of human beings and territories."[44] Further, all efforts to rebuild or refashion an identity manifest themselves in terms of opposition to the colonial discourse and not as components of a post-traumatic identity. Within the context of North of Ireland, the created sense of disorientation manifests itself in terms of the sectarianization of native language, religion, traditional sports, free association and speech, and in terms of a sense of fear and rivalry between the two sides. Specifically, "habitual patterns of social interaction, reinforced by social control . . . maintain social boundaries. It is these that have caused a division in society. And it is the social division that has created a need for distinctive cultural markers so that people can tell which person is on which side."[45] Essentially, the elements that should contribute to an ever-changing coherent cultural identity become predominantly, or at least primarily, sites of resistance or opposition; they become agents in the colonial struggle and not independent and integral cultural components.

The Troubles inform the coming to terms with community identity disrupting in Martin Lynch's and Brian Friel's plays, the former non-traumatic associations of religion and traditional music. Each becomes, rather than a marker of cultural identity and pride, a sign of difference, criminalization, racialization, and violence. In terms of religion, the

role of official Catholicism in defining and sustaining Nothern Catholic identity is widely recognised as having been central since partition until at least the late fifties. For a community that disliked and felt alien from the wider state, the parish became the main civic unit. . . . In the absence of political organisation and because Catholics felt no allegiance to the entity of Northern Ireland, the Church by default was the acknowledged chief source of authority and social coherence of a "state within a state."[46]

However, because religion became the main civic unit, and similar conclusions apply to traditional music, both became the targets of the official state and the primary sites of resistance to the official state, rather than the foundation for a coherent and unified cultural and spiritual identity. Basically, the consequences of the Troubles broke into fragments the former support structures of the Northern Catholic population, resulting in a process similar to what Edward Said calls "chrestomathy."[47] Chrestomathy involves the representation of a culture in "fragmented" form. Essentially, the Catholics in the North embrace their faith and traditions in order to discover a source of meaning and identity and discover instead a source of resistence to power and a stigma that targets them as objects of oppression and violence.

Specifically, in Martin Lynch's play, religion becomes a mark of division and a tool for hatred and oppression. Lynch's references to it demonstrate how the Troubles ruptured religious identity rooted in faith, a potential support in a time of violence, and reinforced old meanings of religion as a divide and a weapon between two peoples. In short, the Troubles highlight and strengthen old prejudices and fears regarding religious differences, contributing to a sense of hatred and suspicion between communities. Religion, particularly the Catholic religion, within the context of sectarian violence and oppression, becomes a mark of difference, a distinction of otherness. Importantly, the distinction is often used by the authorities to mark Catholics as different and dangerous. Essentially, the use of religion as a sectarian divide and tool for hatred severs religion from its bearings and from its source of spiritual comfort and potential as a source of strength in a time of crisis. Consequently, religion becomes disoriented and its sources of meaning become confused. Religion then becomes a mark of divergence and discord. Basically, the "differences between the two communities in North of Ireland are palpable. The lines of division tend to reinforce each other. . . . Although the lines of division are often considered to be religious in character, religion is best seen as a badge of difference."[48]

Lynch clearly demonstrates this point in *The Interrogation of Ambrose Fogarty*, at the time of Fogarty's arrest. When asked his religion Fogarty replies "none."[49] He is told that the officials will "put down RC."[50] Significantly, Fogarty tries to escape a religious label. In saying "none," he does not hide for fear that his religious affiliation would serve as a potential focus for brutality; later remarks by the authorities indicate that he could not in any case hide his affiliation. Further, it is clear that Fogarty chooses to define his religion as "none," rather, to place himself apart from violence and sectarian hatred, and to place himself outside the control of the authorities's labels of difference, their mark of "Catholic" and all that might imply. Moreover, that the authorities label Fogarty so quickly as "RC" indicates that they routinely and easily use religious labels to mark difference, almost as a tool for humiliation. Religion becomes part of the criminalization process. The arresting officers tell Fogarty that for "these puposes" he will be defined as Catholic. For the purposes of arrest, for the purposes of catagorization, for the purposes of control, he will be labeled Catholic. Additionally and significantly, the authories do not use the full term Catholic to label Fogarty. Rather, they use the shortened version "RC." The initials imply that through the use of labels rather than the name, religious difference and faith can be expressed in shorthand. Roman Catholic faith is unimportant and unimpressive as a collection of initials. It is not a threat. However, his faith also serves to remind Fogarty that because it has become part of his label that he too is unimportant and unimpressive.

Essentially, religion becomes a tool of demarcation and criminalization. Further reinforcing the disorientation of religious strength, Fogarty speaks of the night the Troubles broke out in the Lower Falls: "I was supposed to be seeing a wee girl that night, from the Shankill Road . . . . As soon as I saw the mob on the road, that was that."[51] Lynch's remarks indicate that the Troubles recognized boundaries that already existed. The crowd does not indicate that he, as a Catholic, should not go to the Protestant Shankill Road. Rather, the crowd reminds him that religion could be used in the context of violence as a reason for brutality. Religion, in this context, becomes a mark of division and seperateness. The Troubles put religious issues in the forefront of human interaction. Rather than serve as a private source of strength, they become a public mark of difference. Although Fogarty's remarks indicate that the potential of religious conflict has always been a part of life in West Belfast, the Troubles made it an unavoidable and the most notable part of life. Furthermore, Fogarty's remarks imply that the recognition of religious difference as a potential threat to self is a sign that religion is a social divider rather than a mark of spiritual support. Reinforcing the sectarian potential of religious distinction, Peter, a prison official, asks Fogarty, "When were you born, '53?" and remarks that he [Peter], "probably did [play football against Fogarty]. God, I used to hate playing against the Newsboys. All wee tough Fenians from York Street."[52] Fogarty replies that he "wasn't from York Street" and that there were "always" some "protestants in our team."[53] Here, Peter's use of religious difference indicates, as does Fogarty's reference to his abortive date with a Protestant girl, that, although the Troubles did not create the boundaries and suspicions associated with religious difference, they did accentuate them. Clearly, Peter's remarks indicate that he, as a child, feared being beaten by the team from the York Street district. His use of the child's phrase suggests that his adult recollection, informed by the re-emergence of the Troubles and open sectarian conflict, recalled a child's memory; an adult would not consciously use the phrase "beaten up." It is a young boy's phrase. Furthermore, his use of the terms "York Street" and "Fenian" also suggest an old currency of demarcation and fear. The word "Fenian" is used on a number of different levels. By Catholics, it is often a mark of pride referencing the ancient Irish tradition as well as Fenian opposition to British rule in the nineteenth century. However, the Protestests will often use the term as a derisive and demeaning reference to Catholics; Peter uses the term in this sense. Furthermore,

Peter chooses to define Fogarty's team in terms of their "York Street" identification. The place carries a connotation of violence and potential threat. Louis Mac Neice, in *Autumn Journal*, writes "how we used to expect, . . . When the wind blew from the west, the noise of shooting . . . In Belfast in the York Street district" (XVI, ll.21-22 & 24). Significantly, that Peter would remember the Catholic boys as primarily as source of threat, while speaking with Fogarty, indicates that he views all his interactions with Catholics through the Troubles. He does not remember the details of the game nor the fact that the team was made up of both Catholics and Protestants. Rather, he only remembers the sectarian characteristics of the interaction. For Peter, religion is an irrevocable boundary. It marks all cross-community interactions, even the recollection of a boy's game is characterized in sectarian terms. Like all the interactions between the characters of Lynch's play that evoke religious references, Peter's remarks reveal how the Troubles rupture the natural associations of religion and identity so that religious affiliation stands not so much for spirituality and cultural association but for sectarian differentiation.

Whereas Martin Lynch traces the origins and implications of religion as a site of oppression and difference, Friel explores religion as a place of reaction to violence. For Friel there is less intellectualization and more instinctual reaction. Religion in *The Freedom of the City* becomes a signal that faith is used as a response to potential threat and as a form of magical protection. Significantly, in Friel's play, religion becomes part of female expression and identification. In representing women's expression of faith, Brian Friel gives voice to what is a predominantly feminine form of identification with their faith in the context of sectarian conflict. "Women in particular, . . . say that although they have little or no interest in an Irish nation-state, they are forced to describe themselves as nationalist because they think British unionist-majority Northern Ireland will always be sectarian: meaning biased against Catholics."[54] For women in Catholic communities, anti-Catholic bias and prejudice compel them to see themselves as nationalist. Moreover, within their particular expression of nationalism, religious terms and symbols take on a unique significance, confusing their intended and, perhaps, most potentially helpful association with spirituality as a means of coming to terms with violence. Rather, religious expression becomes only a means of reacting to trauma. For Lily, religious expression involves voicing shock and horror at a British military presence. She says, "Jesus, Mary and Joseph there's this big Saracen."[55] Strictly speaking, Lily's words are a religious ejaculation, a short prayer designed to give immediate spiritual comfort. Obviously, however, it is not used here to summon spiritual strength. Rather, she uses it to mark surprise at the power of the force arrayed against her and to emphasize that she is completely physically vulnerable to the armored vehicle. Further, the ejaculation is also meant to be partly humorous, to allow her audience to recognize her physical helplessness in the face of pursuit by this vehicle and the inappropriate application of physical force. Do the British authorities really need a Saracen to get this woman whose only means of protection is an ejaculation? However, on an allegorical level, her use of the ejaculation juxtaposed with the reference to the British armored vehicle as a "Saracen," its military name, also serves to reinforce the ironic use of religious expression in a military and violent context. She uses the religious ejaculation. The British call their vehicle by a name reserved in ancient use for non-Christian warriors. Laid side-by-side, the two reinforce the confused application of religious terminology and phrases in a violent context. Both terms are effective. The British military vehicle does summon, as it is meant to do, the negative connotations of an Islamic warrior to intimidate the populace. Lily's ejaculation does humorously define her shock and hopelessness. However, neither expression summons any spiritual content. Consequently, the lack of spiritual resonance points out a clear disorientation in the use of religious terms. They no longer have their original meaning. They can no longer provide their intended comfort. In a further example, Friel makes manifest the distortion of religious symbols. Lily descibes a friend who "wears a miraculous medal" and "swears" that it's better than a "gas-mask."[56] For Lily's friend, religion serves as a magic charm but not as a substantive guard against violence. The friend is clearly a bit absurd, but that her friend believes it to be true indicates that the friend clutches to religious symbols in an effort to ward off authoritarian danger. She instinctively uses it as a shield, reaches for its, as she sees it, potential magical abilities rather than any spiritual inner strength the object might bring. In this sense, she demonstrates that religion is inadequate to face the real physical danger at hand, but her gesture also shows that she feels some need for protection and instinctively reaches for a religious means of protection, a means that marks her as Catholic. It demonstrates that she wants to reach for her faith in the hope that faith will provide the comforts it ought but that, somehow, the violence surrounding her has dislodged religion from its moorings of true support. Her use of religion points out her need and indicates how, because of the violence, her needs are not met on a spiritual level. She cannot think about those needs, she can only think about physical safety. The medal becomes a disoriented symbol. It should represent her religious faith and a reminder of spirituality. However, she uses a sacramental for physical effects. It becomes a magic charm. The threat around her, the gas and Lily's Saracen, both literally and spiritually block the vision, so that religion is used as a mask, of escape or humor, rather than as a substantive source of strength.

The disorientation of structures and symbols of support in the face of traumatic threat is not limited to religious expression. Traditional music also becomes distorted within the context of violence. Like religious devotion, traditional music can serve as a source of pride and meaningful opposition by affirming the true character of the Catholic populace. However, too often it deteriorates into simply a mark of opposition to British and/or Protestant rule, or it becomes a mark of the internalization of stereotypes and consequently a perpetuation of violence. Essentially, the Troubles rupture traditional music's affiliation, as represented in *The Freedom of the City*, with community pride, support, and identity, and, instead, music finds a disoriented mode of self-definition within the identifiers of the colonizing power. Lily, in an effort to evoke pride asks her companions to "look at [remember] the Nazareth House Ceilidhe Band, thumping away at concerts all over the world, trained armies couldn't stop them."[57] Initially, Lily frames her pride in the traditional band's acceptance throughout the world but, ultimately, focuses on its ability to withstand "trained armies." Her pride narrows into the context of sectarian conflict in the North. Her means of expression of confidence in the band betrays a pre-occupation with the conflict in the North, so that the band's achievements can only be considered through metaphors of the Troubles. Ultimately, Friel represents a more insidious form of traditional music in relation to violence. In the course of the play, a figure appears, identified as the "balladeer," who sings a jingoistic Republican song while the three innocent victims of British violence are surrounded. The balladeer stands for an impression of the Catholic population, and stands, as a specific type of musician, for nationalism and the "minority." He enters with a "glass in one hand, a bottle in the other. He is unsteady on his feet but his aggressive jubilance makes him articulate. . . . . As he staggers across the stage he is followed by an accordionist and a group of dancing children."[58] The balladeer functions on four levels. On one level, he exploits the deaths of the three victims for nationalistic purposes, distorting in his song the lives and affiliations of the three. He makes them Republican martyrs denuding the humanity of the victims and unwittingly supporting the British version of their affiliation. On another level, he exploits the deaths to receive money to feed his drinking habit. On yet another level, he functions as a type of pied piper, demonstrating the insidious effect the disoriented use of traditional music can have on young people by summoning feelings not of ethnic pride but of sectarian hatred. Finally, the balladeer reinforces the stereotype of the drunken and unkempt Irishman. Brian Friel links certain types of representations of ethnic pride to sectarian violence by demonstrating how what should be a source of cultural identification becomes simply a further representation of division, confusion, and violence.

Clearly as Brian Friel's and Martin Lynch's plays reveal the trauma consequence of re-emergent sectarian conflict in the North places in crisis certain fundamental aspects of Catholic identity, which results in a sense of disorientation and loss of self-control. Very often, the forces that rupture Catholic identity come from the outside, from Protestant or British authorities, waging a campaign of brutality. Seamus Heaney, in "Casualty," captures what the Catholic population, driven to extremes by violence can do to itself, becoming an image of authoritarian oppression:

The common funeral
Unrolled its swaddling band,
Lapping, tightening
Till we were braced and bound
Like brothers in a ring. (ll.55-59)

Many in the Northern Catholic community, irrevocably wounded by decades of sectarian conflict, continue to turn to organizations such as the Continuity Irish

Republican Army, hoping to assert their identity in terms of reciprocal violence and brutality. However, many more support the reformed nature of Northern Republicanism, articulated by Gerry Adams in his recent "yes" campaign in favor of the Good Friday Agreement, embracing an identity rooted in positive affirmations of Catholic identity.

NORTHERN PROTESTANT EXPERIENCE

W. R. Rodgers, an ordained Presbyterian minister and native of Belfast, hearing of the re-emergence of the Troubles from his California residence, wrote "Home Thoughts from Abroad" in which he reflects on "the thin thunder/Of far-off invective and old denunciation/Lambasting and lambegging the homeland" (ll.1-3). Rodgers goes on to speak of another Presbyterian minister, Ian Paisley, and to "wish him well from the bottom of my heart/Where truth lies bleeding, its ear-drums burst/By the blather of his hand-me-down talk" (ll.31-33). Within Rodgers's reflections on his home, he reveals insights on aspects of conflict and turmoil, that were at that time, re-emerging within certain factions of Northern Presbyterian society. Indeed, open sectarian conflict traumatized Protestant society at large rupturing long-held concepts of identity and resulting in a sense of anxiety and isolation. Consequently, voices articulating "invective and old denunciation" began to have a new currency in the Six Counties because of the apparent re-assurance they granted. Moreover, Rodgers, in his personal reactions, his sense that "truth lies bleeding" as a result of Paisley's rhetoric and its renewed popularity, anticipates decades of bloodshed and the sacrifice of truth for, as Terence Brown puts it, "the powers of some eschatologically prescient prophet."[59] Indeed, Rodgers accurately perceives the growing mainstream acceptance, and consequence of that acceptance, of the more radical aspects of Presbyterian tradition, what Louis MacNeice, the son of a Church of Ireland bishop, writing a generation earlier, called the "voodoo of the Orange bands/Drawing an iron net through darkest Ulster" (*Autumn Journal* XVI: 25-26).

Within certain factions of Northern Irish Presbyterian society, as represented in Graham Reid's plays, particular cultural and historical myths survive that reveal significant aspects of Protestant identity, including myths of superiority over Catholics, assumptions of security regarding home and work, and values surrounding ideas of masculinity in connection with home and family. Among the myriad of symbols and metaphors,

the Siege of Derry has the most important symbolic significance for Protestants since it evokes for them the idea of wicked, uncivilized, tyrannical people outside the walls confronting civilized, freedom-loving and 'religious' people within. These views reflect the Protestant stereotypes which categorize Catholics as superstitious, untidy and feckless in comparison with the Protestants's rationality, tidiness and hard work.[60]

Within this metaphor, actively commemorated in murals and in marches, the myth of Protestant hegemony and security manifests itself. Specifically, a loose racial distinction between Catholics and Protestants emerges. On the one hand, Catholic populations survive on primitive and uncivilized values, manifesting themselves in irrational spirituality and pseudo-pagan rites. Further, a conception of Catholics emerges, that traces its lineage back to Giraldus Cambrensis and the earliest representations of Irish people in English fictional and non-fictional accounts of Ireland and that represents the indigenous population as incapable of personal self-control and communal self government. The Catholic population, from this perspective, must be kept apart, so as not to contaminate the Protestant settler community, and also must be kept out of positions of authority within government and industry, so as not to allow inefficiency and innate destructive tendencies to interfere with efficient forms of business and law. On the other hand, Protestant society and individuals construct an outpost of civilization, insular and secure, embodying the ideals of rationality and industry. Within this myth, the Protestants establish a community in the North that serves as model and symbol of redemption for their irrational neighbors. Ultimately, Protestant society must remain eternally vigilant, lest their values and outpost of civilization die. Indeed, their "historical self vision is of endless repetition of repelled assaults, without hope of absolute finality or fundamental change in their relationship to their surrounding and surrounded neighbours."[61] Growing from the view of a society as civilizing outpost in a savage land, Protestant values of siege and saving example spread to familial self-conceptions. In this respect, the home and family develop as models of a sacred society. Within such a framework, the father and husband emerges as defender of traditional values.

Moreover, the reemergence of open sectarian conflict in 1968 reenforced the most negative aspects of Protestant identity in some quarters. An exclusive attitude began to emerge that reinforced ancient prejudices and self-conceptions. In order to maintain authority over Catholics and over themselves, "men 'well settled in their religion'" fashioned a God and a self discipline that was "austere and unrelenting" and which embodied "fundamentals of fear, suspicion and triumphalism."[62] From such a perspective, the "Ulster Protestant community is . . . a community which turns inwards upon itself, embodying all the more repressive aspects of Calvinist culture,"[63] including repressive governmental structures. Essentially, in "defence of what they perceived to be their ultimate liberty, they circumscribed the individual liberty of others within the metaphorical city."[64] As each Catholic agitation, ranging from civil rights demonstrations to armed assaults, threatened the metaphorical and literal city, Protestant assumptions about safety and security fell away, resulting in, on a community level, what therapists studying post-traumatic stress disorder diagnose, on the individual level, as heightened anxiety and a sense of loneliness and vulnerability.

Anxiety

Within the context of the North of Ireland Troubles, anxiety resulting from traumatic rupture manifests itself in terms of fears associated with the loss of self identity and with places that once offered comfort. In clinical terms, "anxiety . . . included reports of paralyzing anxiety, fear of death, and thoughts of death. Its association with insomnia suggests the problems casualties had in falling and staying asleep were caused by their fears."[65] In theatrical representations of the Troubles, "anxiety" and a "pre-occupation with death" manifest themselves in a sense of "exile" and insecure feelings associated with "home." Specifically, drama "performs" the result of colonial expansion on the consciousness of the colonized and "performs" an implied pre-colonial landscape, in which notions of home and native land should, and perhaps once did, offer the familiar comforts of safety and security. Essentially, drama highlights the distinction between a view of the colonized territory, as one in which colonial subjects need the matrixes of the colonized power because indigenous support structures are inadequate or non-existent, and an alternative view of the colonized territory, as one in which the native land and people have been so devastated by colonial violence and rupture that an impression of colonial rule permeates even the most essential of basic social and cultural supports. Essentially, the colonized mind becomes a site of traumatic impression upon which an indelible and inescapable mark of violence, death, and anxiety have imposed themselves. In the North of Ireland, playing into the matrixes established by the colonized power, both Nationalist and Unionist factions invent, through visual and narrative myths, a sacred past, whose participants drive sectarian conflict; in order to remain loyal to sacred memory, no compromise in the values of the past can be made. Indeed, it is only through complete devotion to the sacred ideals of the past that the promised future can manifest itself. To achieve that sacred past a "savior" is devised, who "is constructively destructive. His task is to step in and strengthen and reconstruct the body he has come to take charge of."[66] Conspicuously absent from this "sacred" vision is a confidence and security in the present, an alternative view of the North in which people struggle to find a sense that normalcy can exist. Indeed, the view of the Troubles that sees tribal conflict and division as the cause for violence so obscures the present that there is no possible return home, for home "is often portrayed as a place of alienation and displacement" and the "family is sometimes situated as a site of oppression."[67] Through this discourse home and the security of the present become obscured in an official or legitimized pursuit of violence, rupturing the normal factors that condition and stimulate identity. Consequently, the only identities available are notions of exile and displacement.

The connection between the clinical definition and the manifestation of anxiety in Graham Reid's drama involves fear of loss and paralyzing insecurity. Specifically, for Protestants in the North of Ireland, anxiety consequent of the Troubles involves fear associated with the traumatic loss of places that offer security and with masculine self-conception. Within Graham Reid's plays, anxiety permeates a Protestant society whose colonial identity of security and superiority finds itself challenged by the violence that consumes Northern society. Victor, the central character of *The Closed Door*, declares that "[i]t's the troubles, you see. I can't hide anywhere. I've been exposed, flushed out."[68] Victor speaks, specifically, of his cowardice, yet his fear stands as metaphor for a certain group within the Northern Protestant community. The group's insular conception of security did not allow that the prejudice and discrimination directed at Catholics is symptomatic of a society whose security was based on oppression and discrimination, whose privileged position relies on the violence and threat of violence consequent of years of systematic and institutionalized hatred and exclusion. Specifically, within *The Closed Door*, Victor is an "Everyman" of the working-class Presbyterian community. He has a secure job, a nice home, and a wife. However, his circumstances expose the fractures within that community. In a series of violent acts, masked men, whose political affiliation comes from both the Republican and Loyalist communities, destroy his confidence and, metaphorically, Presbyterian hegemony. Specifically, a series of violent acts strips him of his job, of his home, and of his family. Significantly, the site of the Republican attack comes at his place of employment, the location where discrimination against Catholics would have been most manifest. The nightmares that ensue, after witnessing the death of a co-worker, in fact after pointing the co-worker out to the masked men, cause Victor to leave his position with the company and retreat into his home, the symbol of his insular safety. Still, the Troubles follow him there, manifesting themselves not only in his nightmares but also in their very real presence. His mother-in-law declares that she "wouldn't like to be on my own tonight. I've a feeling that this is going to be one of those horrible weekends, riots and shootings and bombing. You wouldn't know who'd come knocking at your door when darkness falls."[69] Her fear, directed against the threat of riots and violence by Catholics, the manifest challenge to Protestant security within their homes, becomes an accurate and ironic prediction of violence that will, literally, appear on Victor's doorstep. An old friend will come to his door seeking refuge from a Protestant paramilitary organization, only to be ignored by Victor. The friend dies, brutally killed just a few feet away from Victor. The Troubles literally invade his home. It is important to note that Protestant violence ruptures his sense of safety. Symbolically, the forces that destroy his life represent the same powers that supported it. In specific terms, as Victor finds himself "sitting down, his back to the door, crying silently,"[70] his safety is ruptured, his identity, vested in his home and all that it represents, is destroyed by the same type of Protestant paramilitary organizations whose use of force and forced segregation and discrimination granted Victor a relatively privileged role in Northern society. In the end, he longs "to be able to sleep at night, without this feeling that I'm sleeping in someone else's skin"[71]; he is left with no sense of self. He has lost his job, the symbol of his authority within his family and the manifest proof of his superiority over Catholics. He, subsequently, loses his sense of security within his home, the symbol of safety and insular identity. Ultimately, any sense of trust between himself and his wife comes to an end as a consequence of his lies and cowardice. The idyllic life of a Protestant "Everyman" becomes exposed to violence and loses its mask of security, superiority, and safety.

Within *The Death of Humpty Dumpty*, anxiety destroys Protestant middle-class hegemony, rupturing an identity based on certainty and power. The father in the play finds himself critically injured as a consequence of witnessing paramilitary violence; the audience never learns the affiliation of the organization performing the violent acts. After his injuries, his family discovers the layers of his false identity. They find out that he had an affair and that his relationship to them based itself in deception and manipulation. In the play's final scene, the father begs his son David for forgiveness: "That night, David, that night. . .I lay and watched all this blood running past my head. . . . I was dying, I was dying son, I thought of your mother and you, I thought of Judith and Mary. No one else entered my head. I thought about the people I really loved. Now I'm back on the doorstep David. You can't just turn your back on me, you can't."[72] As in *The Closed Door*, an authority figure within the family is gravely injured. The home provides no safety or security. Once again, the injured party feels dissociated from his identity. Whereas for Victor, the sense of separation is the result of psychological injuries, the father's wounds, in *The Death of Humpty Dumpty*, are the result of physical injuries; he is paralyzed by a bullet and, consequently, cannot feel his wounds and does not immediately realize that the blood he sees is his blood. However, his plea reveals his still very present sense of superiority. Although he is physically and emotionally vulnerable, he nonetheless rhetorically places himself within his old matrixes of power. He tells his son that he, as father, is on the doorstep, emphasizing not his injuries, and vulnerability within the hospital, but rather stressing the symbol of home and his former position of authority within the home, not realizing that his infidelity destroyed the associations of home and any authority those associations might give him over his son. Further, the father reveals that his "dying" thoughts concerned the people he "really loved," suggesting that the father distinguishes between those he pretends to love, like his mistress, and his family. His appeal to "love" then rings hollow because, although it is an appeal to a natural sense of familial identity, it reveals the father's extra-familial liaison and reveals the father's manipulation of "real" and perceived sentiment in order to achieve physical and emotional satiation. David answers his father by telling him not to "beg me Dad. If you had died that night on the doorstep, I'd never have stopped loving you. But if we bring you home you'll spend the rest of your life begging . . . I couldn't bear it. We can't take you home."[73] Ultimately, the son rejects his father as an individual, embracing not the reality of a vulnerable figure but rather the symbol of fatherhood. As dead martyr, the son would have accepted the father, even though the father's affair would have doubtlessly come to light the same way it came to light as a consequence of the father's injuries. Further, David does not reject his father because he had an affair but because they would "never be able to look each other in the eyes again," because the father would not be an authority figure. Finally, David kills his father which "functions not only as an image of the horror of the violence but also as an image of the absolute necessity of violence for the maintenance and perpetuation of an identity which takes for granted the notion of a fixed position of superiority."[74] Essentially, David destroys his father's life because a paralyzed father would mean the destruction of assumed authoritarian relationships, of a means of familial relation based not on love but on power. By killing his father, David kills the manifestation of weakened authority and assumes the power and hypocrisy once epitomized by his father's cavalier behavior. Once again, as in *The Closed Door*, the ultimate manifestation of violence, which strikes at home and family and the ultimate symbols of secure Protestant identity, does not come from the outside but rather from within. In *The Closed Door*, Protestant paramilitaries strike at the heart of a Protestant's security. In *The Death of Humpty Dumpty*, a son kills his father indicating that the underlying assumptions of family life based on love and trust are false, and revealing its similarity to the society created by Protestant rule, that seems like an ideal world but is actually a world of power, manipulation, and cruelty whose outward sign is the systematic discrimination against Catholics but whose inward consequence is the destruction of the heart of Protestant assumptions of security in home and work. The father in *Humpty Dumpty* then stands as metaphor. Paralyzed and vulnerable, he appeals to the assumptions of his former life, assumptions his behavior proves false and manipulative. In the end, those assumptions maintain themselves through the cruelty of his son just as the Protestant self-conception of a stable, secure, peaceful community maintains itself through violence and hatred.

In addition to the Troubles revealing some aspects of the underlying violence and cruelty of Protestant society and archetypes of home and family, Reid represents the anxiety consequent of violence rupturing masculine archetypes of identification, including the concept of hero, husband, and father. In each play, masculine standards are referred to, evaluated, shown to be useless in the face of the Troubles, and, subsequently, destroyed. In *The Closed Door*, Victor's wife, Doreen, tells her mother that she doesn't "want" her "husband to be a dead hero. Too many men have walked into danger with their eyes open. How many stubborn men would be alive today if they'd listened to advice and not take silly risks."[75] Doreen's comments were prompted by her mother's argument that Victor should be more like her husband who "went right through the war. He stood on the beaches at Dunkirk. Men have to stand up for these things."[76] Mrs. Courtney's insistence that "men" ought to behave in a certain way within the context of a war indicates that she values a certain standard of male behavior in connection with violence. Clearly, in her view, Victor's reaction to the Troubles does not fulfil a standard of male behavior. It is significant also that Mrs. Courtney chooses to demonstrate the masculine ideal by talking about war; her phrase "these things" refers both to heroism and to war. Heroism then, by her associations, exists within conflict; indeed, if it is to manifest itself in certain ways, it must have conflict.

However, Doreen exposes the ultimate futility of her mother's values of heroism by substituting the word "danger" for "war" and the word "silly risks" for heroism. For Doreen, her mother's ideals of heroism are associated with death. She does not mention the word hero alone but rather links it with the word "dead," as if the two words can stand for the same condition. Undaunted, Mrs. Courtney later continues to challenge Victor's masculinity within traditional archetypes by telling him "I'm not afraid of you. If you ever lift your hand to me I'll see you go to jail for it. My daughter's working to keep you. You should be ashamed of yourself. Why don't you go back to work like the rest of the men? They're not cringing behind their wives. Nobody shot you. What are you so scared of?"[77] Mrs. Courtney confronts Victor with the "shame" of having his wife support him. According to her, he is not like "the rest of the men." Victor assumes a stereotypical feminine role while his wife assumes the masculine role. She works. She stands in front of Victor to defend him. Clearly, Mrs. Courtney values the more traditional relationship of husband and wife. She obviously feels that he is not fulfilling his husbandly duties. However, even within her contemptuous statements, she inadvertently undermines her own standards of masculine behavior by demonstrating her true agenda. She tells Victor that he was not "shot" immediately after she tells him that his wife fulfils the traditional masculine role as breadwinner. By associating the prospect of violence with stereotypical masculinity, Mrs. Courtney accepts the likelihood that masculine behavior could end in violence. Importantly, she does not stress Victor's ability to work or to earn a living. Rather, she stresses his fitness within the context of violence, demonstrating that a male figure as combatant is her priority rather than the male figure as breadwinner. She accepts the notion that the role of a husband should be to stand in front of the wife and protect her from the prospect of violence rather than simply earning a living. Mrs. Courtney unconsciously associates masculinity with death in the same way her daughter consciously associates heroism with death, undermining the stated goals of a particular masculine ideal.

The Death of Humpty Dumpty demonstrates the futility of the flawed traditional role of husband within the context of the Troubles. The attending nurse, a Catholic nun, tells Heather that she (Sister) "didn't bring you here to talk about the normal husband you used to have. Have you the remotest idea what those gunmen have done to your husband? They've destroyed him. He's a helpless cripple. He can do nothing for himself, except talk, shout, swear. Do you understand that? You're going to have to be taught to look after him if he is ever to go home again."[78] Unlike Victor, Mr. Samson was not afraid. He opened the door. He was willing to stand in front of his house to protect his family. He fulfils the tradition role of husband. However, the "gunmen," and by association the Troubles, "destroyed" him and made him unfit for "normal" husbandly duties and responsibilities. Consequently, he exists as a "helpless cripple." Metaphorically, because the sister associates Mr. Sampson's role as husband with violence (significantly, she does not refer to him as "George," a referent that would recognise his individuality rather than his role as Heather's husband), and suggests that he can no longer function as a husband, the play posits George Sampson as a type of husband figure destroyed by the Troubles. The play, therefore, creates a link between the values of the archetypal husband as protector and care giver and the destruction of those values within the Troubles. It is as if one leads inexorably to the other. Further reinforcing a connection between archetypal masculine images and violence, in *The Closed Door*, Mrs. Courtney talks about Victor's friend Slabber's creation of his father's identity Mrs Courtney tells Victor that "it's difficult not to sneer at a man who tells you his father was a major in the royal Marines, when you know full well he was a doorman at a local cinema."[79] Slabber creates a more masculine image of his father. Significantly, Slabber's shame lies not so much in his father's economic status (he does not simply make his father a rich industrialist or successful business man) but in his father's lack of masculinity. Within Slabber's fantasy, fatherhood can only be valued as it is measured within the status of warrior. He creates a father who is a military man, an individual capable of skillful violence. Therefore, the role of father not only as protector but as armed perpetrator of violence becomes the most significant aspect of fatherhood for Slabber. He creates an inheritance of violence to compensate for what he sees as his father's shortcomings. However, Mrs. Courtney demonstrates the inadequacy of Slabber's fantasy by "sneering" at him. She dismisses the value of an individual who would use external sanctions of masculinity to legitimize life within a violent society, yet she never questions her rather arbitrary use of masculine ideals to cope with violence. In both plays, Graham Reid structures scenes in such a way as to expose the values of archetypical masculine roles and to demonstrate the ultimate shallowness and inadequacy of those identities in the face of the anxiety consequent of the Troubles.

Loneliness and Vulnerability

In terms of the conflict in the Six Counties and its effect on Protestant identity, the clinical concept of "loneliness and vulnerability," as a consequence of traumatic rupture, manifests itself in terms of loss of authority. Specifically, on the clinical level,

loneliness and vulnerability . . . occur together. The loneliness of the casualties may have resulted from their being away from their homes and families; from being in a new unit; from the loss of friends and buddies in combat; and from the recognition that, however one lives, in death one is alone. The feeling of vulnerability arose from the reality that the soldiers had few means of effectively countering or evading the dangers to which they are exposed.[80]

Theatrical representations of Northern violence "perform" a sense of loneliness and vulnerability that arises when the discourse associates traumatic rupture with the sources of comfort that would normally sustain individuals exposed to violence. Consequently, the discourse that arises from support structures of family and society finds itself in direct confrontation with the colonial power. The alternative discourse offers not only an escape and cure for the pain of violence but also an alternative to violence. However, because the violence associates trauma with the sources of comfort and security, emphasizing the vulnerability to violence of those structures, the alternative discourse finds its ability to counter the colonial power handicapped. Within an Irish context, the colonizer and his agents in paramilitary organizations have focused their attacks on a community as a consequence of its associations with a particular religious inheritance and focus their attacks on people while within their particular community. The people of the North, like Fanon's "Negro," discover that their "metaphysics, or, less pretentiously, . . . customs and the sources on which they were based, were wiped out because they were in conflict with a civilization that [they] did not know and that imposed itself on"[81] them. Consequently, the belief system and cultural support system, with its "imaginative response to the overwhelming burdens of human suffering: disease, mutilation, grief, age, and death,"[82] find their ability to offer a compensation or a counter to trauma hindered. The colonial will associates its violence with a particular cultural or familial support, impressing upon that support the inevitable and indelible reminder of death and violence and an association with trauma. Certainly, it is an attestation to the strength of the various communities in the North that they have maintained considerable resistance to the violence, within the teachings of their respective churches and within their various cultural organizations. However, it is also true that religious leaders and organizations have not been able to offer the comfort they might otherwise have to their communities if the violence had not so ingrained itself into the religious and cultural tradition. Thus, the people in the North of Ireland find the traditional comforts of culture, history, religious community, and religious faith indelibly tainted with violent rupture as a direct consequence of the colonial struggle.

Essentially, loneliness as a consequence trauma tends to result from an individual isolating himself from all that is familiar, and the emotional and social support family, home, and friends can bring. Further, vulnerability results from a recognition of isolation and the consequent inability to come to terms with violence. In connection with Protestant identity in the North, the Troubles do occasionally literally destroy people's homes and families, as was the case with the Enniskillen bomb.[83] However, such traumatic experience is not limited to Protestants. Catholics also lose their friends and families as a consequence of sectarian violence. Significantly, the uniquely Protestant experience of loneliness and vulnerability results from the loss of authority the Troubles can bring, most especially loss of authority as men, as Protestants (non-Catholics), and, for the characters of Graham Reid's *The Death of Humpty Dumpty*, as members of a superior social class. For the Protestants in Reid's plays, familiar comforts such as the concept of position in society, as home as a place removed from Catholic experience, and as life distant from violence and secure in power find themselves destroyed by the Troubles leaving the characters[84] isolated and vulnerable.

As the violence encroaches upon and then invades his life, George Sampson loses a sense of power he formerly associated with his station in life as a man or as a Protestant or as a member of a superior class. In each case, the former components of control and the authority he vested in the individual are referenced, the violence that destroyed the sense of superiority and dominance is associated with the Troubles or the cultural and political dynamic in the North, and the victim's current state of vulnerability and/or isolation is implicitly or explicitly identified with what is considered an inferior type. Clearly, "George [Sampson] conceives of his suffering primarily in terms of a loss of authority," particularly his loss of authority as a man. Indeed, the "torment of George's suffering as a cripple" is "that he now finds himself in the position of helplessness and dependency which he had previously associated with women."[85] Within the play, Doyle, speaking directly to the audience asks, "when is a man not a man?" and answers, "when he's in a wheelchair." He then proceeds to comment on both his and George's situation: "You're going to live, but you'll never walk again, or wash yourself, or shave. Your manhood, your dignity, your self-respect will be drained away. . . . You can talk, some social intercourse, but no sexual."[86] With his lines, Doyle defines what he considers to be the hallmarks of manhood and self-control. They include a sense of dignity and self-respect but not when associated with emotional or physical contact but with sexual contact, and a certain type of sexual contact. Manly self-respect, in Doyle's estimation, involves the ability to be not a receptive or attentive partner but rather the active or aggressive individual. Manhood, then, by association, is vested within a sense of dominance and physically controlling actions. Subsequently, Doyle links the physical disability and the accident of the Troubles to a state of subservience and death at the hands of those who threaten to expose the patient's vulnerability and isolation as a consequence of his no longer possessing his manhood. The gunmen, the "they," Doyle tells an audience, "didn't kill you on the doorstep," the center and symbol of masculine self-control and autonomy. The Troubles did not deal the lethal blow. Rather, they simply revealed an individual's susceptibility. The death blow is dealt by the individual's friends. Doyle does not detail how the friends will engage their lethal potential and, certainly, his remarks ironically anticipate George's actual death. However, it is clear that the disabled patient will have to suffer the kindness and perhaps painful solicitude of his friends. He will no longer be able to physically manage his associations. He can no longer express dominance through sexuality or through overt gestures of power. Therefore, these trappings of dominance stripped away, the patient becomes vulnerable and isolated and subject to the manly control of others.

Likewise, George's position in the hospital ward challenges his sense of control as a Protestant. Indeed, considering that the play "reveals not so much the historical 'facts's of the crisis, but rather the psychological conditions governing much of the conflict: the feeling that violence is terrifying but also necessary for the maintenance and protection of a particular notion of identity based on authority,"[87] and considering that the play reveals that George's injury leaves him, with the exception of Willy, under the dominance and control of Catholics, Sister and Gerry, then it is reasonable to conclude that the allegorical significance of George's injury involves his and the Protestants's potential loss of authority, an authority which bases itself on religious separation and superiority. Certainly, the true isolation of George's condition, as a Protestant in the hospital ward, mirrors the condition of Protestants on the island of Ireland. Indeed, the

protestant state of North of Ireland, a state born amid similar turmoil and conflict, perceives the same inevitability of catholic dominance in unification, which long ago led many protestants to oppose emancipation. The fear of losing their privileged position in such a state is central to protestant thinking and the sense of superiority which the British connection gives to protestants has long explained the considerable reluctance to question it.[88]

Clearly, as a consequence of his injury within the Troubles, George finds himself transported into a world of Catholic dominance. Further, once within this world, George relies on Catholics for emotional and psychological companionship and inspiration. However, the metaphor of his acceptance contrasts with his former world, a world in which Catholics and Protestant/Catholic relations only formulated themselves on the intellectual level, a level in which the reality of the Catholic experience in the North could be ignored. Also, on the intellectual level, George's, and by extension the Protestant community's, superiority and dominance could easily be maintained. Like the border between North and South, an artificial division between a territory with overwhelming Catholic dominance and a territory with limited Protestant dominance, George's intellectualizations create an artificial boundary that can only be maintained by the constant assertion of superiority and authority. Indeed,

Doyle's reference to Belfast's Milltown Cemetery clearly identifies him as a Catholic. As such, George's history lesson about the anti-sectarian gestures of the eighteenth-century Protestant Volunteers seems as irrelevant to Doyle's experience of contemporary Belfast in much the same way that the Sampsons's friendliness to Doyle in hospital contrasts and appears out of place with the pervasive sectarian attitudes outside the hospital which, for Doyle, make such friendships almost unimaginable. The experience of the hospital ward and George's history lessons are similarly isolated from ordinary quotidian reality.[89]

George's injury as a consequence of the Troubles, and his very real physical vulnerability, literally place him in a world of Catholic dominance and control. Metaphorically, George's condition mirrors the Protestant-controlled state in the North, a state whose authority finds itself challenged by the Troubles and the reminder of Catholic dominance on the island. Further, just as George's flimsy intellectual histories are out of touch with the reality of Doyle's experience, then the Protestant state's intellectual justifications of its harsh and authoritarian rule are out of touch with the reality of the political conditions in the North.

George's condition also reveals the distinction between the Protestant working and more privileged classes, a condition Edna Longley recognises as the "demoralisation of working-class Protestants and the apparent indifference of the Protestant middle class."[90] Specifically, George finds himself in a world that, when not under benevolent Catholic influence, is under the control of a dissatisfied and bitter working-class Protestant. The allegorical significance of George's predicament finds a resonance in the politics of middle-class Protestants who find themselves in opposition to, because they are out of touch with, the Protestant working class. For the middle class, Loyalism and Unionism, for the most part, remain a privileged intellectual position; they do not often have to deal with the consequences of the sectarian violence that results from such political views. However, George's privileged position, formally at a remove from the reality of the North, finds itself reduced to a vulnerability to working-class anger, as a consequence of the Troubles. Willie, the attendant, abuses George: "oh, here, getting all la-di-da are we? The point is that you do have to lie there and just listen to whatever I want to say."[91] Willie asserts his control, and metaphorically the control of the working class over the middle class, by referencing what he perceives to be George's sense of superiority. He is "getting all la-di-da." Subsequently, Willie reduces George to a position of inferiority asserting control in a hierarchal-class manner. Willie becomes "the boss." Essentially, sectarian violence destroys George's former authority and places himself in a vulnerable position rupturing his former identity as a superior. Doyle intellectualizes the situation to George by telling him that "it's there mate, it's all there. It's your whole attitude. You feel you're too good to be a cripple, don't you? It's beneath your dignity?"[92] Doyle's remarks reveal the impetus behind Willie's anger and reveal the source of George's true frustration. He feels vulnerable and isolated because the Troubles rupture his identity as an individual apart from sectarian divisions. The violence brings him into the reality of working-class Protestant life, a reality in which sectarian strife is constantly present, a world in which authority and hatred reveal themselves almost on a daily basis along with the very real consequence of maintaining such authority.

Clearly, as Reid's plays reveal, the trauma consequent of the re-emergence of sectarian conflict in the North places in crisis certain fundamental aspects of Protestant identity, which results in a sense of isolation and anxiety, recalling an image from W.R. Rodgers, "Home Thoughts from Abroad." He rationalizes that

... in this day and age
We can't really have giants lumbering
All over the place, cluttering it up,
With hair like ropes, flutes like telegraph poles,
And feet like tramcars, intent only on dogging
The fled horde of history and the Boyne. (24-29)

Rodgers's conclusions regarding the inappropriateness of extreme conceptions of identity and the ultimate harm they can bring seem more than a bit glib considering the decades of violence and thousands of deaths sectarian conflict has brought with it. However, writing in the late 1960s, he could not have forseen the complete tragedy of the Northern War. Nonetheless, he did anticipate the incongruent nature of extreme conceptions of identity in a contemporary society. Indeed, nearly thirty years after Rodgers's poem, many individuals in the Northern Presbyterian community have also begun to see the inappropriateness and extremism of antiquated notions of self and society. David Trimble's recent and more conciliatory and relatively pluralistic vision of the North of Ireland, articulated in his support of the Good Friday Agreement, won a majority, albeit a narrow majority, of Northern Protestant votes, while only a minority supported Ian Paisley's "no" campaign.

CROSS-BORDER/CROSS-COMMUNITY EXPERIENCE

In her *The Statue of the Virgin at Granard Speaks*, Paula Meehan writes of a "November wind sweeping across the border" and warns "its seeds of ice would cut you to the quick." She also writes of "ghost voyagers/on the wind that carries intimations/of garrison towns, walled cities, ghetto lanes/where men hunt each other and invoke/the various names of God as blessing/on their death tactics, their night manoeuvres" (ll.2-3 & 10-15). Within these lines Meehan explores some of the more tragic issues associated with the Northern War: the idea of sectarian conflict bleeding across the border, inter-community war in the North, and the blurred distinction between Northern communities united by common violent means. Meehan's poem goes on to explore an insulated town and its ability to ignore suffering within its borders only to have the traumatic results of that suffering haunt them. Her observations find a resonance with clinical analyses of suffering and reactions to trauma. Specifically, in the North of Ireland, the Troubles rupture formations of identity that bridge sectarian and colonial boundaries. As a consequence of traumatic reactions, "distancing" and "guilt" ultimately reinforce the divisions between Catholic and Protestant communities and between Irish communities on both sides of the border. In terms of "distancing," a retreat or method of relaxation actually seems to unite the two communities. Specifically, in *Catchpenny Twist,* Stewart Parker portrays "a protestant composer and a Catholic lyricist, churning out catchpenny songs alternately for loyalist or for republican buddies while hoping for their big break, winning the Eurovision Song Contest."[93] However, "these former teachers find they can't run far enough, fast enough when the warring factions discover their double game."[94] Music, once sectarian violence intrudes, actually becomes a source of suspicion and, ultimately, death; the fact that the musicians composed songs for both groups made them vulnerable to distrust. Moreover, the Troubles and partition also prompt and augment divisions between the North and the Republic:

Fear of loyalist reprisals is commonly suggested by Northern Catholics as reason enough for Southerners's distance. That seventy years of partition substantially contributed to different priorities and consequent lack of empathy is harder to admit. It is as though the admission would confer legitimacy on the border and the northern state by confirming that they have, in fact, split one people into two.[95]

Essentially, decades of division and a resurgence of violence in the late 1960s bolster a feeling of separation between communities across the border. "Guilty" reactions, produced as a consequence of surviving violence, also reinforce sectarian divisions. Specifically, family members who experience the loss of a brother/father/son will often memorialize the memory of their lost relative within sectarian structures, reinforcing the divisions between the communities. Specifically, in Dungannon, on the eve of the referendum on the Good Friday Agreement, a woman thought of her son who was "literally cut in two by a rocket which went through his car."[96] He goes "about the floor on his bottom using his arms to propel him. . . . His children, their friends are afraid of him because of how he looks."[97] The woman, Anne Slaine, "would like the situation in Ireland very much to change," but she worries that if, by voting yes, she is "betraying him and everything he believes in."[98] Similarly, on a larger scale, communities, out of a sense of duty and obligation to the "glorious" dead of generations past, will construct and bolster detailed yet divisive histories that actively contribute to contemporary violence. These obligations and guilt-inspired tributes, coupled with the failed efforts to distance themselves from violence, serve to rupture national and local non-sectarian identities.

Distancing

Clinical analysis concludes that certain individuals, in response to the threat of violence will imaginatively "distance" themselves from violence by constructing temporary fantasies of life distinct from suffering and death. Specifically, clinical analysis has recorded "reports of psychic numbing, fantasies of running, and thoughts about civilian life. All of these were means by which the soldiers tried to block the intrusion of unbearably threatening battlefield stimuli and/or to distance themselves mentally and emotionally from fighting."[99] "Distancing," experienced by many victims of traumatic violence, finds a resonance in theatrical representations of the Northern War. Specifically, drama "performs" the colonial act of appropriating and transforming the historical and even geographical record of a colonized territory. Drama also "performs" the colonial response; many in the North will fashion an immediate, imagined escape that grants temporary satisfaction but does not function as a long-term or even wholly satisfactory antidote to the traumatic experience of colonial appropriation. Significantly, the refashioned meaning within this context is a fantasy representing only an imagined escape from the tragic realities of colonial violence. Essentially, the colonial acts have so disrupted the colonized's imaginative and literal territory that any more than a fanciful and/or transient escape from violence is, within this context, futile. Consequently, the colonized's effort to "distance" themselves from rupture functions as a temporary numbing of the pain of a troubled history or a simply fanciful, and transitory, escape from violence. Essentially, for individuals in a colonized or recently de-colonized nation or place, such as the North or the

Republic, the past is a prompt for memories of oppression, humiliation, and appropriation; it is a break from the continuity of their history, a continuity disrupted by the colonizer. In addition to marking history,

one of the final moves of conquerors, after conquest, is the dividing up of territories, creating unnatural boundaries and thus ushering in perpetual struggle over space and place. In that context, invasions take on complex meaning. On the one hand, there is the need to reconstruct destroyed historical consciousness and the hierarchies of meaning bestowed there. On the other hand, there is the recognition that once these borders are created and change is instituted, we have entered a stage in which the meaning of location and ownership is already defined and almost irredeemably outside migratory consciousness.[100]

Boyce-Davies's comments find a resonance in the literal arbitrary boundary between the Six and Twenty-Six Counties. In doing so, the British partitioned the historic province of Ulster. Donegal, Cavan, and Monaghan became peripheral counties of a state. Boyce-Davies's observations also find a resonance in the created imaginative boundaries between the colonizer's idea of Ireland and what was the idea of the Irish nation before colonization. The British realized that "any division of this kind automatically leads to a growing apart. Once the two sundered parts of the country start to live their own lives, these fall into new patterns, governed by the specific needs and aspirations of the people living in the two areas."[101]

In Stewart Parker's *Catchpenny Twist* and in John Wilson Haire's *Within Two Shadows*, characters undergo a similar method of distancing that centers around notions of cross-community identity, either between the Protestant and Catholic communities of the North or between the Catholic communities on either side of the border. The characters sometimes attempt to escape violence by constructing a retreat from war through recreation and music. Importantly, the music becomes for them a way to structure a non-sectarian identity. However, the violence of the Troubles inevitably intervenes to destroy the construction, exposing it as simply an imaginative and limited escape. Similarly, the national identities linking North and South, within a Republican consciousness, find themselves ruptured when the prospect of violence compels certain individuals to imaginatively structure the South as a haven from violence, insular and removed from the North. Ultimately, however, the constructions actually cause further violence, demonstrating that such constructions offer only a temporary "block" against the reality of the Troubles.

In *Catchpenny Twist* and *Within Two Shadows*, respectively, Stewart Parker and John Wilson Haire offer the tantalizing possibility of a territory beyond sectarian violence, an area where religious affiliation and political identity matter little. More importantly, the area serves as a place of refuge from traumatic rupture. However, in each play, the possibility of a lasting refuge or identity beyond the Troubles proves impossible. Sectarian hatred and traumatic violence invade all retreats. The most notable yet failed refuge involves music. In *Catchpenny Twist*, Monagh, using her talent to escape the Troubles by going to the South to sing, discovers that she has an engagement. Her manager tells her that her "gig" at first "sounds not-very-exciting, but it's a first-class bill of professional artists and, believe me, very well respected as a booking in the business."[102] The manager's build up suggests that the booking, as a consequence of being "well respected," offers the possibility of leading to other bookings. It, at first, appears that Monagh may escape the Troubles. However, her manager, subsequently, informs her that it is a "Christmas night concert in the Women's Prison. . . . Sure it's full of those Republican girls from Belfast-they'll be delighted with you and your act."[103] Rather than serve as a means of escaping violence, Monagh's talent leads her back to the Troubles. Like the women in the prison, Monagh is held captive by the Northern conflict. Her booking literally sends her to jail, a metaphor which stands for, with its "Republican girls from Belfast," the consequences of the same sectarian violence Monagh sought to escape by leaving the North. Similarly, for Roy and Martyn, Monagh's friends, music offers the possibility of a non-sectarian, even cross community, endeavor. While in the North, they write songs for both parties to the conflict. Their music bridges the sectarian divide. Their inter-denominational partnership succeeds in allowing music to distance themselves from the Troubles. However, for them, the very fact that they did write songs for both Catholics and Protestants raises suspicions of a sectarian agenda. Marie, another friend who is affiliated with the Republican movement, finds their naivety regarding the potential danger of their cross-community efforts astonishing and tells them of the reality of their circumstance:

You're not bluffing, are you-you really don't know what you've gotten yourself into. There was an article in a Protestant paper. Naming you two. It said you'd both been supplying entertainment to their drinking clubs. As a means of gaining information about them. On behalf of the British army. The proof was that you were also doing work for the I.R.A. You're in dead trouble, Martyn.[104]

Roy and Martyn's music does temporarily distance themselves from the Troubles, but, ultimately, serves as the instrument that brings the Northern War directly into their lives; they are eventually killed by a bomb after one of their more successful performances. Marie's warning itself betrays how pervasive is the violence in the North and to what extent it is inescapable. Even within "drinking clubs," places of refuge from the violence, literally barred and gated, the Troubles invade. Even works of "entertainment" serve not only as reminders of the Troubles but as the means by which the Troubles invade the refuge, and, ultimately, the entertainers themselves become servants of a sectarian agenda. Rather than deliver them from the violence of the North, music and entertainment wrench Roy and Martyn back into sectarian conflict and the trauma associated with the Northern War.

In John Wilson Haire's *Within Two Shadows*, internal psychological pressures, rather than external gunman, manifest the power of sectarian conflict within places of refuge. In the play, the father uses his piano as his retreat from the economic and cultural pressures of North of Ireland. The piano helps him to construct an identity independent of the potentially damaging sectarian pressures on his family. His wife is a Protestant, representing one of the "two shadows" of the play's title. He consciously plays classical music, as opposed to traditional Irish or Protestant songs. However, after a series of incidents in which the sectarian pressures invade his home and divide his family, the father destroys the piano, rupturing his contact with a non-sectarian method of identification. Immediately before the father destroys the instrument, his family sits in "silence before the piano starts playing. They do not talk or look at one another."[105] By this time, the piano serves not as a refuge from violence or as a means to communicate effectively outside the context of sectarian brutality, but as a reminder of the father's attempted denial of the reality of his political circumstances. The piano, for the family, is an unwelcome distancing from the reality of the conflict and the symbol of the father's self-delusion. Ultimately, the "piano is playing normally when suddenly it changes to a loud, wild, tuneless sound. A crash is heard, followed by the mad thranging of piano wire as a heavy hammer batters the piano to smithereens along the different scales."[106] Like the emerging violence around him, the father's attempts to control the sound of his music end in a "wild, tuneless sound" standing for the unforeseen consequence of attempted distancing, for attempted blissfully ignorant refuge from sectarian conflict. The piano offered an escape from violence, but in escape, it also offered the temptation to ignore the consequences of traumatic rupture. The problems were not faced but were, rather, ignored. Ultimately, they return with renewed vigor and virulence destroying even the possibility of refuge, of an identity beyond violence. Mary tells her family that "Father is breakin' up the piano. There is goin' to be silence in this house. Only the best silence-the silence of the grave."[107] Unlike *Catchpenny Twist*, which ends in the literal death of its protagonists, the characters in Haire's play, die a metaphorical death. Specifically, as Conor O'Malley observes, "*Within Two Shadows* . . . starkly demonstrated the appalling wastage of human talent. When the father smashes his piano he is destroying all that is good within him. Deep bitter frustration has turned self destructive. *Within Two Shadows* is a play virtually without hope or relief." [108] The refuge from sectarian conflict dies as a result of the continuing and relentless pressures of sectarian conflict, and its death ruptures any possibility of an identity distant from trauma.

The Troubles also distances individuals from a sense of identity that spans the border between North and South. Each community surrounds itself with a cocoon of protective isolation rooted in denial of a national character and the benefits that cross-border identity might bring. Within this matrix, the concept of isolation becomes a fantasy rooted in longed-for distance from violence but manifesting itself, once reality makes the fantasy untenable, in violence and hatred. A dialogue between Martyn and Roy explores what the concept of a national cross-border identity has become:

Martyn: What's another word for 'nation'?
Roy: Country.
Martyn: No good.

Roy: Land.
Martyn: Longer.
Roy: Mausoleum.[109]

As a consequence of the brutality and hatred manifested in the North for both the cause of national British identity and national Irish identity, Roy accurately articulates the belief that any national affiliation ends in death and violence. The Troubles rupture even a desire for affiliation and point out an inherent contradiction within the siege metaphors that each side employs to insulate itself from violence:

It can be called 'walls within walls's or, more simply, the siege metaphor. It is a pattern discernable in all the above descriptions of the province, community, village, farm, home, individual, church, mission, and different degrees of the lodge, chapter, and preceptory. Each of these social units is described as though it were insulated from the evil influences that threaten it from the outside, yet each also seeks to radiate a controlling influence of religion and virtue beyond its bounds.[110]

Like a literal mausoleum, the siege metaphors of both sides seek to set aside a place for death and to separate life from a reminder of death. However, the very presence of a place set aside for death reminds the populace of death. Likewise, insular communities in the North and the idea of isolation between North and South radiates the ideas of separation, distinction, and sectarian notions of superiority to neighboring communities. Consequently, national identity, in part designed as a retreat or protection from violence, becomes an impetus for violence. Nowhere is this concept more apparent than in relations within the Catholic community, spanning the border between the Six and the Twenty-Six Counties. Within Stewart Parker's play, a Southern woman tells Monagh that the North is a "bloody silly place to live" and that she wishes "you'd get on with the bloody killing. Speed it up, hurry it along. Finish each other off, we'll be glad to see the end of you, Protestants and Catholics both, you'll be doing the world a service."[111] Her hatred for the North comes from the belief that Northerners have "crippled our [the South's] tourism" and "blemished the name of Ireland throughout the world."[112] She concludes by telling Monagh that "you're not even a part of it [Ireland]."[113]

In an effort to distance herself from the violence in the North, she removes the distinction between Catholics and Protestants, between British and Irish national identification, in order to argue that the North is a separate entity from the South. The woman insulates herself in a fantasy world in which the Republic can remain apart from violence. However, in doing so, she implicitly recognises the colonial boundary between the North and South, sanctioning the arbitrary division, and, as a consequence, British national identity. Her remarks prompt Monagh to respond by summoning an image of violence. "If you'd had a no-warning bomb in your fibreglass grotto here, you'd know all about real life, and hell slap it onto you."[114] Monagh forces the intrusion of the real violence of the Troubles onto the woman's insular, "grotto," identity. Monagh does so in order to impress upon the woman that she cannot escape from colonial violence, that her imaginative machinations simply reinforce the violence in the North. Monagh sets off an imaginative explosion that ruptures the woman's notions of isolation and security from Northern violence. Moreover, the dispute between the woman and Monagh also demonstrates the illusory nature of another effort to distance oneself from the Troubles. Monagh like many Northerners saw the South, prior to the woman's bias, as a refuge. However, since the onset of manifest sectarian brutality and the Republic's apparent indifference and sometimes open resentment of national affiliation with the North, the South no longer holds the prospect of escaping violence: "At its simplest, the South has lost its chief attraction for Northern nationalist Catholics, the illusion that it was 'home', a friendly, non-Unionist refuge just a few miles down the road where you could 'be yourself'-in the long-lost pre-Troubles days when being yourself was an entirely unselfconscious business." [115] The Republic no longer serves as a refuge from violence, from notions of a cross-border, cross-community identity. The Troubles rupture a sense of national Irish identity apart from violence and destroy any attempt to distance oneself from sectarian conflict with a conjured insular world.

Stewart Parker's *Northern Star* also reveals how characters will adopt masks of seeming comfort and security in order to come to terms with the ruptures they have experienced. The play's setting lays a symbolic foundation for its treatment of these masks. *Northern Star* takes place in a "farm labourer's cottage,"[116] which is a "semi-ruin, half-built and half-derelict"[117] that is "partly-thatched over."[118] The thatched cottage, a common symbol for a romanticized Ireland, find itself half-complete, an image of shelter with no substantive form. Indeed, later in the play, a another romantic image of Ireland proves hollow and inadequate. McCracken, the play's protagonist, considers the "Belfast Harp Festival."[119] He then reflects on the "Irish harpists,"[120] confessing that he "was at a loss as to what the Irish beggars did with their cast-off cloths"[121] until he saw the harpist's cloths. McCracken's comments reveal that he understands both the harpist's efforts to appeal to the romantic image and its ultimate futility. Throughout the play images of martyrdom, heroism, and even the Enlightenment prove hollow and inadequate when adopted as mere masks.

Specifically, McCracken advocates and will sometimes unconsciously associate himself with symbols that prove shallow and ineffective. His false identity, designed to help him escape to America, lists his profession as "Master Carpenter,"[122] a not so subtle allusion to Jesus Christ, and the appeal of a young, heroic death for a cause. Mary, McCracken's lover, sarcastically reminds him that he's "not yet thirty-one years old, our Lord himself did better than that."[123] Certainly, Parker plays with the notion of a martyr's death as a false identity and Mary's sarcasm reinforces the futility of such a gesture. However, McCracken does find some appeal in a martyr's death, at least on some level. He confesses that he and his friends were "high as kites," and "mad keen to fight now. Pledging ourselves for the first time to the republic of United Irishmen."[124] An affiliation with an ideal of country inspired McCracken to want to fight and to die for Ireland.

Other ideals also appeal to him. He sees himself united with "George Washington"[125] and Ireland with the French Republican ideal. McCrakcen also cherishes an image of himself alongside the "men of Reason" and "logic."[126] The images of romance, martyrdom, and even the Enlightenment ideals enable people to link their lives to something larger them themselves, something seemingly invulnerable to violence and rupture.

Unfortunately, they offer little lasting comfort and can, in fact, prove devastating to individuals when people allow their identity to become consumed into the ideal. Ultimately, McCracken realizes the futility of such paths, confessing that the ideals were "heady stuff"[127] and "intoxicating."[128] They were able to animate his life for a moment, and he was "prepared to die for"[129] them. He sees, by the end of the play, all he and the ideals managed to do was to "cram the cells fuller than ever of mangled bodies crawling around in their own shite and lunacy."[130] He and his companions find themselves "trapped in the same malignant legend, condemned to re-endure it."[131] The initial appeal of the prepackaged masks of identity fades into greater rupture and powerlessness. Moreover, by having McCracken express his frustrated revelations using images of prisoners trapped in their own slop, Parker equates McCracken's delusions with the sufferings of Republican prisoners on the dirty protest in the North, suggesting that they too suffer under similarly self-destructive fantasies. Ultimately, then, McCracken speaks from the stage to a contemporary North of Ireland audience, confessing his errors and misgivings and asking the people of the North to consider his warnings; the play was first produced in Belfast in 1984.

Guilt

Clinically, survivors of traumatic events may sometimes experience a sense of guilt as a consequence of living through a violent situation that took the lives of their friends and companions.[132] In the North, the guilt manifests itself in rituals and traditions of a sectarian history that drive further cross-community contacts into the realm of violent interactions. Essentially, to compensate for the guilt associated with not just a personal past but a community past that lies in ruins, individuals live sectarian rites in order to achieve a sense of continuity. Of necessity, Unionists and Nationalists, then, are less the inheritors of a tradition, an indigenous collection of constantly changing and growing customs, beliefs, and teachings, than of a "tradere," of a "carrying or transferring the past into the present and the present into the past . . . laying claim to a supralogical order where something can be *both* what it is and what it is not-the past can be present, the human divine."[133] Specifically, for the Northern Catholic community, there are rituals of fundamental origin that separate them from their neighbors, that function as markers of struggle and endurance. For example, Catholics learn to be "proud" of their Northern heritage because it "was the North [that] fought on against the English until the Flight of the Earls."[134] At "Catholic functions, there was always a sense of daring about playing the Irish national anthem, forbidden under the Special Powers Act; patriotic, and elitist pride for some singing it in Irish, which the masses did not speak."[135] In addition, the "contemporary Northern Protestant's sense of history is markedly similar to that of the Catholic Nationalist." In particular, "Presbyterians have one historical requirement-to uphold the settlement of 1689 and to try to ensure that the principle of Protestant hegemony is recognised and supported. The Siege of Derry in 1689 is their original and most powerful myth. They seem to see themselves in that, and since then, as an embattled and an enduring people." [136] The transcription of the past into the present, which, in turn, catalyzes a transformation of the human into some type of sublime force may, at first glance, seem empowering. However, "tradere" is, by definition, a compensation, a cloak in which an inferiority can disguise itself, in which some vaguely felt shame can be superficially transformed. "Tradere" is a "fictional rewriting of history," the invention of "a sacred prototype which would invest . . . [a] rather shaky rule with an unshakeable, because timeless, authority."[137] "Tradere," as a result, creates a monument of avoidance fashioned not out of a sense of power and independence but rather out of a sense of loss and self blame. In addition, a "tradere" saps the energy of the colonized territory, diverting its intellectual resources from projects of revitalization and growth, diverting energy and resources to the maintenance of a calcified history and an always present sense of sectarian division.

A portion of Northern drama, focussing on the Troubles, consciously performs the absence of any sense of a nonconfrontational or sectarian historical tradition and cultural identity and "performs" the origin of the absence. Essentially, the colonizing force ruptures a feeling of continuity and community with the past, replacing these support structures with a sense of guilt, a sense that the colonial's weakness and inherently flamed character caused the rupture. Specifically, by performing the structures that inform the Northern War, theatre demonstrates that the discourse of tribal conflict conjured and created the "sacred" past of Nationalism and Unionism and that the blame for this created history lies within the inadequate structures of the colonized territory and not as a consequence of the colonial power. Essentially,

the different versions of Irish history are well known to be entangled with ethnic and national identity. One version focuses on the story of the Siege of Derry itself. There are also other narratives from the Williamite-Jacobite Wars, notably that of the Battle of the Boyne. Another set of stories comes from traditional nationalist history. . . . Nationalist history, for example, is nowadays found in Republican writings.[138]

The alternative discourse in much of Northern theater begins to recognize that the sacred past is actually an invented tradition; indeed, there would be no need to attribute blame or guilt for a created past if it were not recognized as created. Specifically, in clinical terms, even within a framework of seeming escape, the traumatized impression remains. For the Irish, Catholic and Protestant alike, both arbitrarily racialized like the black by the colonial gaze, a profound colonial stigma remains infused upon their consciousness for their "inferiority or superiority complex or his [their] feeling of equality is conscious. These feelings forever chill him [them]. They make his [their] drama."[139] In other words, those racialized as inferior by a colonizing power can never fully escape the sense that they are racially different. They are conscious of the stigma, of some imprecise but very manifest shame, liability, or fault that is their inheritance. They carry it with them at all times, even when they seemingly escape from the boundaries of the colonized territory, even when a sense of superiority manifests itself.

A scene from *Catchpenny Twist* demonstrates how those in the North of Ireland who survive after a loved one dies because of involvement in the Troubles will compensate for his absence by creating in his memory a ritual of sectarian division. Essentially, plagued by guilt consequent of surviving the loved one, those who cared for him will attempt to repair the rupture created in their familial/community identity, a rupture created by the death, by honoring the propaganda and publicity surrounding the death. The consequence of such actions involves establishing a connection, through memory, not with the loved one, but with certain facets of his death. Basically, the Troubles catalyze a process by which select and divisive memories replace lost personal connections, resulting in the valuing not of personal connections, which are transitory and subject to the capricious nature of violence, but with the seemingly more lasting and invulnerable sectarian idols and ideals. Consequently, the communities in the North remain further divided, not simply because a sectarian history is honored but because the idea of interpersonal contact becomes subsumed in the idea of patriotic death. Early in his play, Stewart Parker details a communication between a character identified as "Woman," (not to be confused with the "woman" who later challenges Monagh), and Marie. The woman's son has recently been killed as a consequence of his involvement in the Republican movement. Marie shows the woman a copy of the *Irish News*, a Northern-Catholic newspaper:

Marie: There you are. Deaths. Three columns all to himself. It's a credit to you to have borne a son like that.
Woman: It would have made him very proud. He was a good Catholic boy and never did a wrong thing to nobody.
Marie: He died a patriot's death and it'll never be forgotten.
Woman: God bless you, Marie. I'll take this home and clip it out to keep.[140]

The woman initially identifies her son as "a good Catholic boy," indicating that she attempts to come to terms with her loss and her sense of duty (guilt) regarding her obligation to honor his memory through traditional religious means. If she could come to terms with her son's death through a traditionally religious grieving process, the son's memory would enable her to come to terms with her grief over the loss of her son and come to terms with her personal relationship with him. However, Marie, almost rebuking the mother for a solely religious reaction to grief, argues that his was "a patriot's death" and that it will "never be forgotten." Marie substitutes the ideal of sectarian involvement for the idea of the son. Essentially, the mother's personal grief becomes irrelevant to the memory of the son because of the circumstances surrounding his death. His memory does not belong to the mother on a personal level. His memory belongs to the Republican cause, a memory in this context that will "never be forgotten." The mother, confronted with Marie's contextualization of the son's death, agrees to "take this home and clip it out to keep." Basically, the mother takes the newspaper account of her son's life and death home with her. She makes no further comment on the reality of her personal relationship with her son, does not tell Marie a story about her son. Rather, the newspaper account of his life becomes the primary means of recollecting the son's presence. Significantly, the mother intends to save the news story, to honor and cherish the public version of his life and death. Consequently, the mother achieves contact not with her son but with the idea of her son represented in the newspaper. Inevitably, the public account of her son supersedes her personal recollection of his relationship to her. Consequently, the manner in which personal grief subsumes itself in public memory and homage to the ideal of an individual, rather than to the reality of his life, values the public ideal rather than individual suffering and grief. As a result, personal grief and a personal relationship with the son or any individual becomes less important than violence and sectarian ideals, a consequence that drives inter-community conflict and reenforces inter-community division by preserving the sectarian ideal. Therefore, with each death a sectarian history is created that honors division over reconciliation and violence over human interpersonal contact.

When the sectarianization of personal memories becomes habitual, a community history builds up based on resentment and bitterness, resulting in conflict between the two communities in the North. Essentially, a history manifesting itself in sectarian rituals and a sense of habitual repression demands the attention of the current generation, which pays homage along the prescribed means out of a sense of duty and obligation to the suffering and dead that have come before. To the surviving generation, not to honor their dead in the prescribed way somehow results in a betrayal of their idea of the past. Specifically, in *Catchpenny Twist*, Marie and Roy exchange comments about their concept of an Irish identity:

Marie: I know where I stand. On eight-hundred years of history, eight hundred years of repression, exploitation and attempted genocide . . .
Roy: I live in the twentieth century, love.
Marie: . . . this time we're going to put an end to that for all time. There's unfinished business in this country . . .
Roy: You know, the twentieth century-aeroplanes, spin dryers. Pinball machines.
Marie: . . . and you're involved as much as any other Irishman which is right up over your ears whether you want to be or not.
Roy: You can keep your history. You belong in it. They should build museums for you instead of prisons. The rest of us want shot of it.[141]

For Marie, repression and violence mark history. She speaks of centuries of brutality, "repression, exploitation and attempted genocide." She also speaks of her obligation to the past, "the unfinished business" that so occupies her thoughts. Without doubt, Irish Catholics, particularly in the North have been and continue to be victims of prejudice, brutality, and violence. However, Marie's present and future become an act of revenge as means of commemoration, as means of fidelity to the dead. Her life structures itself, not around contemporary events and practices, but around finishing the "business" of previous generations. As a consequence of her sense of duty and obligation to the memory of the dead, she dehumanizes herself and Roy, speaking of what she sees as their history, as unavoidable and inevitable: "You're involved as much as any other Irishman which is right up over your ears whether you want to be or not." In the process, she dismisses Roy's vision of the present, a practical present that marvels in technology and convenience and that has time for the leisure of a "pinball machine." In rejecting Roy's vision of the present, Marie spurns any idea of progress or freedom or pleasure. Marie writes a history directly related to her version of ethnicity and ethnic identity.

When history is fashioned out of a sense of guilty obligation to an imagined past and devotion to the abstract notion of ethnicity, it is never used to recognize the human element in the past to establish a sense of continuity over time. Rather, history becomes sectarian and when

history is directly related to ethnicity it is used in at least three differentiable ways: as rhetorical commentary that either justifies or condemns; as a blueprint or 'charter' for action; and as a focus for alliance.... When history is used as political rhetoric, it typically upholds the claims of one's own 'side' to power, prestige, and influence in the present while stigmatizing one's opponents. Rhetoric of this kind seems usually to have one of two forms. The first consists of a list of past grievances awaiting redress. The second makes an assertion of the superiority of one's own group.... History's second major use is as a 'charter.' Here, a set of archetypical situations provides rules or guidelines for acting in the present.... In the third of these uses of history, commemorations of historical events in, for example, processions or rituals, can provide a focus for ethnic allegiance. They thus form part of the interactive process whereby ethnic boundaries are daily defined and recreated.[142]

Clearly, Marie's version of history lists wrongs that need to be redressed and is used as a justification for sectarian action. However, Marie's republican history is not the only sectarian history in the North. *Within Two Shadows* details the Protestant/Loyalist form of ethnic, sectarian history:

The sound of a lambeg drum can be heard in the distance. In the street, outside the McGreevys's household, is erected a wooden arch reminiscent of an ancient gateway to a walled city. The arch is decorated with a series of open work, five-pointed metal stars and the short, symbolic ladders of James II, who unsuccessfully gave siege to the walled city of Derry in the seventeenth century. There are also orange lilies, Union Jacks, the red hand flag of the province of Ulster, red, white, and blue bunting, and on the top of the Arch a large painting of King William III, sword upraised, mounted on a white horse, crossing the Boyne

River to victory. On the Arch are written the slogans: "Remember 1690," "No Pope Here," and "No Surrender."[143]

John Wilson Haire details history as a form of ethnic allegiance that takes as one of its primary goals hatred of Catholics. The Protestant march, designed to intimidate Catholics as much as to rally Protestants around a sacred commemoration of the past, honors the siege metaphor, reducing to symbols the individuals who gave their lives in defence of Protestant ideals. Further, it is a vision of a calcified history that seeks to transplant the slogans and meanings of a far distant past into the present to lend vitality to a cause, not through any indigenous value the present cause might have, but through an association with the past. Clearly, the march asserts the supposed superiority of Protestants and aggressively lays claim to dutiful commemorations of the long dead.

Essentially, the march and Marie's history become a permanent, unchangeable monument speaking for what its inventors, Unionists and Nationalists, feel they lack: a stable inheritance beyond transience. Basically, "what is at stake in all these forms of history is not historical truth. What people find interesting is the way the facts are put into rhetorically useful frames, each partially structured by the siege metaphor but each defining a different rhetorical conclusion."[144] However, like all permanent structures, a "tradere" needs constant attention and fidelity, the attention and devotion of a savior figure. If it should change, then its fissures would become even more manifest. By exposing itself to revision, the "tradere" subjects itself to possible discovery as invention. The constant effort to maintain the seeming invulnerability and permanence of this structure, conjured from a sense of internalized shame and liability for a history of oppression, creates a sense of fatigue, draining a society's or an individual's resources, and reinforcing sectarian divisions.

Importantly, even in the years approaching and following the 1994 ceasefires both communities in the North produced cultural statements in wall murals that indicate elements on neither side want to relinquish a sectarian history. Specifically, in the Loyalist Fountain area of Derry, a 1993 mural depicts Michael Stone, the bomber who killed funeral mourners, as a King Billy crossing the Boyne.[145] Stone finds his features, posture, and gestures transformed into a frozen likeness of mural representations of King William. Stone's depiction endorses a calcified sectarian view of history that subsumes the identities of individuals within an historical reference. Similarly, a mural in Belfast's Short Strand depicts the faded likenesses of local Republicans dwarfed and subsumed by a feminized and militarized image of Ireland and by the words "I measc laochra na nGael go raibh a nainmeacha" (Their names are among the heroes of the Gaels).[146] The murals, themselves indications that the Troubles and continuing sectarian violence divide communities in the North and that any cross-community identity would be difficult to accomplish, did not bode well for the success of the Good Friday Agreement. Nonetheless, when a majority of both communities voted for the Agreement, they endorsed a Northern Irish concept of identity and form of government that recognises a nonsectarian identity. Within the agreement, each side relinquished divisive components of their identity in favor of a more inclusive and reconciliatory vision of the future. Moreover, even though the Agreement, and by their overwhelmingly affirmative vote the people of the South, call for the relinquishing of an absolute constitutional territorial claim to the North, the people of the South, within the Agreement, once again affirmed the right of Irish people on both sides of the border to call themselves Irish and assumed, for the Republic, a greater role in the affairs of the North. In doing so, both communities in the North and communities across the border accepted a new identity that does not include a guilty homage to the dead through a calcified and sectarian history, nor does it include an isolated and insular program of government and national conception.

Through the Good Friday Agreement, the peace process attempts to discern the formations of identity that can effectively respond to violence and that do not attempt to reinforce or sanctify the violent. Indeed, old forms of identity, within the Protestant community, tend to vest security and authority in terms of hegemony over Catholics, an identity that, threatened by violent insurrection, responds with brutality to violence. Likewise, many of the structures of Catholic identity sanctify sectarian history and Irish traditions and beliefs as a response to threat and, in consequence, further threatening Protestants and the peace in the North. Basically, the Agreement struggles to define Northern Catholics and Protestants in terms that do not assert themselves only at the expense of the other. Like Catherine Harper's bog figure, the peace process seeks to discover the buried distortions of human identity long hidden by sanctified and ritualized conflict. Moreover, the peace process seeks to convert the inhumanly brutal expressions of identity into cooperative assertions of individual and community worth within a framework of mutual understanding and recognition.

NOTES

[1] Fionnuala Ó Connor, *In Search of a State: Catholics in North of Ireland*, (Belfast: Blackstaff Press, 1993), 334.

[2] Marianne Elliott, *Watchmen in Sion: the Protestant Idea of Liberty*, (Derry: Field Day Theatre Company, 1985), 5.

[3] Ed Cairns, "Social Identity and Inter-Group Conflict in North of Ireland: A Developmental Perspective," *Growing Up in North of Ireland*, ed. by Joan Harbison, (Belfast: Stranmillis College, 1989), 129.

[4] Ibid.

[5] Ó Connor, *In Search*, 356-57.

[6] Declan Kiberd, *Inventing Ireland*, (London: Jonathan Cape, 1995), 32.

[7] Edward Said, *Culture and Imperialism*, (New York: Random House, 1994), xix.

[8] Ibid.

[9] Kiberd, *Inventing*, 32.

[10] Paddy Hillyard, "Law and Order," *North of Ireland: Background to the Conflict*, ed. John Darby, (Belfast: Appletree Press, 1983), 46.

[11] Jonathan Bardon, *A History of Ulster*, (Belfast: Blackstaff Press, 1993), 723.

[12] J. Bowyer Bell, *The Troubles: A Generation of Violence, 1967-1992*, (Dublin: Gill and Macmillan, 1993), 432.

[13] W.D.Flackes, and Sydney Elliott, *Northern Ireland: A Political Directory, 1968-1993*, (Belfast: Blackstaff Press, 1994), 99.

[14] Bell, *The Troubles*, 268.

[15] Ibid., 270.

[16] Bardon, *A History*, 688.

[17] Zahava Solomon, Nathaniel Laror, and Alexander Mc Farlane, "Acute Posttraumatic Reactions in Soldiers and Civilians," *Traumatic Stress: The Effects of Overwhelming Experience on Mind, Body, and Society*, ed. Bessel Van der Kolk, Alexander Mc Farlane, and Lars Weisaeth, (London: The Guilford Press, 1996), 106.

[18] Ibid.

[19] Arjun Appadurai, *Modernity at Large*, (Minneapolis: University of Minnesota Press, 1997), 162.

[20] Kevin Boyle, Tom Hadden, and Dermot Walsh, "Abuse and Failure in Security Policies," *Troubled Times: Fortnight Magazine and the Troubles in North of Ireland, 1970-91*, ed. by Robert Bell, Robert Johnstone, and Robin Wilson, (Belfast: Blackstaff Press, 1991), 52.

[21] Brian Friel, *Freedom of the City*, (London: Faber and Faber, 1974), 117.

[22] Martin Lynch, *The Interrogation of Ambrose Fogarty*, (Dondonald: Blackstaff Press, 1982), 89.

[23] Friel, *Freedom*, 133.

[24] Ibid.

[25] A.M. Gallagher, "Civil Liberties and the State," *Social Attitudes in North of Ireland: The Second Report, 1991-1992*, ed. by Peter Stringer and Gillian Robinson, (Belfast: The Blackstaff Press, 1992), 89.

[26] Flackes and Elliott, *Northern Ireland*, 448.

[27] Friel, *Freedom*, 111.

[28] Ibid.

[29] Ibid., 169.

[30] Ibid.

[31] Ibid., 162.

[32] Edward Said, *Orientalism*, (New York: Random House, 1978), 109.

[33] Lynch, *Interrogation*, 98.

[34] Allen Feldman, *Formations of Violence: The Narrative of the Body and Political Terror in North of Ireland*, (Chicago: University of Chicago Press, 1991), 114.

[35] Lynch, *Interrogation*, 95.

[36] Ibid., 97.

[37] Ibid., 126.

[38] Ibid., 97.

[39] Ibid., 99.

[40] Feldman, *Formations*, 111.

[41] John Osmond, "Clash of Identities: The Ulster Theatre of Graham Reid and Martin Lynch," *'Standi. Their Shifts itself. . .' Irish Drama from Farquhar to Friel*. ed. By Eberhard Bort, (Bremen: European Society for Irish Studies), 245.

[42] Michael Etherton, *Contemporary Irish Dramatists*, (London: Macmillan Publishers Limited, 1989), 34.

[43] Solomon, Larorr, and McFarlane, "Acute Post-traumatic Reactions," 106.

[44] Said, *Orientalism,* 123.

[45] Anthony Buckley and Mary Catherine Kenney, *Negotiating Identity: Rhetoric, Metaphor, and Social Drama in North of Ireland*, (Washington: Smithsonian Institution Press, 1995), 9.

[46] Ó Connor, *In Search,* 274.

[47] Said, *Orientalism*, 128.

[48] Edward Moxon-Browne, "National Identity in North of Ireland," *Social Attitudes in North of Ireland*, ed. by Peter Stringer and Gillian Robinson, (Belfast: The Blackstaff Press, 199), 23.

[49] Lynch, *Interrogation*, 94.

[50] Ibid.

[51] Ibid., 108.

[52] Ibid., 107.

[53] Ibid.

[54] Ó Connor, *In Search*, 341.

[55] Friel, *Freedom*, 114.

[56] Ibid., 115.

[57] Friel, *Freedom*, 131.

[58] Ibid., 118.

[59] Terence Brown, *The Whole Protestant Community: The Making of an Historic Myth*, (Derry: Field Day, 1985), 9.

[60] Osmond, "Clash of Identities," 248.

[61] Brown, *Whole Protestant Community*, 8-9.

[62] R.L. McCartney, *Liberty and Authority in Ireland*, (Derry: Field Day, 1985), 22.

[63] Fran Brearton,"Dancing unto Death: Perceptions of the Somme, the *Titanic* and Ulster Protestantism," *The Irish Review*, 20 (Winter/Spring 1997): 93.

[64] McCartney, *Liberty*. 24.

[65] Solomon, Larorr, and McFarlane, "Acute Posttraumatic Reactions," 106.

[66] Buckley and Kenney, *Negotiating,* 68.

[67] Carol Boyce Davies, *Black Women, Writing and Identity: Migrations of the Subject*, (New York: Routledge, 1994), 21.

[68] J. Graham Reid, *The Closed Door*, (Dublin: Co-op Books, 1980), 55.

[69] Ibid., 26.

[70] Ibid., 29.

[71] Ibid., 43.

[72] J. Graham Reid, *The Death of Humpty Dumpty,* (Dublin: Co-op Books, 1980), 55.

[73] Ibid.

[74] Lionel Pilkington, "Violence and Identity in North of Ireland: Graham Reid's *The Death of Humpty-Dumpty*," *Modern Drama* 33, 1 (1990): 26.

[75] Reid, *The Closed Door,* 21.

[76] Ibid.

[77] Ibid., 26.

[78] Reid, *Death,* 19.

[79] Ibid., 23.

[80] Solomon, Larorr, and McFarlane, "Acute Posttraumatic Reactions," 106.

[81] Frantz Fanon, *Black Skin, White Masks*, trans. by Charles Lam Markmann, (New York: Grove Press, 1967), 110.

[82] Benedict Anderson, *Imagined Communities: Reflections on the Origins and the Spread of Nationalism*, (London: Verso, 1991), 10.

[83] On 7 November 1987, during a Remembrance Day ceremony, the Irish Republican Army exploded a bomb in Enniskillen, killing eleven people and injuring sixty three. The bomb "was placed in the speaker's platform. At the appropriate moment the local establishment, the veterans, soldiers, and all those who wanted a close view of events would gather there. There was no prospect of limiting any explosion to military or even security figures. The bomb was set to go off exactly at the moment of remembrance in a crowd that . . . would have civilians, innocent of anything but location, as well as proper targets." Bell, *The Troubles*, 750.

[84] Pilkington, "Violence," 20.

[85] Ibid., 21.

[86] Reid, *Death*, 15.

[87] Pilkington, "Violence," 26.

[88] Elliott, *Watchmen*, 25-26.

[89] Pilkington, "Violence," 18.

[90] Edna Longley, "What Do Protestants Want?" *The Irish Review*, 20 (Winter/Spring 1997): 117-18.

[91] Reid, *Death*, 20.

[92] Ibid., 25.

[93] Claudia Harris, "Stewart Parker," *Irish Playwrights, 1880-1995*, ed. Bernice Schrank and William De Mastes, (Westport, Conn.:Greenwood Press, 1997) 283.

[94] Ibid.

[95] Ó Connor, *In Search*, 227.

[96] Warren Hoge,"The Troubles," *New York Times Book Review*, 15 March 1998, National Edition, A6.

[97] Ibid.

[98] Ibid.

[99] Solomon, Larorr, and McFarlane, "Acute Posttraumatic Reactions," 106.

[100] Boyce-Davies, *Black Women*, 16-17.

[101] Garrett Fitzgerald, "Steps towards Reconciliation," *Troubled Times: Fortnight Magazine and the Troubles in North of Ireland, 1970-91*, ed. by Robert Bell, Robert Johnstone, and Robin Wilson, (Belfast: Blackstaff Press, 1991), 20.

[102] Stewart Parker, *Catchpenny Twist*, (Dublin: Gallery Press, 1980), 32.

[103] Ibid.

[104] Ibid., 40.

[105] John Wilson Haire, *Within Two Shadows*, (London: David-Poynter, 1973), 103.

[106] Ibid.

[107] Ibid.

[108] Conor O'Malley, *A Poet's Theatre*, (Dublin: Eco Press Ltd., 1988), 98.

[109] Parker, *Catchpenny Twist*, 17.

[110] Buckley and Kenney, *Negotiating*, 65.

[111] Parker, *Catchpenny Twist*, 26.

[112] Ibid.

[113] Ibid.

[114] Ibid., 27.

[115] Ó Connor, *In Search*, 229.
[116] Stewart Parker, *Three Plays for Ireland*, (London: Oberon Books, 1989), 13.
[117] Ibid.
[118] Ibid.
[119] Ibid., 39.
[120] Ibid.
[121] Ibid.
[122] Ibid., 37.
[123] Ibid., 28.
[124] Ibid., 55.
[125] Ibid., 25.
[126] Ibid., 51.
[127] Ibid., 65.
[128] Ibid.
[129] Ibid.
[130] Ibid.
[131] Ibid.
[132] Solomon, Larorr, and McFarlane, "Acute Posttraumatic Reactions," 106.
[133] Richard Kearney, *Myth and Motherland*, (Derry: Field Day, 1984), 63.
[134] Ó Connor, *In Search*, 339.
[135] Ibid., 340.
[136] Brown, *Whole Protestant Community*, 8-9.
[137] Kearney, *Myth and Motherland*, 62-63.
[138] Buckley and Kenney, *Negotiating*, 41.
[139] Fanon, *Black Skin*, 150.
[140] Parker, *Catchpenny Twist*, 41.
[141] Ibid., 51-52.
[142] Anthony Buckley, "Uses of History Amongst Ulster Protestants," *The Poet's Place: Ulster Literature and Society*, ed. by Gerald Dawe and John Wilson Foster, (Belfast: Institute of Irish Studies, 1991), 260.
[143] Haire, *Within Two Shadows*, 66.
[144] Buckley and Kenney, *Negotiating*, 50-51.
[145] Bill Rolston, *Drawing Support 2: Murals of War and Peace*, (Belfast: Beyond the Pale, 1995), 2.
[146] Ibid., 54.

4

"Ubertratung":
The Mask of Protection/Projection

Locky Morris, a sculptor born and working in Derry, constructs modern "masts,"
"files," and a "trophy" from discarded televisions, wood, and paper, moulding them
into forms that have resonance in a culture sometimes void of individual,
indigenous natural expression. His forms take shape in the received images of
television and film, the violence of the Troubles, and the mass-produced consumer
society. Locky Morris writes that he "will be moved from border checkpoint into
a New Europe along a path I haven't chosen,"[1] as a consequence of Ireland's
integration into the European community. Indeed, his work speaks of a society,
traumatized by years of violence, that takes prepackaged forms of identity and
applies them to the surface of its conceptions in order to be "taken" into the future
"along a path" that does not fully articulate the internal desires of its members.
Essentially, the identity of many individuals traumatized by violence and brutality
can only express itself through masks of identity. In the sense that masks stand for
personas created by individuals seeking refuge from violence, it is a "useful
metaphor"[2] because the "noun persona had originated as the designation for the
masks worn by Greek actors and later adopted by their Roman counterparts. Thus
the phrase *per sonare* referred to the mouthpiece of the theatrical mask through
which the actor's voice was projected."[3] Ultimately, "the term persona slowly
evolved to a more abstract designation indicating the dichotomy between
appearance (the mask) and the actor."[4] The vocabulary of the mask, applied to the
North of Ireland and to Morris' work, finds a resonance in those ostentatious
trappings of identity assumed in order to come to terms with a society consumed
with the Troubles.

Essentially, the mask, in the North of Ireland, indicates the dichotomy between
the traumatized identity and the assumed identities of traumatized individuals.
Basically, the traumatized identity then becomes "a structure within the body, a
non-assimilable alien, a monster, a tumour, a cancer that the listening devices of the
unconscious do not hear."[5] The traumatized identity remains hidden and subsumed
within the individual's personality while the assumed trappings of identity interact
with the violent environment. The dramatic representation of the masking process

in Northern Ireland manifests itself chiefly in terms of the disruption of social contacts, the adoption of media archetypes, and the interaction with historical and traditional myths of identity. Within the context of social contacts, the adoption of a persona through which to come to terms with the world prevents individuals from forming lasting social and community relationships. Individuals exposed to trauma will have difficulty establishing interpersonal contacts because of the "intrusion of traumatic recollections,"[6] and because of their "inability to control responses to stress."[7] In a further effort to defend themselves against violent and traumatic memories, many individuals will adopt media archetypes to inure themselves against the brutality of their environment. When the masks of archetypes replace the reality and when "the real is no longer what it used to be, nostalgia assumes its full meaning."[8] Essentially, the "figurative," as represented in the "alterations in personal identity"[9] masks the traumatized identity of the victim of violence and replaces it with a self conception, taken from the media, that seemingly offers a more stable identity; basically, the individual takes the "signs of reality for reality." Further, in "an escalation of the true," in an effort to validate the assumed identity's authenticity, individuals will expose themselves to the "lived experience" of violence by "compulsively expos[ing] themselves to situations reminiscent of trauma."[10]

Similarly, many traumatized individuals will turn to their historical and cultural inheritance for identities through which to experience their violent surroundings. Specifically, individuals will come to terms with a portion of their history by forgetting their more recent and traumatic experience. What Heidegger wrote of Western thought is true of the individuals who adopt the myths of convention in place of their identities:

The history of Western thought [traumatized experience] begins, not by thinking what is most thought-provoking, but by letting it remain forgotten. Western thought [traumatized individuals] thus begins with an omission, perhaps even a failure. . . . The beginning of Western thought [traumatized recollection] is not the same as its origin. The beginning is, rather, the veil that conceals the origin-indeed an unavoidable veil. If that is the situation, then oblivion shows itself in a different light. The origin keeps itself concealed in the beginning.[11]

The "veil that conceals the origin" of the traumatizeds's response to their environment includes the masks of history and tradition, even demeaning representations, taken in order to "avoid specific triggers of trauma-related emotions"[12] or because individuals "suffer from generalized problems with attention, distractibility, and stimulus discrimination."[13] In terms of psychoanalytic theory, the masking process in Northern Irish drama is akin to what Carl Jung called "Ubertratung," which he used to describe as the "carry[ing] something over . . . from one form into another."[14] Specifically, for Jung, in "projection" illusion becomes reality for the individual[15]. Applying Jung's theories to the traumatized focuses attention on the way victims of violence project masks of protection (against dealing with trauma or against possible further trauma) onto their identities. The victims unconsciously associate alien identities with their own and cannot distinguish between them; they assume the identities to be their own. Many never come to understand that they are actually living an illusion and never fully recover from trauma.

SOCIAL RELATIONSHIPS

In "The Bullaun," Fleur Alcock writes of two trusting boys in County Antrim asking for a photograph to be taken and then mailed to them. She, subsequently, reflects that they "would soon mistrust" (1.36) people who want to take their pictures. In the poem, Adcock accurately observes and predicts a characteristic of people in time of war and trauma. In relatively peaceful or naive times, like childhood, the boys are trusting and carefree. However, as war encroaches, like the girl at the train station in Belfast, another character in the poem, they will become suspicious of strangers and their apparently innocuous gestures. Shortly, Adcock observes, after they have experienced the brutality of conflict, apprehension will replace trust, hostility will replace playfulness. The boys, indeed many individuals, exposed to trauma will wear masks of mistrust in their dealings and interactions with other individuals, permanently damaging their social interactions.

In terms of social relationships the masking process functions to misdirect efforts to preserve and refashion identity. Specifically, the intrusions of traumatic recollections and the inability to control responses to stressful situations prevent individuals who have been exposed to trauma from regulating their responses to their environment. Consequently, those individuals tend to perceive threats to their identity coming from sources that offer little or no real threat. In response to the perceived threat, people, who have been exposed to trauma, will often embrace identifiers that seemingly insulate them from violence. Their reaction does grant some limited and temporary protection, but, ultimately, it shields those individuals from potentially more fulfilling aspects of their identity, including communal, interpersonal, and familial relationships. In Christina Reid's *Did You Hear the One about the Irishman?* and Anne Devlin's *Ourselves Alone*, the two clinical factors that determine the response to perceived threat (i.e. the intrusions of traumatic recollections and the inability to control responses to stressful situations) manifest themselves in terms of the characters's relative relation to power and authority. For those characters in positions of authority, even if the authority is limited in terms of the overall environment, the inability to control responses to stressful situations manifests itself in terms of physical and psychological abuse perpetrated against those in positions of relative subservience. For those characters in positions of relative subservience, traumatic recollections intrude on their reactions to stressful situations, and they misdirect their anger at sources of perceived weakness around them or even at themselves. Essentially, individuals exposed to trauma will produce their own realistic responses to their environment. Moreover, their "[r]ealism is more than an interpretation of reality passing as reality; it *produces* 'reality' by positioning its spectator to recognize and verify its truths."[16] The reactions of individuals exposed to traumatic threat mask fulfilling factors that inform individual contacts behind a mechanism of self preservation that verifies and validates itself as a consequence of its extreme reactions. Essentially, the reactions to stress provide temporary escape from apparently stressful factors. However, those same responses will produce greater stressful and threatening situations that require a heightened response to stress which in turn provides protection, on a limited basis, and which, in turn, produces even more stressful circumstances, ultimately, disrupting social contacts.

Intrusions of Traumatic Recollections

In *Ourselves Alone* and *Did You Hear the One about the Irishman?*, traumatic recollections inform the characters' response to interpersonal contacts, disrupting and damaging familial and communal relationships. The characters' behavior mirrors the clinical reactions of those exposed to violence who "experience persistent intrusions of memories related to the trauma, which interferes with attending to other incoming information."[17] Representing the Troubles on stage, Irish theatre "performs" the conflict between individuals' desperate attempts to escape from violence by constructing a mask of seeming avoidance. However, the mask actually ritualizes the pain and trauma. Specifically, many people cannot filter out the traumatic act, or continuing violent acts, from their everyday lives. Essentially, the normal circumstances for such people involve violence and rupture, and, for them, the altered state is what those outside trauma would consider normalcy: lack of trauma and stable social and interpersonal connections. In terms of Freud's theories, "the shadow of the object fell upon the ego, so that the latter could henceforth be criticised by a special mental faculty like an object, like the forsaken object. In this way the loss of the object became transformed into a loss in the ego, and the conflict between the ego and the loved person transformed into a cleavage between the criticising faculty of the ego and the ego as altered by the identification."[18] Here, Freud describes the loss of a loved one to natural causes, but his principle could easily be applied to a general sense of loss in the North of Ireland. Applying Freud's theories to trauma in general, individuals incorporate the means of dealing with the world within trauma into their consciousness in order to reconstitute their identity, but instead of reconstituting their identity, they graft a sense of loss onto their identity. Basically, the mask of violence becomes part of their concept of identity, and this previously alien sentiment informs their lives and interactions with their society and with themselves. In the North, the habitual violence manifests itself in the manner that many individuals cannot escape the sense of traumatic loss that informs their lives, and, even when they do make an effort at peaceful reform, with "a ballet box in" one hand, they, inevitably have "an armalite in" the other[19] Essentially, in the plays, the characters attempt to assert their identities in the face of traumatic circumstances or recollections. However, their identities, so informed by the violence, force their assertions of identity to become violent, resulting in even more violence and subsequent traumatic response.

Family members, in *Did You Hear the One about the Irishman?*, in response to distrust and severed intimacy, as a consequence of violence or the threat of violence, between parent and child and brother and sister, use humor laced with the threat of the Troubles as a tool for retaliation and revenge rather than in an effort to reestablish social discourse. When her mother asks, with an obviously disapproving tone, to whom her daughter was speaking, Allison answers, "You know very well who it was, mother. And yes, I'm serious about a lot of things, but you don't want to know about them. Particularly at seven o'clock on a Saturday morning. What are you doing out of bed this early anyway? Is there a bomb scare in this select suburb?"[20] Allison is initially hurt by her mother's questions about the nature of the relationship with Brian. The mother's concerns are sparked, partially, in response to the potential violence that can result from a cross-community affair. Allison, however, responds by humorously pointing out her mother's vulnerabilities. Allison tells her mother that she "doesn't want to know" about the things her daughter finds interesting. She, in her comments, suggests that her mother never takes an interest in her life unless it is to attack and ridicule. Allison strips her mother's mask of pretence, revealing her vulnerability. However, rather than respond with a gesture of trust, Allison exploits her mother's vulnerability by introducing the Troubles into their interaction. She sarcastically argues that her mother woke up early in response to a "bomb scare." In doing this, Allison strips her mother's pretence once again, exposing her snobbery and position of relative security within the Province. Money, the implication is, can purchase a certain level of security. However, by using humor with sectarian violence as the punch line, Allison also strikes at the heart of her mother's fears about the potential consequences of a relationship with a Catholic. Allison's joke pushes her mother away from her, further disrupting familial contacts, and raises the threat of violence in order to hurt her mother's sensibilities, in regard to her relatively elite social position, but also in regard to her fears for her daughter's safety. Consequently, rather than restore a sense of familial and social identity to her interactions with her mother, Allison actually disrupts familial contacts through aggression and the threat of violence.

Likewise, Brian's sister has concerns about the consequences of his relationship with Allison, and, similarly, humorously raises the threat of the Troubles to attack him. Marie asks Brian, "how is little miss wonderful this morning? Nobody's put a bullet through her head yet, I take it?"[21] Marie, like Allison, forces a confrontation with a family member through humor. Marie's jokes strips Brian of any pretence that his relationship with Allison could result in anything but sectarian violence. However, her aggressive humor results in further increasing Brian's sense of alienation rather than producing a sense of intimacy and concern. He tells his sister that he is "sorry to be such a disappointment to you and your friends."[22] Essentially, Marie, in response to her concerns about the threat of the Troubles to her brother and his girlfriend, does not express her love for her brother but rather forces her brother away from her as a consequence of using the Troubles as a weapon against him. Like Allison, Marie hides her sense of vulnerability and fear behind the threat of force, humorously using violence to retaliate against her brother for making herself feel vulnerable, as a consequence of the threat to her brother and her love for him. However, the joke actually further disrupts social discourse and familial relations. For both Allison and Marie, violence intrudes on their interactions with, respectively, their mother and brother, informing their interaction and familial concern and disrupting the social bond.

In another context of Reid's play, humor also functions as a tool for hatred and division. Ultimately, the "Irishman" uses the device of a joke to introduce the threat of violence, mirroring the demeaning verbal force used by the "Comedian" throughout the play. Essentially, the "Irishman" and the "Comedian," a representative of English bigotry, use humor as a weapon against one another. Throughout the play, the "Comedian" has been punctuating the scenes between Allison and Brian with racist, anti-Irish humor. The comedian tells his audience to "grow your own dope. Plant an Irishman."[23] Later, he asks, "What do you call a pregnant Irishwoman? A dope carrier."[24] The "Comedian" and the "Irishman" function as a type of choric element. Not directly involved in the primary action of the play, they provide subtle commentary on the events. In the final sequence between the two, the "Irishman" uses a joke to strike out against the "Comedian." His action suggests a possible motivation for sectarian conflict and disruptive social interactions.

The Irishman tears the news bulletin into shreds. [announcing Brian's and Allison's death and] (turns to the bigoted comedian)
Comedian: Hallo Paddy. You still here? (He walks to the Irishman.) Have you heard the Irish knock-knock joke? You haven't? Right, you start.
Irishman: (expressionlessly) Knock. Knock.
Comedian: Who's there? He laughs and begins to walk away.
Irishman: (quietly) What do you call an Irishman with a machine gun?
Comedian: I don't know, Paddy. What *do* you call an Irishman with a machine gun?
Irishman(warily): You call him sir.[25]

The "Irishman," consumed by grief over the death of Brian and Allison, becomes the victim of the "Comedian'"'s tasteless humor. The "Comedian" preys on the "Irishman'"'s vulnerabilities to achieve a sense of triumph and victory. Like Allison and Marie, the "Comedian" strikes out at someone in an obviously vulnerable position. However, unlike the interaction between family members in the play, the interaction between the "Comedian" and the "Irishman" directly results in the perpetuation of sectarian violence and division. Essentially, humor becomes a means for violence to manifest itself. Humor becomes a mask behind which individuals can hide their sense of vulnerability. Allison's joke, like Marie's and like the "Irishman"'s and, perhaps, even the "Comedian"'s series of jokes, becomes a marker that points out "a hole, a fault, a point of rupture, in the structure of the external."[26] In the words of Lacan, humor, in Christina Reid's play, becomes the "psychotic fantasy," the force a part removed from reality, that "patch[es]"[27] over the pain consequent of sectarian hatred. Humor marks the intrusion of traumatic recollections of violence. It is the way violence recalls itself to the individual consciousness. However, rather than exposing the fault, the "hole," caused by trauma, humor patches it over, and perpetuates the social division caused by the Troubles.

In both plays, anger becomes a tool for revenge. However, in both, the characters vent their anger at targets either not responsible for the original act of violence or only remotely connected to it, resulting in a greater cycle of anger and desire for revenge. Essentially, the circumstances of the Troubles invade their efforts to counteract the threat of trauma. Brian tells Allison a story that highlights the cycle of violence, response, and frustration that permeates Northern society:

One of the kids came up to me in school yesterday. 'Here's your watch, sir', he said. 'And my big brother says to tell you if you ever have anything else pinched, just let him know.' How do I explain to a nine-year-old boy who's never known anything better, that I don't want his big brother threatening to knee-cap some other little boy, if he doesn't give the teacher back his watch? How does anybody explain anything about law and order and individual rights to a child whose earliest memory is of his mother screaming when armed soldiers broke down the door at four o'clock in the morning, and dragged his father out of bed and into a landrover. Why should that child respect the law that allows the army and the police who terrorize in the name of catching terrorists. His father was interrogated for two days simply because he was the secretary of a Gaelic Football team, and made regular trips across the border to arrange matches in The South. And after his release when he tried to sue them for wrongful arrest, they harassed his wife and children until he dropped the case. Now his oldest son organizes big league games for the I.R.A. and the nine year old can't wait until he's old enough to shoot a man in uniform. The British never learn, do they? Men with guns create other men with guns. And that child learned very early on that the men with the most guns win.[28]

Brian's remarks demonstrate how anger, sublimated and projected outward, creates further violence and anger. Essentially, violence becomes a weapon used to compensate for a sense of vulnerability in every circumstance and situation. Initially, the police use force to counter the terrorist threat. However, because they use force arbitrarily, the authorities create the desire for revenge and actually, unwittingly, advance the cause of terrorism and rebellion, further contributing to social unrest and sectarian division. Ultimately, the victims of violence, trauma and force having so informed their lives, can only turn to violence as the curative for any social disruption. In order to counteract a schoolboy's prank, the Republican movement must use the threat of violence. The use of force in this situation teaches the lesson that "the men with the most guns win," rather than the lesson that social discourse must be rebuilt in order to end sectarian division. Essentially, the memory of trauma informs the interactions of individuals on all levels of conflict in the North.

Anne Devlin's play also demonstrates how violence when misdirected results in further conflict and misunderstanding rather than in reconciliation and intimacy. After her boyfriend is beaten up by her father, Frieda "gets down on her knees to face John, who is propped against the wall" and tells him that he is a "stupid, thoughtless, reckless, insensitive, selfish bastard! . . . I could murder you! You've blown my one chance! Walking in there tonight and brazenly exhibiting yourself. . . . My head aches and my stomach's heaving-I think I'm going to be sick."[29] Furious at her father for his violent outburst, Frieda directs her anger at the victim of her father's violence, blaming him for its provocation and effects. Frieda feels threatened by her father's attacks on John; because she cares for him, she too is injured by the attack. However, rather than respond with intimacy and kindness, Frieda blames John for making himself vulnerable. She comes to John, aligning herself, through violence, with her father's violent outburst. She positions herself with his strength in the face of threat to counteract her sense of vulnerability. However, rather than granting her a sense of invulnerability, her actions make her ill. She manifests physical symptoms as a consequence of the attack, as both a type of sympathetic victimhood and as an act of self destruction aimed at punishing herself for feelings of intimacy that made her vulnerable to violence. Basically, Frieda, her actions informed by violence, can only express intimacy through the use of force, which results not in the expression of intimacy and the building up of a trusting and mutual relationship within conflict but in the building up of a relationship of violence and hatred as the only means of expression. Ultimately, John will hit her in response to feelings of vulnerability.

Similarly, one of Frieda's friends, Josie, describes her interaction with her lover. "His arrival is the best time. It's his mouth on my neck, his cool fingers touching me-I make it last right up until he has to leave. And then I row, I fight, I do everything I can to keep him with me and when I hurt him I hurt myself. It's as if we're driven, that bed is like a raft and that room is all the world to us."[30] Like Frieda, Josie expresses her feelings of vulnerability through violence, hurting her lover to hurt herself, to have a physical proof of her emotional pain. Violence has so informed her psychology, that she can only express intimacy through the use of force. Further, her impulse for violence seems uncontrollable. Josie feels "driven" to it. Essentially, the prospect of her lover leaving her room makes her feel abandoned and hurt. The social relationship is disrupted. In an effort to heal her pain, Josie and Frieda both respond by donning the mask of violence. They establish control over the situation utilizing the only means they know to be productive. Informed by an environment that offers violence as the curative for all ills, the women see violence as the source of power. However, their behavior actually contributes to the destruction of intimacy, resulting in a greater sense of vulnerability and the greater need for violence. Essentially, the "subject who utters the socially injurious words [or commits socially injurious actions] is mobilized by that long string of injurious interpolations: the subject achieves a temporary status in the citing of that utterance, in performing itself as the origin of that utterance.

That subject-effect, however, is the consequence of that very citation; it is derivative." [31] The women, and the boy in Brian's story, reach for violence to receive a type of invulnerability to pain. However, because their reaction is "derivative," informed by the traumatic intrusion of violence, they cause a further rift in the social discourse, actually driving intimacy away and increasingly the likelihood of the need for further violence to counteract a greater sense of susceptibility to emotional distress.

In Devlin's *Ourselves Alone*, anger against oneself also becomes a tool to regain self-control in the face of violence and abuse. Specifically, Donna, a young woman under thirty, turns her anger back onto herself, actually reinforcing the intrusions of traumatic recollections rather than countering them. When Liam accuses her of infidelity, telling her that "in the Kesh [in Long Kesh prison] they told me about you after the dances. They all had you." [32] She deals with her sense of outrage not by striking out violently against Liam, but by asking him to do violence to her.

(Donna takes up a knife from the table, and hands it
to him.)
Donna: Take it. Kill me, love. Kill me. Kill me.
Liam: No!
Donna: Kill me. You want to kill me. Please.
Liam: No! (He throws the knife away.) [33]

Donna, informed by the dynamics of violence, can only express her vulnerability and pain through violent means. Clearly, Liam's remarks are meant to hurt her. She, in an effort to take herself out of the vulnerable situation, actually makes herself more vulnerable. Essentially, she attempts to gain control of the situation by hurting herself, or by telling Liam to hurt her physically. Likewise, when she hears the "sound of Landrovers screeching to a halt and doors slamming, followed by heavily shod feet running. Donna takes up the bottle of pills in time to face the first of two armed soldiers who come through the open door." [34] Subsequently, she tells the soldiers that, "if you don't leave me alone I'll take these pills. I mean it. I'll swallow the lot! (She puts the bottle to her mouth and begins to swallow the pills)." [35] Her only method of self preservation in the face of threat is the threat of self annihilation. Basically, Donna's mask of violence is similar to Frieda's and Josie's, and the boy's in Brian's story. They all use violence to protect themselves from violence. However, Donna's mask of violence is more transparent than the others. Clearly, her methods lead to self destruction and actually destroy any real hope she had of escaping violence. Basically, the other individual's use of violence grants, at least to them, the temporary illusion of invulnerability. However, Donna's use of force grants her a sense of control by making herself completely vulnerable to violence. In Donna's case, there are no illusions of security, no masks of escape through the use of force. In Donna's case, as in the case of many victims of colonial and sectarian trauma, the "violence was consecrated in the language of those who had been annihilated. We should not under rate the horror of this ventriloquy: the implications of a liberation that cannot be glorified except in the language of the former [or current] master."[36] Donna attempts liberation from trauma by mimicking the force of those oppressing her; she takes control and intimacy away from herself by destroying herself.

Inability to Control Responses to Stress

Trauma victims also, oftentimes, deal with their lives through a mask of brutality and anger. Their behavior is, quite clearly, a "primal representation" characterized by "the ability of the speaking being [the abuser], always haunted by the Other [trauma, violence, brutality], to divide, reject, [and] repeat."[37] Women's shelters in the North of Ireland are filled with stories of wives and children who are beaten by fathers/brothers/sons. Typical of these stories is that of the wife of a Loyalist paramilitary: "Before he [her husband] was imprisoned, he used to wind down from a night's work of killing Catholics by screaming abuse at her, then beating and raping her."[38] The story is also repeated in paramilitary Catholic households. Moreover, when studies reveal that "men who batter tend to have poor self-esteem, to hold a rigid view of masculinity, and have poor impulse control,"[39] then it can be concluded that the poor self-esteem is a product of the individual male's seeing his position in relation to the overall hierarchy in the North. He then asserts his dominant, although limited in terms of the society at large, position in his personal milieu to rebuild his self-esteem. His rigid view of masculinity is the internalisation of the received male role. His poor impulse control is symptomatic of his underlying lack of self-esteem; it is a product of the mask. Essentially, the men, often victims themselves, attempt to compensate for feelings of vulnerability with brutality. Further, the trauma and stress associated with sectarian conflict conditions their bodies to be in a heightened emotional state. They are, after repeated exposures to violence, incapable of "modulating" their physiological responses to trauma and function in a prolonged state of stress and emotional/physical excitement from which they cannot escape and which they can only satiate with further brutality. Unfortunately, their brutality takes its toll on victims both within and without their community, and within and without their homes.

In the plays of Christina Reid and Anne Devlin, individuals respond to threats against their identity with a disproportionate level of violence or with prejudice. In essence, according the clinical definition of traumatic response, characters "lose the ability to modulate their physiological responses to stress in general, which leads to a decreased capacity to utilize body signals as guides to action."[40] Basically, the characters take almost insignificant or minor challenges as direct and threatening tests of their identity. In response, the characters assert their identity, through physically or verbally violent means. However, in doing so, although the characters defend their rigid definitions of identity, they disrupt more stable and flexible identifiers, including family relationships. Significantly, the characters, however, feel their response is appropriate. The Troubles have so conditioned their lives that they lose any sense that their actions or hatreds are serious threats not only to their familial identity but to the community. Specifically, Christina Reid relates a story of an individual, not only unaware of her prejudice but also unaware of her threatening intellectual position. A friend of Reid's was delivering "wine and spirits" to the Mackie family

the week after Mackie's Foundry on the Falls Road was attacked by an angry crowd who were quite rightly protesting that this workplace in the heartland of the Catholic Community only employed Protestants. . . . On this particular day, Mrs. Mackie, who had known him since he was a boy, took him to one side and said, 'You're a Catholic. Could you explain to me why this rabble are attacking our Foundry now? I mean, we have never employed Catholics.' When I asked him what he'd replied, he said, 'Nothing. I was too dumbfounded by how she appeared to have no perception that she had said was so insulting and offensive." Says it all really.[41]

For Mrs. Mackie, as well as for the characters in Reid's and Devlin's plays, their actions and long-held beliefs seem the natural and appropriate response to living in their environment. None perceives how their prejudice or violence threatens the community.

In *Ourselves Alone* individuals in situations of power when faced with violent or stressful circumstances, and unable to control their reactions, focus their efforts at regaining control in acts of violence directed against individuals in weaker positions, consequently, increasing the stress and trauma of the moment and driving further divisions between themselves and their family members, friends, or other members of the community. Specifically, when confronted by his friends with a challenge to his masculinity and power, Frieda's father responds with violence:

Second Man: Have you no control over your daughter?
(McDermot is pushed roughly towards the door by
Gabriel and the Second man. They exit. Malachy has
caught Frieda by the wrist to restrain her from
following. He now pushes her across the room.)
Malachy: You stay (Frieda is struck on the back of the
head by Malachy.) You'll not make a little boy out of
me! I'm sick to death of hearing about you. . . . All
I get is complaints . . . bringing that hood in here.
Frieda: (Recovering) What do I have to do or say,
Father, to get you to leave me alone.
Malachy: I'll leave you alone all right. I'll leave
you so you'll wish you'd never been born. (He makes a
race at her. She pushes a table into his path.)[42]

Malachy feels that McDermot's presence challenges his masculinity; he has been made into "a little boy." In addition, his friends question his paternal authority. He responds by pushing his daughter across the room and by striking her. His position of power reasserts itself through violent means. However, his relationship with his daughter is irrevocably damaged. The father opts for a mask of violence to assert his masculine control, and the mask shields him from criticism but also shields him from intimacy with his daughter. Later in the play, McDermot, when faced with a challenge to his ideological authority, also responds with violence:

Frieda: I think you're becoming something of an
apologist for your tribe. (He leaps out of bed and
slaps her across the head.)
McDermot:How dare you! (In a rage, HE HITS HER AGAIN.)
How dare you! (Hits her again!) I've spent my life
fighting sectarianism. (She falls into the corner,
putting up her hands to protect her face and head. He
hits out again.)
Frieda: Stop it! Please! (He is standing over her
breathing deeply, while she is crouched on the floor
holding her head, unable or afraid to look up at him
or move. He begins to pace the room.)[43]

Frieda challenges McDermot's identity as a nonsectarian peacemaker, accusing him of being not only a member but a defender of his "tribe." He violently asserts a nonsectarian identity by striking out against Frieda. McDermot, consequently, reveals that his identity is as violent as any sectarian identity. He too is subject to the rules of violent behavior dictated by his environment. In an effort to escape from those identifiers, he fashions a mask of nonviolent, nonsectarian communism. However, Frieda's challenge strips away his mask and reveals another layer of his self conception. In striking out against Frieda, McDermot re-establishes his self control, but betrays both his non-violent mask and his relationship with Frieda. Both Malachy and McDermot face a relatively minor stressful situation. However, each male character cannot modulate his response to stress and interprets any challenge, however minor, to his position of authority as a major threat to his identity. In order to restore his identity, each man strikes out violently against the object of his affection, a daughter or a girlfriend. Each man does re-establish his masculine identity and control. However, each remains unable to establish control or intimacy outside the context of violent action. Each, essentially, further disrupts his essential identity as a consequence of violence. Basically, the men, rather than establish coherent, non-traumatic relationships, become masks of violent masculinity.

In Reid's *Did You hear the One about the Irishman?*, characters also respond with violence to threats to their identities. They strike out with racial prejudice in an effort to maintain their masks of superiority. However, in their repeated efforts to bolster themselves with racial hatred and stereotypes, the characters so limit their own identity that any threat to their sense of hegemony must be faced with increasing levels of violence, even if that threat comes from members of their own families. Essentially, an important feature of colonial discourse is its dependence on the concept of 'fixity' in the ideological construction of otherness. Fixity, as the sign of cultural/historical/racial difference in the discourse of colonialism, is a paradoxical mode of representation: it connotes rigidity and an unchanging order as well as disorder, degeneracy and daemonic repetition. Likewise the stereotype, which is its major discursive strategy, is a form of knowledge and identification that vacillates between what is always 'in place', already known, and something that must be anxiously repeated.[44]

Indeed, the members of Allison's family vigorously and anxiously repeat the prejudices against Catholics in an effort to retain their familial identity. Unfortunately, their efforts so limit their identities that they drive a wedge within their family, alienating their daughter. Specifically, Mrs. Clarke asks Allison,

You're not serious about this person, are you?
Allison: He has a name mother. Brian Rafferty. He
was here only last week. Remember? Eye-patch.
Wooden leg. Parrot on his shoulder.
Mrs Clarke: He is most unsuitable.
Allison: Why?
Mrs Clarke: His background . . .
Allison: Is exactly the same as Susan's.
Mrs Clarke: His family . . .
Allison: Is Catholic, and Susan's is not.
Mrs Clarke: His brother is a terrorist.
Allison: So is Susan's. Or are there terrorists and
terrorists, mother? theirs and ours?[45]

Allison humorously acknowledges her mother's prejudicial notions by describing Brian as a pirate and degenerate. She further repeatedly exposes her mother's politely unspoken bias by stating that Brian's religion makes him unacceptable in her mother's eyes. The mother responds by damning Brian because of his family's participation in the Republican movement. Allison responds by, once again, stripping away her mother's prejudicial mask. Indeed, Allison's direct manner reveals that her mother's concern, at this point in the play, is not motivated by apprehension regarding her daughter's safety. Rather, Mrs. Clarke's impetus is the preservation of her familial identity as non-Catholic. She tells her daughter that "whether you like it or not, you are the niece of a loyalist politician. You marry a Catholic and it will be headline news."[46] Clearly, Mrs. Clarke seeks to preserve her "tribal" integrity. However, in doing so she promotes rifts in her familial identity, alienating her daughter and revealing her true bias. In response to stress, the mother does not respond by appealing to her daughter's love. Rather, she vents, however subtlety, her prejudice and bigotry. Essentially, the mother reinforces her mask of prejudice and elitism at the expense of her identity as parent, rupturing the familial identity she sought to protect. Mrs. Clarke "fixes" her identity as a Protestant but, simultaneously, "fixes" it so rigidly and so anxiously maintains it that her self definition and identification allow no room for her daughter. The mother's act disrupts the communal, familial identity that potentially serves as a counterpart to the violent and traumatic circumstances of her daily life in Belfast. Mrs. Clarke reaffirms an identity based in sectarian violence, which reenforces the underlying cause of the Troubles rather than shields one from it.

Obviously, the intrusions of traumatic recollections and the inability to regulate responses to stress inform the social interactions of many people exposed to trauma. For those individuals, their violence or threatening posturing functions as a guard against potential danger. Their reactions to seeming threat become part of their identity at the expense of familial, interpersonal, and communal relationships. Ultimately, many of the factors that compel individuals to seek social interaction become symptoms of vulnerability and weakness that need to be purged in order to protect oneself against the perceived threat of danger and violence. Essentially, emotion and the tendency toward relationships becomes a type of defilement, and "defilement is what is jettisoned from the '*symbolic system*.' It is what escapes that social rationality, that logical order on which a social aggregate is based, and then becomes differentiated from a temporary agglomeration of individuals and, in short, constitutes a *classification system* or a *structure*." [47] Basically, emotion is eventually "jettisoned" from some individuals exposed to trauma, and, in its place, a new "structure" or mask arises based not on communal interaction but on mistrust and violence, which, of course, perpetuates the violence and traumatic nature of the environment. In the North of Ireland, as Fleur Adcock observes in "The Bullaun," and as Christina Reid and Anne Devlin observe in their plays, the Troubles initiate traumatic responses so that, in time, trust turns towards suspicion and violence becomes not only a component of identity but the primary fashioning tool of identity. In the poem about the Troubles, Fleur Adcock writes of the young trusting boys's inevitable inheritance of distrust. For them, their inheritance is not only the violence of the North, as much a part of the landscape, according to her poem, as the ancient stone structures that punctuate the Antrim countryside, but also the prospect that the Troubles will be a omnipresent fixture in their conscious experience. In her correspondence, Christina Reid writes that her drama "was written out of love and despair for my family and my country during the height of The Troubles there." She adds that she has

been back home a couple of times since the ceasefire, and have been overwhelmed by the feeling of hope in Belfast. The Majority of people want peace. I'm not naive enough to think the process will be easy or simple, but the desire is there. And I believe that can, and will, overcome the blinkered attitudes of the violent minority groups on both sides who continue to think in . . . bigoted extremist terms. [48]

Reid expresses the hope of many people in the North of Ireland, that violence and the masks of fear and brutality can give way to more trusting and fulfilling social and inter-communal contacts. Indeed, the recent referendum supports Reid's notion that many people have a desire for peace and reconcilement and recognize the danger of masks of seeming self protection.

MEDIA ARCHETYPES

In Belfast, in the early-to-mid 1980s, a generation was coming of age that knew nothing but war. In this generation's struggle into adulthood, the entire Northern community, Protestant and Catholic alike, began to reassess itself: its values, its violence, its legacy. Writing in 1987, Ed Cairns observed "a veritable clamour of voices [that] began to express anxiety about the moral development of Northern Ireland's young people forced to live in an apparently amoral society."[49] Individuals on both sides of the Peace Line saw the image of what the Six Counties had become in the normal struggles of adolescence distorted into the patterns of the Troubles. The Irish Council of Churches/Roman Catholic Joint Group on Social Questions, even a decade earlier, began to question the effect of the "catastrophic and terrifying decline in respect for the sacredness of human life"[50] on pre-school and early-school-aged children born in the years shortly before and after the resurgence of sectarian violence in 1969. Essentially, the Northern War had inexorably altered the values of a generation of young adults. In response to this crisis in self-definition and self-characterization, drama explores some implications of the conflict.

Specifically, in Kenneth Branagh's *Public Enemy*, characters come to terms with violence by, using the clinical vocabulary, fashioning identities seemingly invulnerable to conflict or by compulsively exposing themselves to traumatic circumstances or, sometimes, both. Specifically, the characters fashion identities that seem more powerful in the face of sectarian conflict than their own. The Hollywood gangster films of the 1930s offer Tommy Black, the young protagonist, and Thompson, an older police detective, insular protective shields through which to experience danger, emotional vulnerability, and life. Through these masks, the characters come to terms with their environment, but the more fulfilling aspects of their identities remain submerged beneath the masks of Hollywood film. Consequently, they can never fully come to terms with their environment because they can never fully incorporate the traumatic events of their lives into their consciousness. Rather, they filter violence through an alien identity, subsuming both the referent (the Hollywood identity) and their consciousness into a hybrid state which does not satisfy. In essence, the referent, appropriated by the wounded consciousness of the victim of trauma, loses its context and its attendant meaning while the appropriating consciousness loses itself within the referent. It is as Barthes suggests, in certain language, "haunted by the appropriation of speech, the voice gets lost, as though it had leaked out through a hole in the discourse."[51] In Branagh's play, the characters's voices "get lost," their identities disintegrate, through the "hole" of trauma and the response traumatic experience sometimes necessitates.

Altered Identities

Many victims of trauma tend to assume ready-made masks of individual identity from their society. Essentially, the real [that which the traumatized see as their identity] is produced from miniaturized units, from matrices, memory banks and command models-and with these it can be reproduced an indefinite number of times. It no longer has to be rational, since it is no longer measured against some ideal or negative instance. It is nothing more than operational. In fact, since it is no longer enveloped by an imaginary, it is no longer real at all. It is a hyperreal.[52]

Basically, victims of trauma find themselves stripped of their identities as a consequence of violence and, sometimes, adopt identities in which to place their frame of reference. They consider these identities their "real" consciousness. However, these identities are simply models assembled from their environment without any reference to individual consciousness. In Northern Ireland, cases have been reported in which young people and adults will adopt the patterned persona of a television or movie character and come to terms with the world through that character's consciousness, as a means of protection. Specifically,

one can watch nightly the innumerable melodramas, generated by the producers of television programs and Hollywood films, in which worthy social institutions and virtuous women are regularly saved from destruction by rough, tough young men with hearts of gold. This is, of course, an ancient pattern. . . . In all these tales, a saviour is not merely, or even primarily, a destructive force. Nevertheless, both the creativeness and the destructiveness are vital.[53]

Essentially, children learn to model themselves on a hero who both destroys and creates to preserve good; he exists outside the law to preserve the greater good of communal identity. Furthermore, there is

growing evidence that the consumption of the mass media . . . often provokes resistance, irony, selectivity, and, in general, *agency*. Terrorists modelling themselves on Rambo-like figures. . . . Housewives reading romances and soap operas as part of their efforts to construct their own lives. . . . Where there is consumption there is pleasure, and where there is pleasure there is agency. Freedom, on the other hand, is a more elusive commodity.[54]

The process that Appadurai recognizes in universal terms reads like a critique of the situation in the North. Traumatized individuals find in the media identities seemingly immune to violence and then assume these identities, obscuring their own consciousness in the process. The pattern is a familiar one, and social workers practicing in inner cities around the world can share stories of young men taking gangsters or the gangster lifestyle as a model.

Played out on the stage, in Kenneth Branagh's *Public Enemy*, are the efforts to legitimize or give form to the instinctual drives Patrick White articulates in his study, *The Needs of Young People in Northern Ireland*. In his work, White attempts to "draw" from studies of "psychologists, sociologists, and educationalists" in order to "establish a comprehensive list of needs that are common to young people in Northern Ireland"[55] and, indeed, throughout the world. However, White deals, specifically, with "the needs that are accentuated in Northern Ireland as a result of the political and social conflict in the province."[56] He outlines five areas of need which include a desire "to come to terms with sexual development, to explore sexuality and to clarify gender roles," to "secure relationships with parents and other adults through which emotional independence can be achieved," to achieve "recognition and acceptance from peers which fosters emotional independence from parents and gives the security of social status," to "develop intellectually and to foster vocational skills which will lead to a sense of achievement and eventual economic independence," and to undergo "adventure and new experiences in which beliefs and values can be tested in order to make the transition to adult morality."[57] In essence, the main characters of *Public Enemy*, even though they are in their mid-twenties, are thrust, by circumstance, into a prolonged adolescence in which the demands Patrick White articulates become the chief needs of their young-adult life. Tragically, the means of fulfilment for Branagh's characters, involves channeling needs through fictional characters. The emotional distance allows Tommy Black and his friends and family to protect themselves from vulnerability, but the distance also prevents them from fully exploring or satiating their needs. Essentially, in response to trauma, "they have alterations in their psychological defence mechanisms and in their personal identity."[58] Consequently, the mask of 1930s Hollywood, that Tommy Black adopts, grants temporary satisfaction but long-term frustration.

In *Public Enemy*, Branagh's main character, Tommy Black, attempts to "foster vocational skills which will lead to a sense of achievement and . . . independence"[59] by expressing his needs through a fictional character. Tommy's sense of achievement comes vicariously. He expresses his worth by transferring himself into the identity of another. He makes the logical leap that involves the assumption that Jimmy Cagney's character has worth. Therefore, Tommy Black playing Jimmy Cagney has worth. Consequently, Tommy never directly comes to terms with his needs and, consequently, never finds fulfilment. Specifically, Robert asks his brother, "have you got one sentence of your own?"[60] Robert confirms the true unreality of Tommy's psychosis. Indeed, Tommy's values are the values of the movie gangster. He tells his friend Davey that they need "a way out of Chicago."[61] Tommy no longer lives in Belfast but in a fictionalised hybrid of a Chicago taken from film and the Belfast of the PIRA and the UDA. Within his fictionalised dynamic, the values are "money,"[62] "broads and booze,"[63] and fine clothes and guns. His prize is "the winner's whisky"[64] and "twenty pounds."[65] The values are those of virulent masculinity. Tommy knows what to do with women, can get money, dresses like a man, and drinks. He is no pampered, upper-class schoolboy. However, Robert is quick to point out Tommy's fiction as "this Cagney thing."[66] In addition, Robert taunts Tommy by asking if he is "thinking of leavin' the house during daylight?"[67] Robert rhetorically transfers Tommy's vocation into the dark, into the underworld of criminals and dishonesty, into the world of a Hollywood fiction. Tommy does not go into the daylight. He is not employed in Robert's idea of a vocation. The reality of Tommy's world explodes in Robert's anger and story of the price of Tommy's debts: I've just been trying to get the money for a paper bill from Brian Best. Remember him, your local friendly video-shop owner. Well, he's not so bloody friendly any more, I can tell you. Cos you owe him that much bloody money that I'll be paying for it before he pays for the papers-are there no other lives you can disrupt?" [68] Tommy's fiction has not yet brought him the currency of economic independence. Robert must pay the price, literally, to sustain Tommy's fiction. Robert pays Tommy's video bill. Even though Tommy rhetorically emasculates his brother, Robert holds the masculine currency. Tommy does not have the ability to communicate as a man because he does not have enough money. Robert reveals the reality of his values. He condemns Tommy over money. Robert's central value is the trappings of wealth.

Both brothers misdirect their efforts far away from their actual needs, and they misdirect their need to foster vocational skills that would lead to a sense of economic independence and a sense of vocation. In two moments of candor, Tommy, still within his Cagney-esque persona, reveals his frustration and the conflicting nature of life in Belfast that forced both him and his brother to misdirect their energies. Tommy tells his brother that "You got book learnin' and poems and all that fancy stuff you need for good jobs. That's you. *I'm* the mutt."[69] Robert has fulfilled society's expectations for appropriate behavior. He has sought out an education, but his education has done nothing to prepare him for the reality of an environment in which practical skills and ability to produce marketable goods is more in demand than intellectual curiosity. Robert continues to pursue the goals fostered in his educational environment, continues to read, continues to work, continues to move. His movement, however, brings him no closer to acceptable employment or an acceptable level of confidence because the society, in reality, does not foster Robert's sort of skills. The skills society rewards are those skills best represented by Tommy's Cagney persona-money and stereotypically masculine behavior. He asks Kitty, "Is there anyone in this town ready to give you a break? I've spent my life stayin' *away* from those bastards and tryin' to keep some self-respect together in a town where they don't let you breathe and hardly anybody gives you credit for a bit of sense." [70] In short, Tommy is able to grasp society's true values but can only do so by adopting a film persona, and Robert grasps society's posited values but is unable to grasp the reality of his society. Reality and unreality meet. Society pretends and educates the young to adopt the values of education and industry. However, beyond this mask of respectability lies society's true values, the violence endemic to 1980s Belfast. These are the values of the gangster, the values Tommy attempts to escape. Essentially, Tommy's "bit of sense" makes him see the face of society's lie, but the society will not give him "credit" because to do so would involve a societal-realisation of its self-deception. Tommy uses the word "credit" to consciously mean an attempt to follow the standards of society and his ability to see for what society really stands. Credit can also be seen in the sense of money. Therefore, both brothers deceive themselves into channelling their efforts at fulfilment into non-constructive efforts. For Tommy, the sense of achievement comes through the assumed persona of a gangster. In Tommy's mind, the Cagney persona will enable him to find success in a society whose surface values contradict its substantive values. For Robert, who cannot see through society's self-deception, his needs are channelled through society's prima facia values. He can no more find fulfilment and vocation than can his brother. In essence, he has created a mask equal to his brother's Cagney persona only Robert's mask is acceptable to society and not seen as a persona. Tommy's character, however, comes closer to fulfilling society's standards even though it is fictitious because it attempts to fulfil the unspoken values of society. Neither brother, though, can see through the next level, can see the necessity to throw off all of society's standards. Tommy comes closest when he instinctually longs to escape from Chicago. It is true that he creates the fictional hybrid of film-Chicago and PIRA and UDA dominated Belfast, but his fiction more clearly represents the real Belfast than does Robert's image of society. This creation and deception fosters the brothers's misdirected sense of vocation. The sense of misdirection manifests itself in the characters's need "for opportunities for adventure and new experiences in which beliefs and values can be tested in order to make the transition to adult morality."[71]

Essentially, Branagh's play indicts the violent society of Northern Ireland. Kitty tells Tommy that she does understand his circumstances. "Look, I do understand. I do. And I know you're angrier inside than you let on. But I just feel a bit insecure. I hardly know you, mister, but I do care for you."[72] Kitty's words reveal that she sees Tommy's hidden anger, sees his turmoil, and sees what fuels his efforts to escape from his frustration. She also reveals her need to care for him perhaps because, in his hidden anger, she sees herself and can care for her needs by trying to care for his needs. She "knows" that he is angrier inside than he lets on. She receives this knowledge after sexual interaction, after symbolic union. She feels insecure because she confesses her love and consequently makes herself vulnerable, because she in reality does not know him well, and because she sees herself in him, in their sexual union. Tommy, himself, betrays the same tendency to express concern for himself by caring for others. He tells Davey that he will "do for you all right."[73] He will take care of Davey, will "do for" Davey. Tommy's actions will create no need for Davey to act, will replace Davey's actions. Tommy will become like Davey, will, in essence, become Davey in order to alleviate Davey's suffering. Tommy, Kitty, and Davey find emptiness inside themselves, find a void, and, consequently, are unable to find internal, conscious sanction for their instinctual needs to care and show love. Tommy's mother tells the policemen that there is

Nothin' in their lives. Is it something we've done? I was brought up when there was no work about, you know. I was never unhappy the way I see my kids are. Somethin' in their eyes. Somethin' lost in their eyes. I keep thinkin' is it my fault? . . . What *do* you do for kids now? They've got everything. Television, video. Most of the things we never had, but their lives are empty. Empty.[74]

She too makes a connection between her suffering and the young peoples's suffering. She too identifies with them. However, she is able to diagnose their problem, able to see that they are empty, that they exist in a void.

The internal emptiness manifests itself in external violence that corrupts the instinct for tenderness and contact. When the young people try to care for themselves by caring for another, they never answer their internal desires, never come to terms with their needs. In an effort to give himself and his actions sanction, Tommy tries to give Robert a cigar. Robert tells Tommy, "I don't want your cigars. . . . And I don't want you takin' the rise out of me."[75] Robert also tells Tommy "You're half the reason people aren't interested in me. I've got your stench reeking off me"[76] Earlier, Tommy decides that in order to take control of his life that what he and Davey "need is a gun" because "I've [Tommy] gotta be Jimmy Cagney. You've [Davey] gotta be the best mate. We need the equipment."[77] In the latter case, control of own's life means violent control of others and violent conformity to another's identity. In the former case, Robert reacts with violence to the suggestion that he sanction Tommy's actions. In each case, violence follows the efforts at contact; violence substitutes for compassion. Even when Kitty, Ma, and Tommy say they will show compassion, they cannot. Each of their acts of compassion serve to isolate the object of their concern in similarly violent manners. Kitty throws Tommy out. Ma gets drunk and laid off. Tommy gets a gun and fights with his brother. The rhetoric of interaction also betrays a twisted desire for contact that expresses itself in distorted sexual terms. Tommy tells Davey that they need the "equipment" of masculine discourse to survive, that they need guns, the extension of the male organ. In addition, Tommy also finds an exaggerated expression of maleness in the cigar he offers his brother. Robert, subconsciously, recognises Tommy's need to control the masculine symbols and refuses to allow Tommy to dominate him. Further, Tommy takes "the rise" out of his brother's successes. These plays for dominance, these misdirected impulses for contact result in conflict and confrontation, result in violence.

The sense that the needs and impulses of life lie beyond the control of the young characters's of Branagh's play carries forward into their efforts to obtain "recognition from their peers which fosters emotional independence from parents and gives the security of social status."[78] Branagh's play, for all its overtones of violent interaction, actually details a relatively non-violent relation among peers. Their interaction is cloaked in rituals designed to protect each individual from vulnerability, but rather than betray violence, these interactions betray a latent need for intimacy. Like almost all Tommy's activities in the play, the Cagney persona is used to manipulate opinion in his favor. He uses it in his interactions with Davey and Kitty to gain their affection and admiration because he lacks confidence in his real personality. In fact, Tommy's interactions with Kitty and Davey reveal that his real personality is now long hidden under his mask of the Cagney persona. Specifically, Tommy begins conversations with both of his friends using the Cagney-esque phrase, "Whaddya hear, whaddya say?"[79] Davey is fairly quick to catch on. After all, in the play's initial scenes, the two young men are fairly inseparable. Consequently, it is not surprising that Davey recognises Tommy's eccentricities. Unfortunately, Davey all too quickly plays along, and their dynamic takes on a rather unreal quality in which they play out scenes from various gangster films:

> Davey: Where the hell have you been? Must be off my head waitin' here. Anythin' could have happened.
> Tommy: Well, whaddya hear, whaddya say, if that old yellow streak ain't shown up in Matt one more time.
> Davey:Yellow, me arse. I'm waitin' round late at night on a dark street in Belfast for someone who used to be my mate before he lost his marbles.[80]

Davey does not seemingly play along with the game. He answers Tommy in a Belfast accent and with "arse" and "lost his marbles." However, he does answer to "Matt," and their dynamic becomes much like the dynamic of friends in a Cagney film. Tommy controls Davey's behaviour, Davey's responses. Tommy can get Davey in a dark alley and call him "yellow." Tommy is the controlling partner.

Unlike the interaction between Davey and Tommy, in which Davey is very quick to respond to Tommy's film persona, Kitty is initially baffled. She asks, "What do I what?"[81] Tommy then reveals his method to her, asking, "Hey, you crazy mixed-up chick. Can't you understand plain old American/Irish/English?" The subsequent banter reveals the result of Tommy's assumed persona.

> Kitty: Is that what it is?
> Tommy: Sure. Plain as the nose on that pretty little face.
> Kitty: Watch it.
> Tommy: Hey kid, I know you're sore about losin'.
> Kitty:No, I'm not. I thought you were brilliant.[82]

Tommy has made contact. His persona has disarmed Kitty. She feels safe within this banter, safe enough to tell Tommy that she enjoyed his performance, that she thought it "brilliant." Under normal circumstances, Kitty probably would not have been as enthusiastic, but the Cagney-esque phrases have allowed her to show her true feelings. Eventually, she assumes her own persona, telling Tommy as "Garbo", "I vant to be alone."[83] The two continue their courtship ritual of playing at being different personalities. Kitty ultimately reveals that Tommy "can have a wee bit of family history thrown in for nothing."[84] Kitty drops the persona and in her Northern accent uses the word "wee." She does not use the American idiom, does not speak in "American, Irish, English." Rather, she reveals details about her family to Tommy. Tommy obtains the intimacy he so longs for but never drops the Cagney persona; in fact, he steals the drinks they were enjoying as part of their date. Consequently, his interaction with Kitty is never fully realized, just as his interaction with Davey is never fully realized because of the persona.

The consequence of adopting a mask of interaction is a sublimation of Tommy's real personality to the mask, actually frustrating any real efforts at contact and only lending credibility to the mask. Psychologically, the mask is then reinforced through the interaction amongst peers. It is his method to make contact with Kitty and to gain a position of dominance over Davey. However, any empathy, any affection Tommy receives psychologically reinforces the persona and further distances Tommy from his genuine character. Therefore, he does not obtain emotional independence but an emotional dependence on the persona.

In Branagh's play, the characters come to terms with adult society, the world of parents and the world of other adults, through confrontation and avoidance. Specifically, Tommy and Davey play games of confrontation with George Pearson. Significantly, Pearson belongs to the UDA, an organisation practiced in dominance and brutality. The pattern of these contacts involves initial displays of dominance and control by Tommy and Davey, private expressions of disdain and contempt for Pearson, and, ultimately, complete submission to Pearson's acts and threats of violence. Davey tells Pearson to "c'mon and sit down. Have a wee drink and we'll sort it out." In the next sentence, Tommy tells Pearson to "now listen here."[85] Later, Tommy assumes a personal tone with Pearson and tells him that in "Two minutes, Geordie. I'll be right with you."[86] Both Tommy and Davey attempt to control Pearson. They invite him for a drink and treat him with seeming deference, but their casual tone and commanding language betray a subtle impulse for dominance. In offering an invitation for a drink, Tommy and Davey manipulate Pearson's actions. They are in charge of him. Their private conversations reveal their subtle disdain and hatred for Pearson and the motive for their attempts at control. Tommy tells him that "he's the biggest mouth there ever was and thick with it. A couple of pints and a bit of brown-noisin' will do it. You've heard him shoutin' his mouth off. We'll know where to get a gun after a session with him. Then we "borrow" it for half an hour. Do the pictures. Take it straight back. No sweat. No strain. Whaddya hear, whaddya say?"[87] Tommy paints Pearson as weak and susceptible to manipulation, vulnerable to "brown-noisin." In this imagination, Pearson is the character Tommy and Davey attempt to manipulate. However, despite the stated certainty of control, Tommy knows that Pearson has the gun, the instrument for freedom and independence. Pearson really holds the key for Tommy's realization of his adulthood. For this reason, because Pearson controls Tommy's independence in Tommy's mind, the young men mock and attempt to assert their control over Pearson. Rhetorically, Tommy illustrates his lack of control. Not only does Tommy close his speech with the lines of Jimmy Cagney's gangster, an obvious defense mechanism. He proceeds the Cagney line with a series of short imperative statements, desperate in their commanding tone. Tommy gives commands to "do" and to "take" speaking out clearly that he feels no pressure, no "sweat" and no "strain." However, that Tommy has to articulate that he feels no pressure and that he has to articulate that he is under control, clearly means he has no control because thoughts of expressing control are foremost on his mind. Rather than acting with control, Tommy acts as Cagney. In just the same way his persona protects him from intimacy, Tommy's persona protects him from fear and the appearance of weakness. Tommy even mocks Davey's fear of the UDA. "What, you think we'll have the UDA bangin' on the door again, eh?"[88] The Ulster Defense Association should be feared. As an umbrella organisation for loyalist vigilante groups, the group charges itself with protecting Protestant interests. If Tommy and Davey go counter to those interests, then they make themselves susceptible to retribution. In fact, both Tommy and Davey, when confronted with the reality of violence, yield any pretext of dominance and control. Pearson calls Tommy a "cheeky git" and warns that "They'd be dead men if they started messin' with me and the organization."[89] Later, Pearson tells Tommy that "Ay, sure, your old man was a cocky bastard, too. Never saw him eye to eye with him either."[90] At this threat that recalls Pearson's act of violence that resulted in Tommy's father's death, Tommy yields even the pretext of control. He tells Pearson that his wishes are "no problem" and answers that "Christ . . . I've got my ma to look after."[91] Not only is Tommy submissive and respectful, he does not assume his persona. His fear penetrates into his real experience when the memory of his father's death is recalled. In the face of the reality of violence, Tommy becomes dependent on the control of violence. His sudden submissiveness provides a framework for understanding the construction of the Cagney persona. Violence has so penetrated Tommy's life that his only path to independence is to master the violence. Because he cannot master it in reality, he masters it imaginatively by assuming the persona of a character who controls violence and gains control over the violent gangs of Hollywood's Chicago.

His clear dependence extends to his interactions with Kitty, in his effort to clarify gender roles and to come to terms with an image of himself as an ideal sexual partner. Tommy, rather than fully come to terms with his internal impulses and needs, acts according to a code of sexuality received from the movies. Tommy expresses his desire to provide for Kitty's material needs: "She's gonna have everything."[92] Significantly, Tommy does not tell this to Kitty. He tells it to Davey. It becomes part of a macho exchange, bragging among men. Kitty becomes a "she," an impersonal pronoun, an object. Following this remark, there is a quick exchange between Tommy and Davey:

Davey: You amaze me the way you keep this up. You're a case Tom.
Tommy: I'm keeping it up cos it'll keep me sane.
Davey: You really mean that.
Tommy: I know where I'm goin' now, Dave. And I ain't goin' nowhere for people like Robert. Some chick sure ain't gettin' a bargain with him.[93]

Tommy "keeps up" the Cagney image. His romantic relationship with Kitty does not allow him the freedom to express himself as himself. He assumes the gangster persona. In addition women become "chicks," using the American idiomatic expression, a further objectification of the feminine, a further defense against the intimacy of the feminine. In addition, Tommy brings in his older brother and points out his inability, compared to Tommy, to attack and take care of a woman. Tommy defines himself in terms of sexual prowess. Even the phrasing of his exchange with Davey summons images of sexual force. Tommy is able to "keep it up," to keep up the persona and its attendant sexual prowess, its attendant sexual attraction.

Tom's positional superiority extends itself into the realm of genuine, as opposed to rhetorical, sexual interaction. Tommy takes possession of Kitty, literally, in harsh unromantic gestures of dominance in which his brutality and gangster persona fully manifest themselves. Kitty asks Tommy, "What's inside you, mister?" She seems more curious than displeased, but she does address him as mister, as a servant would address her master. Clearly, her words represent an act of submission. In addition, she senses an alien presence, one not present in their earlier, candid and honest exchanges of romantic love. She senses something other from Tommy from Belfast. She describes it as "more than just lust or love or whatever. I could feel something really strong inside you. Something on fire."[94] The fire, the burning rage, the destructive impulses of the violence and the dominance of the gangster warrior manifest themselves in the sexual act. She feels not the Tommy that reveals himself with confidence in the face of his mother's insults, nor the Tommy that exposes himself in an intimate exchange. Rather, she feels the sexual prowess and bravado present in Tommy's exchanges with Davey. She has been taken, literally, into the possession of Tommy's persona and the psychosis that drives him toward destruction. The dominant impulse clearly manifests itself in the masculine impulse and in the sexual impulse. The gender roles offered by the gangster films and the violent Northern society allow Tommy to reconstruct the mask of the gangster, to build his invulnerable masculine image. Branagh's representation of a young man adopting a gangster as a role model in order to come to terms with a violent society certainly has resonance with young American men, growing up in the inner city, who also idolize the gangster lifestyle and model their behavior on the representation of gangsters in contemporary films. The vulnerabilities of both young men from American inner cities and young men from Belfast find expression in a violent archetype that can guard themselves against vulnerability. Moreover, that actual gangsters would find inspiration in film representations of gangsters also has a resonance with the American experience. Specifically, John Gotti modeled his public persona on the gangster from *The Godfather* films, and many involved in the drug trade find inspiration and a model in the Cuban gangster from *Scarface*. The model allows for a sense of distance from not only the societal prohibitions against organized violence but also from emotion and sensitivity on the individual level. Moreover, the cinematic archetypes offer an alternative societal ethos in which violence and the criminal code substitute for societal prohibitions against illegal activities. The "street" adaptations of film rolls subsequently become models for further film representations of gangsters, feeding the cycle of violence and its disconnection from the "reality" of genuine human interaction.

Compulsive Exposure to Trauma

Some people cope with trauma by making masks of rauma a part of their identity that informs the actions of their everyday lives. They transfer the memory of trauma into action, ritualize violence, and use the methods and aims of violence to infuse their lives with meaning. Essentially, their identity constitutes itself around the loss associated with trauma. To compensate, the traumatized deal with the world through the mask of violence. Their manner of interaction leaves them dissatisfied; their dissatisfaction reveals to themselves the absence inside of them created by trauma. They respond with further violent means of coming to terms with the world, in order to compensate for the loss caused by trauma; are further dissatisfied; and respond with further violence. In the context of the North of Ireland, children's and young adult's games and dark humor manifest patterns learned from the violent environment. Children and young people fashion their identities within and around these games and verbal acts of play, ritualizing the Troubles. Clearly, in one way, these games and dark humor help children and young adults come to terms with the violence, to control the violence. However, in another way, the games and jokes reinforce the structures of violence that have already taken hold of their consciousness. The violence of these games and jokes escalates until the children and young adults progress from modelling the world around them in play to acting out the violence in real life, having also been desensitized to the consequences of violence through repeated play exposure to its matrixes. Essentially, "the playful punches and the threats [of the games] can become a metaphor. They can exemplify the mildly rebellious, rough and tough kind of person that the participants claim to be in real life."[95] The children and young adults create a mask of invulnerability. Basically, in order to compensate for their sense of loss consequent of trauma, children invent games and jokes. The games and jokes desensitize the children and young adults to violence, confusing the distinction between fantasy and reality. Subsequently, the children and young adults come into adulthood and carry forward their "games" but with very real consequences. The focus of the adult "games" creates more victims. In fact, it seems to focus on creating victims and inflicting terror rather than on achieving military or political objectives. Essentially, the "range of those who kill, maim, and rape seems to be tied up with a profound sense of betrayal that is focused on the victims, and the betrayal is tied up with the relationship between appearance and reality. . . . This sense of treachery, of betrayal, and thus of violated trust, rage, and hatred has everything to do with a world in which large-scale identities forcibly enter the local imagination and become dominant voice-overs in the traffic of ordinary life."[96] Thus, in the North of Ireland, to apply Appadurai's principles, children who mature with the structures of violence and trauma around them, learn to confuse the real and the imagined ("appearance and reality"), seek compensation for violence within structures that model violence, feel betrayed when those structures do not offer compensation, and focus their sense of betrayal in rage directed at their intended victims; they widen the circle of violence and further confuse appearance and reality, creating a world in which identity, formed in violence, is confused, angry, suspicious, and cannot distinguish the real from the imagined.

   Public Enemy does not allow for easy distinctions between   clinical definitions of "altered identity" and "compulsive exposure to trauma."   Thompson, the character who most clearly manifests the latter clinical category also experiences an altered identity modeled on a media archetype, in his case the film detective. However, whereas Tommy uses his archetype in an effort to fashion a new identity invulnerable to conflict, Thompson uses his altered identity to gain access to areas of conflict. Indeed, he will "sometimes compulsively expose . . . [himself] to situations reminiscent of trauma"[97] in order to satisfy his effort to refashion his identity. Essentially, Thompson's character functions in three ways. In part, his experience to trauma is similar to Tommy's; he fashions a new identity based on 1930s American film. In addition, like Tommy, the new identity cannot fully satiate Thompson's emotional needs because he fails to fully integrate the new identity into his personality; it remains a protective shield. Finally, within his protective shield, Thompson engages in potentially traumatic experience but at a part removed from the actual conflict. In total, Thompson's character comes to terms with society, through his altered identity, in a different way than Tommy. However, his compulsive exposure to traumatic situations brings him no closer than Tommy's attempted masculine refashioning does to a fully conceptualized image of self within conflict.

   Specifically, as Tommy struggles with this image of the masculine game player, Thompson stands in the background, not struggling, supremely confident and assured in his role as the isolated, the emotionally insular, the fighting, and the physically agile and appealing masculine teacher/detective. Moreover, he finds himself compulsively attracted to violent scenes and traumatic occurrences. Kenneth Branagh, in his introduction to *Public Enemy*, describes Thompson's role and considered presence in the play, telling the reader that the

character of Thompson is more open to individual interpretation [than is Tommy's character]. In our production we saw him moving dreamer-like on the fringes of the action. In Act Two, Scene Thirty-six he did not in fact join Ma in the "Blacks" set but played to her, as if re-enacting a scene from his memory. He was always an observer, unable to interact with other people. We even thought about leaving him on stage throughout, though in the end he did occasionally exit after certain scenes.[98]

Thompson functions as a type of chorus, commenting on the progress of the scene and the character of Tommy Black, and as a type of deity, omnipresent and omniscient about the characters's   motives and actions. However, Thompson maintains his separateness from the action. Consequently, he finds himself, like Tommy, isolated from the police and the paramilitaries and the real community of Belfast The consequences manifest themselves within the dynamic of emotional insularity. He observes of Tommy, after the talent contest, that

they sure couldn't touch them that night.
Nobody could.
The kid was on his way.
He took'em all in.
No sweat. No strain.
Everybody on his side.
Everybody in the same dream.[99]

Thompson sees into the hearts and minds and motives of Tommy's audience at the Hall. His words, picked up later by Tommy to describe his act of violence, demonstrate Thompson's complete control of his emotions because he is able to rationally diagnose emotion and understands its usefulness in controlling the audience while remaining above its effects. In addition, Thompson refers to "everybody" being "*in* the same dream." Thompson is not in the dream but he recognizes that Tommy's persona is a spell that exists outside the real. Further, Thompson seems quite at ease and comfortable placing everybody inside the dream. His judgement, unaffected by emotional consideration, diagnoses the condition of the spectators, as a detached scientist would diagnose the condition of the subject of a study. Basically, Thompson, trapped within his persona, is able to perceive emotion, but only to come to terms with it as an observer. His archetypal identity grants no lasting emotional satiation. Moreover, the consequence of Thompson's non-emotional condition is the same as the consequence of Thompson's isolation from the real Belfast. He is apart, an outsider, to use Branagh's word. However, unlike Tommy, Thompson is quite comfortable in his emotionally insularity; interestingly, Thompson's name indicates an evolution, a "son," a descendant from Tommy at the same time it seems to indicate a formalized, "Thom" as opposed to Tommy, version of the younger man. Thompson is at ease discussing the "romantic madness in" the hearts of the UDA and the PIRA saying "They just don't know when to stop. It's the Irish way."[100] Significantly, such emotion is not Thompson's way. He does not say it is "our" way. Thompson identifies the nationality of both sides as Irish as an outsider would identify both sides as Irish. He is apart from each. Further, the form of the first speech with its short, direct, abrupt phrases so obviously reminiscent of Hollywood's detectives, demonstrates how natural is Thompson's rational, Hollywood detective identity. In addition, the speech itself is laid out as if it were verse-lines ending after every sentence, the syntax building towards conclusion as it builds in complexity, indicating Thompson's role as choric witness, dispassionate and aloof. Further, he is able to correctly diagnose Tommy's calculated use of the persona rhetorically linking Tommy's Cagney as Cohan and Tommy's Cagney as gangster. Tommy uses the same words to describe his violent act as Thompson uses to describe the act of entertainment: "No sweat. No strain." Essentially, Thompson characterizes even the most innocuous of Tommy's imitations as violent, revealing as much about Thompson's character as about Tommy's imitation. Thompson compulsively uses the descriptives of violence; he is attracted to them, drawn to them and unable to escape, even within his aloof persona, from violence.

In keeping with the distinction between Tommy's efforts to affect a film persona and Thompson's natural role as film detective, Tommy as fighter enters into a delirium of movement and affected overblown confidence. In this role, he possesses a relentless, effortless discipline and a mindset that, again, places him in the context of film detectives more so than the real Belfast of the mid 1980s. Again, in a form laid out as if it were a poem and in short direct, "American" words, Thompson speaks. This time he describes his technique. First,

I *scour* the thing.
Professional discipline of course.
Years of that.
Too many.
But even so. I'm still a copper.
Was.
I'd always tried to look further than anyone else.
Read the signs early for trouble. Be ahead of myself.
Be ahead of everyone.
Be good.
Know what I mean.[101]

Thompson's lines read as a soliloquy by a 1930s Hollywood detective, outside the regular force because of some secret or hidden reason not associated with his abilities as a detective; later, the reader learns that the case of Tommy Black drove him from the force. In fact, Thompson's abilities as a detective set him apart from the other detectives. He would always "look further," be "ahead of everyone." However, also like the American film detectives, Thompson worked for "too many" years, but he goes on. He refuses to let "the rules" or other's inadequencies stop him. He, like Tommy, is possessed by a frenetic spirit that pushes him to fight, but, whereas Tommy fought for appearances, Thompson fights for internal, personal integrity. Simultaneously, Thompson's fight takes him, repeatedly, into moments of violence and trauma, as if his assumed identity needed violence to maintain itself. Indeed, as much of Thompson's role functions as a memory of events, Thompson seems doomed to relive his experiences over and over again, compulsively exposing himself to traumatic circumstances and functioning within those matrixes through his persona:

The race was on.
A three horse race. The IRA, the UDA, and the police.
That must be a record. Whoever it was had killed the
wrong guy with the wrong gun. All for £130.
If he'd known that he wouldn't have started.
Unless that's what he wanted?
I'd given up lookin' for logic.
I saw a guy rattlin' the mobs.
And a way to nail some evil for good.
If I played it right. And made this one work for

me.[102]

Thompson fights for himself, to retrospectively validate his sense of right and wrong. He separates himself, with confidence, from the society that drove Tommy to his psychosis. Thompson's behavior reinforces his internal morality. He does not rely on external sanction for validation. His certainty and position are complete. However, so is his isolation. His persona does not allow meaningful contact with the objects of his scrutiny, resulting in continuing isolation that, in turn, feeds his persona as the "rugged individualist." Thompson's character seems caught in a repeated cycle of memory and violence, uncontrollably attracted to and yet unable to directly interact with the objects of his scrutiny. Clearly, Thompson's compulsive memories and equally compulsive re-constructions of events and his persona-informed commentaries on events reveal an individual obsessed with the moments of brutality that preceded the sectarian violence inspired by Tommy Black. Thompson is traumatized and utilizes the identity of a film detective to repeatedly revisit the sites of his trauma. However, because he only comes to terms with his traumatic recollections through the persona, he is never adequately able to come to terms with the violence, which, in turn, ensures that the violence will always haunt his recollections, which, consequently, ensures the perpetual need to revisit the violent situations.

Tommy Black and Thompson, in the process of building alien identities as their own in the face of traumatic threat, essentially sever their consciousnesses from contact with the world. In the process, both have settled for what Jung would characterize as "inadequate or wrong answers" the life's basic questions.[103] Each lives in a world of symbols, and "to live and experience symbols presupposes a vital participation on the part of the believer, and only too often this is lacking in people today. In the neurotic it is practically always lacking."[104] Indeed, in the case of Tommy Black and Thompson, neither experiences the vitality of the symbolic figures they fashion themselves into. Rather, each experiences his newly fashioned identity as a type of shield, protecting each from trauma, but also preventing each from experiencing the world around him, essentially, in response to traumatic threat, shutting himself off from life. In response, the "unconscious" brings up further symbols, taken from the Hollywood gangster films, and more fully incorporates those symbolic elements into the characters's various identities. In Tommy Black's case, the Cagney persona allows him to commit and then come to terms with murder. In Thompson's case, the detective persona allows him to explore the implications of Tommy's life, without ever having to become personally engaged in that life. Kenneth Branagh's play raises serious questions about individual, especially young people's, responses to traumatic threat. Many in the North have been robbed of their "language" as a consequence of sectarian strife and must fashion a new one.

Documenting this crisis in the North of Ireland, trauma researchers produced an explosion of analyses and creative works that explored these themes. Most notably, Joan Harbison published a series of three studies in the 1980s beginning with "A

Society Under Stress," a volume that made "available information on a number of research studies dealing with children and young people in Northern Ireland" studying "the impact the violence in Northern Ireland had been having on the young people living and growing up in that society."[105] Three years later, with the assistance of the Learning Resources Unit of Stranmillis College, Belfast, Harbison put together a "follow-up volume" that sought not only to "examine the prevailing psychological view of research on and with children and young people in Northern Ireland" but also, and perhaps more importantly, to stress "the importance of research leading to constructive strategies of intervention by individuals, professional groups or agencies."[106] A third volume, published in 1989, sought to "add further detail to previous work, reflect on the past, or present new work, all of which relate to the impact of growing up in Northern Ireland on its young people."[107] Though extraordinary influential and valuable to research on children growing up in violent societies, Harbison's volumes represent only a portion of the plethora of inquiries on the effect of the "troubles" on young people in the Six Counties. Other significant studies include the work of Ed Cairns, the Quaker Peace Project, and Youth Link. Specifically, Cairns's book seeks to show that the children of Ulster "have lived through the longest period of concentrated civil disturbances to have hit the western world in modern times."[108] The study sought to answer the following questions:

Has growing up against a backdrop of bombs, explosions, assassinations and riots produced a totally amoral generation of potential psychopaths, a shell-shocked amoral generation of neurotics or has it had any effect at all? And what of the hatred that apparently fuels violence in Northern Ireland. Has that been passed on to the next generation or has the horror of the past, the continuous violence, led to a war weariness and made the young people of Northern Ireland turn away from violence to seek a more peaceful solution to their age-old quarrel?[109]

In 1984, the Ulster Quaker Peace Education Project, under the auspices of Magee College in Derry, began a ten-year project that sought to apply the lessons and analyses of researchers like Harbison and Cairns to direct acts of intervention with Northern Ireland's young people, to avoid the situations that make the likelihood of a Tommy Black a reality. The Project not only involved workshops in Derry and Belfast but also teams of workers trained by the Project who went into schools and churches throughout the Six Counties to confront the effects of a generation of war on the development of young people and to help them grow into adulthood with an awareness of their power to counteract the continuing cycles of violence and hatred. In addition, the Project also published a series of pamphlets and other studies designed to assist young people. Similar organisations, modelled on the work of the Quakers, began to intervene directly in an effort to counteract the process of socialisation towards violence. The results of their work can be measured in the overwhelmingly affirmative response to the referendum on the part of the young adults Cairns and Harbison and Branagh wrote so movingly about in the 1980s.

INHERITED MYTHS

In "Belfast on a Sunday Afternoon," Donald Davie writes of the Orange Lodges and their rituals that include "Sashes and bearskins in the afternoon" (1.3). In his poem, Davie captures the essence of historic commemoration within some quarters of the Protestant community in the North. He further details a parade with particular attention to historical symbols. However, he also juxtaposes a sense of violence and brutality with these symbols. Moreover, he emphasizes how isolated each marcher is despite functioning within a communal ceremony. Similarly, John Montague in "Heroics" writes that

In an odour of wet hawthorn
arm-swinging heroes march,
eyes chill with yearning.
they sport dark berets and
shoulder rifles as forthrightly
as spades. Spider webs
lace their sparbled boots.
A burst of automatic fire
solves the historical problem.
They drop to one knee. (ll.1-10)

For Montague's Republican honour guard, the innocence and solemnity of "hawthorn" and "spades" and mourners "drop[ping] to one knee" is juxtaposed against the "arm-swinging" militarism of men in "dark berets" who "solve" the problems of a brutal past and traumatic present in a "burst of automatic fire." Moreover, the macabre image of "spider webs" spun by human hands serves as a counterpart to the marcher whose movements resemble a "bat" in Davie's poem. Both Davie and Montague explore an aspect of the nature of history and historical commemoration in Troubles's era Northern Ireland. Rather than offer an alternative within a meaningful counter to violence and traumatic disruption, the identities taken from history often substitute for a genuine coming to terms with the violence of the present through the symbols of the past. Essentially, rather than a sense of reassurance through continuity, the brutal and "crippled" commemorations of history offer a perpetuation of traumatic reaction.

In an similar way,three plays Patrick Galvin's *We Do it for Love*, Brian Friel's *Volunteers,* and Frank McGuinness's *Observe the Sons of Ulster Marching Toward the Somme* explore the use, confrontation with, and manipulation of historical and political symbols as symptoms of a society, as a consequence of traumatic threat, unable to discriminate between the appropriate use of inherited myths and standards and the inappropriate use of traditions and values. In addition, the playwrights detail the manner in which inherited myths involve the sometimes conscious and sometimes unconscious adaptation of comedic stereotypes designed to numb the responsiveness to traumatic threat. Essentially, when some characters from the plays adopt comedic or historic masks as their reality, they tend to use them as a method for perpetrating violence; the masks then become sources of violence and brutality rather than temporary guards against trauma. In the sense that characters come to terms with their traumatic circumstances through masks of historic or comedic identity, the plays function as allegories for the more contemporary violence in the North. Many of the same factors that informed these myths and traditions culminate in the violence of the Troubles. Both sides look to history for martyrs and ideals that sustain and even demand violence in order to satiate the masks of traumatic reaction. Furthermore, both sides will, in coming to terms with trauma, adopt negative attributes with the intention of hiding from violence. Essentially, the myths and stereotypes provide a sense of stability and security within which characters hope to recover from trauma. In their representation or in the coming to terms with their uses and misuses on the Troubles's era stage, Friel, Galvin, and McGuinness reveal how stable these myths continue to be and how "useful" they are in perpetuating violence.

Basically, the masks of comedy and history allow individuals to live in a state of neurosis because of undeveloped feelings.[110] The inherited forms void emotional contact and interaction with the environment or with other individuals within the environment. Rather, they focus emotion through masks of representation distancing the practitioners of violence from the immediate consequences of traumatic threat. Moreover, as Jung suggests, the individuals still suffer because the comedic and more serious masks of history are not integrated into individual identity. Rather, they remain external masks that demand, in order to sustain themselves, constant reinforcement. Within *Volunteers* and *Observe the Sons of Ulster*, the constant reinforcement takes the form of the perpetuation of violence. The plays suggests that the uses of history and stereotypes endemic to some groups in the North perpetuate violence as a means of coming to terms with violence. Utilizing the language of clinical studies of traumatic response, the characters within the plays manifest symptoms akin to "numbed responsiveness" and "stimululus discrimination."

Numbed Responsiveness

In an effort to control their reactions to their environment, with the intention of avoiding violent circumstances and traumatic recollections, many victims of trauma will unconsciously but "actively attempt to avoid specific triggers of trauma-related emotions, and experience a generalized numbing of responsiveness."[111] Another way of dealing with trauma involves the adoption, by individuals, of a mask of non-feeling or non-emotional involvement with their community and environment in an effort to insulate themselves from the further consequences of trauma. Deprived of stable emotional connections, these individuals both isolate themselves from the factors that could actually help them come to terms with the violence around them and, simultaneously, desensitize themselves to violence and human suffering, insulating themselves from the emotional repercussions of their own actions. In the North of Ireland, some individuals will turn to the packaged emotion of ideological groups in order to achieve a type of emotional satiation to compensate for the lost emotional satisfaction of personal contact. Nationalist/Republican or Unionist/Loyalist displays, marches, and rallies can grant participants and spectators a type of emotional reward that gives a sense of belonging without having to relinquish individual control. Specifically, "organizations and networks devoted to the cultivation of such activities . . . ensure that the members of the ethnic group have a focus-or, indeed, an array of competing foci-for their allegiance."[112] Basically, the individual can experience the range of emotions (affiliation, love, fear, hatred, anger, vulnerability) through the group, sealing the self from the personal cost and reward of such emotions. In terms of Julia Kristeva's theories on personal emotional satisfaction, such an individual is a "*deject*" who "places (himself), *separates* (himself), *situates* (himself), and therefore *strays* instead of getting his bearings, desiring, belonging, or refusing."[113] In other words, individuals who embrace an ideology to experience emotion seal themselves off from the long-term rewards of emotional interaction in order to protect themselves.

In Brian Friel's *Volunteers* and Frank McGuinness's *Observe the Sons of Ulster Marching Toward the Somme*, avoidance and numbed responsiveness take the form of the adaptation of comedic stereotypes. Characters will create a comic persona in order to represent themselves as nonthreatening individuals, in the hopes of avoiding the wrath of the authorities and the forces that potentially represent violence or traumatic recollections. In addition, the comic persona becomes a mask behind which individuals protect themselves against violent circumstances. Ultimately, the mask does temporarily shield the individual from truama but also forces repeated associations with truamatic circumstances.

Particularly characters from *Volunteers* and *Observe the Sons of Ulster Marching Toward the Somme* adopt a comic and demeaning stereotype, which is in some cases reminiscent of the stage Irishman, in part to represent themselves as non-threatening to figures in authority and, in part, to distract attention from a potentially traumatic situation. In doing so, they subsume their identities into the stereotype and numb their individual responsiveness to their environment, consequently, never fully coming to terms with their own identities. Of the negative comedic stereotype, Christopher Murray observes, "there were two types of stage Irishman. One, the uneducated servant whose mistakes, verbal and logical alike, provide the basis of popularity."[114] In Friel's play, Keeney plays the part of the uneducated servant, slyly sneaking past his guardian to obtain contraband:"Keeney slips past GEORGE and into the office. There he quickly gathers up cigarette butts from the ash-trays. His eyes dart around for anything else he might forage."[115] Keeney, here, becomes a type of comic thief, obviously stealing luxuries from his supervisor's office. When Keeney realizes that he needs to explain his behavior, he says, "Thank God Professor King smokes. Positive life-saver these. May the giving hand never fail. Pity he isn't an alcoholic-with a harem. . . . True as God, George, at this very minute I'd give an arm for a large, neat whisky and a large, loose woman."[116] His comedy deflects from the nature of his actions and presents himself as a prankster unable to control his impulses. His wistful reflections on whisky and women also play into the stereotype of the drunken and licentious Irishman. Keeney emphasizes these qualities so that he can, without much suspicion and resentment, rob from those charged with guarding him. Under normal circumstances, an IRA prisoner would be seen as a threat and any effort, on his part, to obtain special privileges or to subvert authority would be met with the harshest repercussions. However, because Keeney accentuates certain qualities indicative of the stage Irishman, including notions of "ungovernability," "wildness and unreliability,"[117] he presents himself to the authorities not only as a non-threatening entity, but presents himself in such a way as to appeal to those latent prejudices in those watching him. Consequently, he is able to circumvent the rules and to gain special considerations because his captors think, because of his exhibitions within the stereotype, that his inability to control his impulses, his trickster attitude, and his ungovernability is endemic to his nature. Moreover, his nature, as a consequence of the association with the buffoon, becomes benign and not threatening. Therefore, Keeney successfully transforms his character from an association with violence, and the consequent punishment and resentment that might bring, into an association with seemingly harmless buffoonery, and the consequent reinforcement of the guards's sense of superiority that might bring.

In a like way, Pyper, from *Observe the Sons of Ulster*, plays the comic buffoon, invoking images of laziness and trickery. He tells his associates that he "once nearly starved rather than do a day's work. In fact I did starve. You wouldn't think that to look at me, would you?"[118] Earlier, he banters with another member of the company, playing against the military discipline and camaraderie expected of those who volunteered for the trenches:

Craig: Who the hell are you?
Pyper: Pyper, sir, Kenneth Pyper.
Craig: Are you sure, Pyper-
Pyper: Call me Kenneth.
Craig: Kenneth, are you a fit man for this life?
Pyper: Yes, sir, I wish to serve, sir.
Craig: I'm not sir. I'm the same rank as you. I'm
Craig. David Craig.
Pyper: David-
Craig: Call me Craig.
Pyper: I prefer sir.
Craig: You're a bit of a mocker, aren't you, Pyper?
Pyper: Me, sir?
Craig: They'll soon knock that out of you.
Pyper: I sincerely hope so.[119]
Pyper reinforces his comic type in a subsequent introduction.
Craig: I'm Craig. David Craig.
(Moore and Craig shake hands. Millen goes towards

Pyper.)
Pyper: David's the name, David Craig.
Millen: That's funny. Two boys with the same name.
Craig: His name's Pyper.
Millen: Then why does he call himself-
Pyper: I have remarkably fine skin, don't I? For a
man, remarkably fine.[120]

Clearly, like Keeney, Pyper plays against expectations, drawing himself as a trickster and a harmless buffoon, disarming his fellow soldiers with his wit and apparent nonchalance in the face of impending violence. He, in his interactions with Craig, subverts military hierarchies and protocols, referring to him as an officer and insisting on the appellation, even after the error is pointed out. With Millen, Pyper mocks the forced masculine familiarity of the trenches in favor of mockery and femininity. He mirrors Craig's response to Millen and then reflects on the quality of feminine, "fine" skin. Pyper's characterizations and actions place himself in a subservient, non-threatening position with his fellow soldiers. However, unlike Keeney, his motivation is not inspired because of the manifest physical threat of his associations; Pyper is not in the IRA. Rather, as "the only member of the Northern Protestant Ascendency, Pyper, . . . overbred, effete and nihilistic,"[121] in part mocks them to mock the society and, in part, mocks the situation to both disarm fear surrounding service in the War and to disarm any suspicion, resentment, and fear that might attend his rank in society. Essentially, Pyper creates an identity, in the face of violence and mistrust, to hide his real identity, so as to appear non-threatening. In doing so, he aligns himself with another version of the stage Irishman: "The second version of the stage Irishman was more socially elevated. He was a landowner, a man of means, with military experience. . . . [He] was ignorant by English standards and used the language ineffectively and at times ridiculously." [122] Indeed, Pyper creates a mask of a military-style stage Irishman in order to blunt and, even, numb his response to a potentially violent situation and to disarm his fellow soldiers.

Keeney too draws himself as a comic type of soldier playing directly against the fears of the effective Republican military volunteer. "As soon as KEENEY begins his march PYNE falls in behind him. Their wellington boots make the march ridiculous."[123] Further, Keeney utilizes ridiculous and ineffective language, another aspect of the stage Irish persona: "Paddy the Irishman is above all the archetype of mistranslation. By concealing the labour of translation, the difficulties that many Irish people faced in learning English as a foreign language, coupled with mother tongue interference and with apparent idiosyncrasies of accent and idiom, were presented as the undistinguished hallmarks of stupidity." [124] Keeney, at times in the play, will assume a broader accent and speak utilizing stereotypical expressions. Specifically, he tells his friends that, "'Once upon a time'-ah sure thanks be to God, lads, its only an aul' yarn,"[125] and "Ah, shure I can schmell a dishaster comin'."[126] In doing so, Keeney characterizes himself as a type of wandering clown, in the tradition of Dion Boucicault's *The Shaughraun*, in order to distract his friends's attention from their impending assassinations. Keeney, then, like Pyper, seeks to blunt and, even, numb his colleagues's response to a traumatic situation and their inevitable fate. Indeed, he even says that "fools have a long and impressive history of immunity."[127]

Indeed, within the play, Keeney will often adopt various comic personas in direct response to violence or traumatic recollections. In one scene, his fellow prisoners discuss Smiler's "night terrors."

Knox: Did any of you hear anything last night?
Pyne: Hear what?
Knox: Noises.
Pyne: Noises! What sort of noises?
Knox: Sounded like. . . (dry chuckle) . . . screaming?
. . . Maybe five or six screams. That kind of sobbing.
Pyne: I'd watch that Knoxie, if I was you.
Knox: You must have heard it, Butt. It was terrible.
Pyne: It was the big blonde I had. I gave her money
but he kept yelling for an overtime bonus.
Butt: I heard it. . . . It was Smiler.
Pyne: Jesus. Did they-?
Butt: No. In his sleep.
(Pause)
Pyne: It's almost every night now. Jesus, he must go
through agonies.
Knox: I knew I heard it. I knew. I knew.
Pyne: Jesus, the bastards-the bloody bastards.
(A very brief silence. Then suddenly KEENEY leaps to
his feet.)
Keeney: (very rapidly) Good afternoon, children, and
welcome to our dig. Your teacher tells me. . .[128]

For the first time in the play, the characters verge on seriously discussing their predicament and their traumatic experience. In order to avoid the discussion, Pyne attempts a joke and fails to distract attention from the traumatic recollection. Subsequently, Keeney "very rapidly" assumes a comic persona and ultimately succeeds in avoiding any discussion that might give rise to traumatic recollections. Keeney's behavior is not surprising. Often,

in traumatic neurosis, and particular in those brought about by the horrors of war, we are unmistakably presented with a self-interested motive on the part of the ego, seeking for protection and advantage-a motive which cannot, perhaps, create the illness by itself but which assents to it and maintains it once it comes about. This motive tries to preserve the ego from the dangers the threat of which was the precipitating cause of the illness and it will not allow recovery to occur until a repetition of these dangers seems no longer possible or until compensation has been received for the danger that has been endured.[129]

Consistent with Freud's theories, Keeney, like many of those exposed to the brutality of war, will, in an effort to preserve identity, to protect the "ego," will create an "illness." In Keeney's case, and in Pyper's, the "illness" assumes the form of the comic persona, adopted by those "seeking protection and advantage," in order to avoid impending danger or the recollection of past trauma. Moreover, as Freud suggests, the "illness" will persist until "the danger seems no longer possible or until compensation has been received."

In utilizing stereotypes to avoid trauma, Keeney and Pyper do subtly undermine its authority and the authorities of those individuals and forces wielding power in violent situations -the guards, the ethic of war, or male camaraderie in the face of violence. However, in the end, they subsume their identities in the stereotype. Essentially, the stereotype allows them to ignore conflict and traumatic recollections but it does not remove the potential for danger nor does it compensate for past trauma. Rather, the mask of the comic Irishman merely numbs Keeney's, Pyper's, and their friends's responses to conflict. Curiously, in this way too, the characters's behavior also mirrors the stage Irishman: "If the stage Irishman may, like a court jester, challenge the audience's superiority . . ., he must, like a court jester, ultimately confirm it, be made to acknowledge the hierarchical order of things. In this manner, his presence may in fact serve to defuse or sublimate the ongoing political conflict of which his nationality is a reminder." [130] Keeney and Pyper do, momentarily, comically undermine the forces arrayed against them, not only in the persons of the guards or the fellow soldiers, but also the forces of impending violence and trauma. Ultimately, however, the comedy confirms the authority of those forces because it proves ineffective as a definitive and permanent counter to trauma. Essentially, the comic mask of the stage Irishman, as utilized by Keeney and Pyper, becomes a "'structure' that is skewed, a topology of catastrophe. For, having provided itself with an *alter ego*, the Other no longer has a grip on the three apices of the triangle where subjective homogeneity resides; and so, it jettisons the object into an abominable real, inaccessible." [131] The comic persona jettisons the true identity of the trauma victim so that, even though the confrontation of a traumatic past or violent present is avoided, the true identity of the individual becomes lost and "inaccessible." The stage Irish character type replaces, through performance, the true identity of the victim, and a

performative utterance will, for example, be in a peculiar way hollow or void if said by an actor on the stage, or if introduced by a poem, or spoken in a soliloquy. This applies in a similar manner to any and every utterance -a sea change in special circumstance. Language in such circumstance is in special ways -intelligibly- used not seriously, but in ways parasitic upon its normal use-ways which fall under the doctrine of the etiolations of language. [132]

Keeney's and Pyper's persona, ultimately, proves both "hollow" and "void" in the face of violence and not intelligible as a source of true security and relief from trauma. Indeed, in the beginning of McGuinness's play, Pyper asks the power that forces his recollection and repeated performance of his traumatic memory: "Why does this persist? What more have we to tell each other? I remember nothing today. Absolutely nothing. (Silence.) I do not understand your insistence on my remembrance. I'm being too mild. I am angry that you demand that I continue to probe. Were you not there in all your dark glory? Have you no conception of the horror? Did it not touch you at all?" [133] Pyper remembers "nothing." His recollections and confrontations through his comic persona do numb him, yet he is compelled to face the traumatic circumstances again and again. Ultimately, Pyper reflects on his post-war experience, on his subsequent creation, not of comic stereotypes but of stone idols: "I turn people into stone. Women and men. Into gods. I turned my ancestors into protestant gods, so I could rebel against them. I would not serve. I turned my face from their thick darkness. But the same gods have brought me back. Alive through you. They wanted their outcast. I have returned with you to worship Enniskillen and the Boyne. My life has been saved for their lives, their deaths. I thought I'd left the gods behind. But maybe they sent me away, knowing what would happen. I went to Paris. I carved. I carved out something rotten, something evil." [134] Pyper's images, like his comic persona, help him to avoid directly confronting trauma but it is those "frozen" images that compel him to visit and revisit the scenes of his traumatic experience. Originally, the sculptures were figures of "rebellion" and avoidance. However, ultimately, rather than feed his need to be an "outcast," to numb his response to trauma, the figures "return" him to his traumatic recollections. In the end, Pyper's sculptor and comic persona, and Keeney's comic masks become

no longer a question of imitation, nor of reproduction, nor even of parody. It is rather a question of substituting signs of the real for the real itself; that is, an operation to deter every real process by its operational double, a metastable, programmatic, perfect descriptive machine which provides all the signs of the real and short-circuits all its vicissitudes. Never again will the real have to be produced: this is the vital function of the model in a system of death, or rather of anticipated resurrection which no longer leaves any chance even in the event of death. [135]

The comic persona substitutes "signs" of response and numbing for response, apparently avoids the "vicissitudes" of traumatic experience, and seemingly replaces the forces of trauma and authority. However, as Pyper's plea of "again. And again" [136] rings out in his repeated cycles of masking and avoidance, and in Keeney's repeated productions of various stage Irish character types proves, the persona, ultimately, only delivers a sense of repetitive and "orbital" circling of violence.

Patrick Galvin's *We Do It for Love* also offers numerous examples of "numbed responsiveness," including the stereotype of the drunken Irishman; the stage directions often indicate that "Moses has a bottle in his hand." [137] He admits that he frequently will "feel like" [138] taking a drink. However, Moses's most dominant illusion, constructed to escape the violence, involves his Merry-Go-Round. As if to reinforce the illusory nature of his diversion, the stage directions reveal that "most of the center of the stage is taken up with a make-shift Merry-Go-Round. The horses on the Merry-Go-Round don't look like real horses and the figures on the horses are made of cardboard. The faces are the faces of the cast in the play" and change "as the characters move on and off."[139]   That the Merry-Go-Round takes up "most" of the stage indicates the central nature of the delusion to the characters and to the plot and reveals its dominant role in the play. That it is not a real Merry-Go-Round allegorically suggests the absence of reality in the lives of the characters that gather near it. Finally, the temporary faces, changing as the characters change reveals that all of the characters in the play fall into the device's trap of self delusion at one point or another. Ultimately though, Moses Docker's character finds himself at the center of the Merry-Go-Round's delusory promise. It offers him a temporary escape from the Troubles. Moses reflects that a "thousand people could die out there, but the Merry-Go-Round goes on."[140] It offers a sense of permenance within the capricious life of the Troubles. Moses acknowledges that it is not real, telling a child that it's "just make-believe"[141] but also retreating into its possibilities of escape. When the child asks Moses if he "hate[s] Brits."[142] Moses "turns on the Merry-Go-Round music."[143] Moses later admits that the illusion is "becoming part" of him. It offers him the opportunity to shield himself from hatred and violence. However, it offers a false reality, one that does not guarentee an escape from the Troubles but rather only an escape from reality. Moses begins to understand this when he observes that "every day the faces begin to look more and more alike."[144] Ultimately, the escape from violence and into child-like delusion, takes Moses away from the reality of life, from his ability to distinguish individuals.

Eventually, the Merry-Go-Round becomes the center of staged violence. Moses explodes in anger at the war around him. His tensions, built up over the course of the play, first vent themselves in a speech that indicts all parties to the violence: "They had the nation right here in their hands and they split. Divide. Break off into factions. And for what? A principle a dying man wouldn't give death to. And while they're out there killing each other the politicians are rubbing their hands and falling over each other to maintain power." [145] His speech makes little distinction between British and Irish, even less between Catholic and Protestant. Just as the faces on his device become indistinguishable, his ability to respond to individuals and individual factions becomes indistinguishable. He becomes numb to the differences around him. In his numbness and quickly escalating rage, he burns his delusion, chanting "Tears falling like rain/Keep out the rain, ease out the pain/Troubles away."[146] He has projected the violence onto his device, making it a scapegoat for the Troubles. Burning it, he burns the symbol of his delusions but does not escape from the violence. Rather, the violence remains; its force intensified by the addition of the burning Merry-Go-Round. Moses's delusion, with its allegorical connection to all illusory constructions of escape, like *Volunteers* and *Observe the Sons of Ulster*, serves to indict all temporary constructions that do not deal directly with the underlying causes of the conflict and of trauma but rather simply offer a perpetuation of the violence.

Stimulus Discrimination

Many victims of trauma also "suffer from generalized problems with attention, distractibility, and stimulus discrimination,"[147] which manifests itself, in terms of the North of Ireland, in narrow definitions of national identity and affiliation. In addition, while it is true that "states and empires provide an effective context for internal redistribution [or recovery from trauma by channelling an individual's need for non-traumatized identifiers], they are vulnerable if there is little to distribute, or if there is little diversity in what is produced; or if they contain inner contradictions, inadequate social control mechanisms, or are unable to protect themselves from the destabilizing effect of connected systems or more encompassing ones."[148] Furthermore, such narrow definitions of nationhood also create "a web of guilt, pride, superstition, and premonition."[149] Trauma victims, in order to compensate for their loss of identity, will often organize their ideology around the performance of a limited, narrow interpretation of its origins, going so far as to elaborate a myth and structure of foundation, opposition, and exclusivity. However, because the groups order their traditions and ideology on so narrow a ground, their organization is, by necessity, intolerant of views that deviate, even slightly, from the orthodoxy, producing an "utterance" that "is then, we may say, not indeed false but in general *unhappy*."[150] The groups invent their history around basic truths; the groups's "unhappiness" bases itself in its inherent instability and consequent intolerance. In the North of Ireland, for example, around the basic structures of Nationalism/Unionism, groups will splinter and re-form over the most subtle difference in interpretation of ideology, causing some of the most violent intra-community conflict, let alone subsequent competition between the newly formed groups to achieve legitimacy and to prove themselves "truly loyal" to the genesis of their community's formation ideology by striking out against their neighbors across the peace line. Each group strives to prove that it possesses the most accurate mask of genuine orthodoxy. "The phenomenon of the intolerable arises when the experience of radical novelty threatens the possibility of the social groups recognizing itself."[151] In the Six Counties, there seems to be an endless supply of martyrs and prophets welcoming their self-sacrifice and the sacrifice of their followers in order to maintain their "limited" version of a national ideology. In more recent years, however, this seems to be changing.

However, for the characters of Brian Friel's *Volunteers*, the restricted national identity manifests itself in the limited nationalism of the prisoners's colleagues, who plan the death of the "volunteers" after the dig is over. Friel, within this context, plays on the variety of meanings associated with the word "volunteer." It can mean both a "volunteer" for the dig or active affiliation with the Republican movement. Within the play, Friel explores the restricted Provisional Irish Republican Army (PIRA) notion of "volunteer" and uses it to demonstrate the inability of the PIRA to properly discriminate between those siding with their cause or those siding against their cause. In terms of Frank McGuinness's *Sons of Ulster*, the narrow definitions of national consciousness express themselves in terms of two archetypes of Ulster Protestant history. In part, the play explores "the whole question of unionism and the Empire, and the fate of the Ulster Division at Thiepval on the Somme on 1 July 1916 when the division lost 6000 men in one day."[152] Within the context of the play, the "'Somme' in the title can symbolise more than the battle itself: the sons of Ulster are marching towards doom, sterility, political stagnation, attrition, the deserted temple (of Ulster) at the play's close. One can, it might be inferred, watch them marching towards a (metaphorical) Somme even now."[153] Moreover, McGuinness explores more than the images of the War. Specifically, if "the Somme can be appropriated as a symbol of the Ulster Protestant 'fate,' so too can that other 'archetypal event in Loyalist history,' the sinking of the RMS *Titanic* on 15 April 1912."[154] McGuinness, in exploring the loss of the *Titanic*, manufactured at Harland and Wolff's Belfast shipyard, unearths a primal image from the Ulster consciousness because

like the Somme, the loss of the *Titanic* has come to symbolise unconsciously the thwarted nationhood of Ulster Protestants, that at the level of community dreamwork the foundering of the ship and the foundering of Northern Ireland were intertwined, that the ship *became* Northern Ireland, a statelet that invited the pride in which it was fashioned, but was always in danger of being sunk by the chilling impersonal 'iceberg dynamics's of Irish nationalism.[155]

The archetypal images and vocabulary of Ulster history, invoked by Friel and McGuinness serve as an example of the inability of many who have been exposed to trauma to discriminate appropriately between threatening and non-threatening images and variations of assumed national standards. The characters, within the plays, reconstruct their identities in terms of these archetypes only to discover that those identities fail to provide adequete conpensation for violence and traumatic rupture. In this sense, the historical archetypes prove as inadequate as surrogate identities as do the comic archetypes of the stage Irishman.

In part the Ulster Protestant identity articulated in McGuinness's play proves so limited in its imaginative identification that it cannot adequately maintain a national identity for its enthusiasts; in short, "there is too little to distribute."[156] Consequently, the identity relies on violent motivations and references in order to maintain its stability, offering its adherents not an escape from violence but a perpetual need for violence in order to support itself. Essentially, the Protestant historical identity, represented by *Observe the Sons of Ulster*, demands that its enthusiasts restrict their interpretation of national character to such an extent that all stimuli are taken in not in terms of themselves but only in the context of Ulster Protestant history. Pyper, the comic trickster, at the end of the play seriously contextualizes Ulster identity at the Somme in terms of Presbyterian history. He prays,

God in heaven, if you hear the words of man, I speak to you this day. I do it now to ask we be spared. I do it to ask for strength. Strength for these men around me, strength for myself. If you are a just and merciful God, show your mercy this day. Save us. Save our country.

Destroy our enemies at home and on this field of battle. Let this day at the Somme be as glorious in the memory of Ulster as that day at the Boyne, when you scattered our enemies. Lead us back from this exile. To Derry, to the Foyle. To Belfast and the Lagan. To Armagh. To Tyrone. To the Bann and its banks. To Erne and its islands. Protect them. Protect us. Protect me. Let us fight bravely. Let us win gloriously. Lord, look down on us. Spare us. I Love-. Observe the sons of Ulster marching towards the Somme. I love their lives. I love my own life. I love my home. I love my Ulster. Ulster. Ulster. Ulster. Ulster. Ulster. Ulster. Ulster. Ulster. (*As the chant of 'Ulster' commences rifles and bayonets are raised. The chant turns into a battle cry, reaching frenzy.*)[157]

Pyper cannot imaginatively come to terms with his contemporary experience. Rather, he rallies his regiment by imaginatively transporting them to Ulster. Rather than articulate the need to fight the Germans, he re-articulates the memory of past victories, "when [God] . . . scattered our enemies." The archetype of Protestant identity he chooses, in order to come to terms with the violence laid out before him, offers only the comfort of past battles and violent reinforcement of a version of national consciousness so limited in its scope that the experience at the Somme becomes both an imaginative war and a literal war. Imaginatively, the men of the Ulster Division, as represented in Pyper's speech, are fighting on the fields of their North of Ireland homes, transporting the literal battle against the Germans to the imaginative landscape of Ulster. Consequently, Pyper and his fellows dissociate themselves from any contemporary conception of identity. Rather, they create a narrow fraternity of national comradeship limited to only battle and death. Pyper's Ulster then, is not a real community, does not offer a real identity. Rather, "it is imagined as a *community*, because, regardless of the actual inequality and exploitation that may prevail in each, the nation is always conceived as a deep, horizontal comradeship. Ultimately it is this fraternity that makes it possible, over the past two centuries, for so many millions of people, not so much to kill, as willingly to die for such limited imaginings." [158] As Benedict Anderson observes of imaginative national identities similar to Pyper's Ulster identity, "such limited imaginings" offer a restricted identity but one incapable of growing away from violence and, therefore, incapable of offering its enthusiasts any identity beyond a shared traumatic experience. Consequently, the trauma endures both for the individual and for the community.

In addition to granting a restricted notion of national identity, many individuals, when faced with trauma, will adopt so narrow a definition of membership within national identification that they allow for "little diversity"[159] among their fellows. Consequently, in order to maintain discipline within the group only a limited number of external variations remain so as not to distract members from the specific goal of the national identification. Unfortunately, because the national identification allows so little variance amongst its members, its mask of identity must maintain itself through an equally restricted means; the restricted ends is the narrow mask of identity. The restricted means involves violence. In terms of the North of Ireland articulated in *Volunteers*, the PIRA requires its "volunteers" to adhere to a strict non-cooperation agreement. When the "volunteers" for the dig break ranks, they are initially met with cold hostility. Wilson and George discuss the PIRA's reaction:

Wilson: . . . Would you believe it, George, since the
day they volunteered to work here five months ago-May
3, am I right?
George: Correct.
Wilson: Not one of their mates back there has broken
breath with them.
George: I know. You've told me.
Wilson: Not one. What about that for solidarity?
George: Remarkable.
Wilson: An outside it's the same thing-they're a dirty
word with their mates outside, too.[160]

Wilson and George both marvel at the discipline of an organization that would so easily and effectively exclude individuals from membership. Indeed, their code of silence requires that once a "volunteer" has deviated from the official organizational command, they are to be ostracised. Moreover, the deviants are to be sought out and killed. Keeney explains the situation to his fellow "volunteers":

Yes. Well. All I've got to tell you is this. That our fellow internees held a meeting the night before last-no, not really a meeting-a sort of kangaroo court. And they discussed again our defection in volunteering for this job. And they were unanimous that being sent to Coventry wasn't an adequate punishment for us. So the court ruled that a punishment to fit the crime of treason be meted. And the assembled brethren decided that the only fit punishment would be . . . capital. . . . So there is to be a contrived riot in Block C probably next Monday night. And in the course of that riot they're going to take care of us-a fall from a roof-a tumble down the stairs-you know how accidents can happen in a chaotic situation.[161]

In order to purge deviants from its ranks and to maintain its uniform identity, the PIRA plans a prison riot to mask the assassinations of the prisoner "volunteers." Significantly, the PIRA plans a deviant act, a riot, as a performative setting to punish deviants. It is as if the PIRA plans to dramatize the state in which its ideology is left after some members break ranks as a background for punishment and to restore order. The prison riot, within this context, becomes an elaborate masque, or performance, within which order, and the mask of identity, can be re-established. Certainly, the deaths of the "volunteers" will temporarily affirm the old order. However, the violent manner in which members are excluded creates a reliance on rituals of violence in order to maintain the integrity of the organization. Therefore, the organization can only be maintained by forces that could disrupt it. Within this trap, Friel introduces the term "volunteers." He consciously calls the prisoners, and titles the play, using the appellation usually applied to Republican "volunteers." The former leave violence behind them and begin to unearth aspects of an Irish historical heritage that defies easy and restrictive national classifications. They uncover a Norseman in Ireland. Conversely, the loyal Republican "volunteers" enforce their strict discipline through violence, reaffirming an even stricter national identity. The result is the rejection of a deeper more integrated understanding of national identity in favor of the violent suppression of diversity in a segregated and restricted nationalism.

In *Observe the Sons of Ulster*, Frank McGuinness provides his readers with an image of heroism and a pedigree of nationality that is at once insular and seemingly pure but simultaneously contains "inner contradictions."[162] It is a play that is a "humane study of cultural confusion and military heroism."[163] Consequently, its heroes trumpet a past that does not "discriminate," differentiate, between those components that support its isolated bias and those elements that suggest a more integrated past. The consequences involve the adoption of a mask of national consciousness that, while it contains components that have the seeds of a unified, though diverse, society, reinforces a restricted version of nationalism and nationality that promotes dissension and, ultimately, violence in order to avoid confronting its contradictory elements. In his extended prologue Pyper speculates that

there is a type of man who invites death upon himself. I thought once this is the type of stuff heroes are made from. I enlisted in the hope of death. I would be such a man. But mine was not the stuff of heroes. Those with me were heroes because they died without complaint for what they believed in. They taught me, by the depth of their belief, to believe. To believe in you. What sense would you make of their sacrifice? I at least continued their work in this province. The freedom of faith they fought and died for would be maintained. There would be, and there will be no surrender. The sons of Ulster will rise and lay their enemy low, as they did at the Boyne, as they did at the Somme, against any invader who will trespass on their homeland. Fenians claim a Cuchullian as their ancestor, but he is ours, for they lay down for centuries and wept in their sorrow, but we took up arms and fought against an ocean. An ocean of blood. His blood is our inheritance. Not theirs. Sinn Fein? Ourselves alone. It is we, the Protestant people, who have always stood alone. We have stood alone and triumphed, for we are God's chosen.[164]

Within Pyper's apologia for his lifelong devotion to an exclusive Protestant hegemony and inheritance in Ulster, he unwittingly reveals contradictions in his ideological stance. Specifically, he declares that he and those like him will fight all who "trespass" on his "homeland," most notably Catholics. However, he subsequently legitimizes Catholic claims on the exclusively Protestant "homeland" by using Catholic metaphors to assert his title to an ancient past -the figure of Cuchullain and the concept of "Sinn Fein." It is true that he appropriates them for a Protestant heritage, but in invoking them, he gives them and, by connection, their supporters licence to use them in invoking a claim to Ulster. Further, he undermines an exclusive Protestant heritage by summoning not the sacred figures of Presbyterian history, but a Celtic hero, and by expressing his thoughts through the Irish language. Each of these components (Celticism and Irish) contradict the exclusive notion of inheritance perpetuated by some Protestants. When Pyper suggests Irish and Celtic heroes are appropriate metaphors and an appropriate means of expression for articulating a right to an Ulster homeland, he allows for diversity inside the myth of a pure Protestant identity. Essentially, because the Protestant myth "is a myth of origination and consists of the notion that a kind of Eden was perfected by the planters out of the rough paradise which already existed before their advent and which has ever since been imperilled by the Catholics,"[165] any acknowledgment of an origin within ancient Celtic or Irish language tradition threatens that myth. In addition, when he declares his defence of the ideologically pure Protestant claim, he praises those who would "die without complaint for what they believed in." A complaint could very well recognize those contradictions. Furthermore, out of a "sense of sacrifice," he "continues their work" by diving into action rather than by reflecting on the meaning of their ideology; again, reflection might point out contradiction. When he does associate thought with their deaths and ideology, he speculates on "freedom" to do violence, a freedom of "no surrender" and an image of a people who will "lay their enemy low." For Pyper, the proof of the legitimacy of his argument, and the disproof of any maculate components within Protestant identity, involves the actions of its members in support of that identity. Essentially, within "a sense of dutiful allegiance to the claims of father and fatherland" a "continuous link" is invented which legitimises the "fictional rewriting of history."[166] The rewriting offers, in Kearney's words, a "Pietas" or mask "which provides a story of foundation, with a narrative of origination" and a "sacred prototype which would invest the present with an unshakable, timeless authority."[167] However, the mask does not reconcile the inner contradictions of the identity, it simply disguises them within a code of action and "no surrender." Ultimately, it is only through violence that the mask can maintain its integrity because its inner components suggest diversity and because lack of action would force consideration and, ultimately, acknowledgment of this diversity.

Significantly, the characters of *Observe the Sons of Ulster* eventually confront their immediate past and recent historical inheritance, through the *Titanic*, revealing "a web of guilt, pride, superstition, and premonition."[168] The *Titanic*'s implications for Belfast's Presbyterian community involve "the end of the Victorian and pre-dating that, Enlightenment, dream; the decline of Ulster Protestant political and economic power; the disappearance, literally, of large numbers of people from the face of the earth -the workers from the yard, the passengers from the ships, the soldiers in the Great War." [169] Locked within the hull of the *Titanic*, according to Brearton, McGuinness's characters, and a numbers of scholars and critics, is the Ulster Presbyterian notion of invincibility and pride, the mask of national identity, and the ability to focus on the goal of a pure Protestant heritage manifesting itself in the "unsinkable" labor of Protestant hands. Indeed, McIlwaine speaks of the haunting memories of the ship:

McIlwaine: Know what I'm thinking about?
Millen: Keep taking your breath.
McIlwaine: That boat.
Moore: I see nothing before me.
Anderson: The *Titanic*?

Millen: The end's in sight.
Anderson: What brings the *Titanic* into your mind?
McIlwaine: The drum. The noise of it. It's like the
sound she made hitting the Lagan.
Anderson: We weren't to blame. No matter what they
say.
McIlwaine: Papists?[170]

McIlwaine's reflections indicate an imagination haunted by the traumatic memory of a lost ship. The noise of the drum, another symbol of Protestant pride, reminds him of the *Titanic* hitting the water out of dry dock. His imagination recalls the rupture created by its loss in a discussion with his friend:

Anderson: The bloody *Titanic* went down because it hit
an iceberg.
McIilwaine: The pride of Belfast went down with it.
Anderson: You're not going to meet any icebergs on the
front, are you? So what are you talking about?
McIlwaine: The war is our punishment.
Anderson: There's more than Belfast in this war.
McIlwaine: But Belfast will be lost in this war. The
whole of Ulster will be lost. We're not making a
sacrifice. Jesus, you've seen this war. We are the
sacrifice.[171]

The loss of the ship, recalled by the sounds of Ulster Protestant celebration, and reinforced by the death and violence of the War, indicate that the loss of the *Titanic* ruptures McIlwaine's concept of identity. Logically, if Ulster Protestant legitimacy's external sign involved the goods it produced, in this case the most luxurious and seemingly sturdiest ship ever built, then if that external sign sank, certainly, the symbol of Protestant identity and the mask of worthiness sank with the ship. The result involves not simply a sense of guilt associated with the foundering of the *Titanic*, although Anderson's denial that Protestants "weren't to blame" does suggest guilt. The loss of the ship involves the loss of identity and is accompanied by premonitions of death and "sacrifice" and inevitability: "the war is our punishment." Moreover, McIlwaine's conscious recognition of the *Titanic*'s role in the formation of Protestant identity and its implications for Belfast and Ulster suggest devastating consequences for Presbyterian concepts of hegemony. Essentially, the *Titanic* becomes a symbol of disintegration and chaos, and the

transition from signs which dissimulate something to signs which dissimulate that there is nothing, marks the decisive turning point. The first implies a theology of truth and secrecy (to which the notion of ideology still belongs). The second inaugurates an age of simulacra and simulation, in which there is no longer any God to recognise his own, nor any last judgement to separate truth from false, the real from its artificial resurrection, since everything is already dead and risen in advance.[172]

Ulster Protestant identity, wrapped up in the rituals and certainty of past military triumphs involves "signs which dissimulate something." Indeed, the "theology" of "truth" surrounding Protestant myths of origination and purity, as fragile as they prove, remain a mask of identity. Whereas, the *Titanic* is a "sign which dissimulates that there is nothing." It is a mask not of identity but the mask of loss and emptiness. The *Titanic* becomes a myth, a simulation, of the absence or the end of history. Within this mask, trauma and violence become inevitable markers of the passing of an inheritance. The historical legacy then involves doubt and uncertainty.

The myths of the Great War and the *Titanic* and even the archetypes of the Stage Irishman offer some historical context for understanding the trauma and violence of Northern Ireland. Each of these symbols becomes, in Brian Friel's *Volunteers* and Frank McGuinness's *Observe the Sons of Ulster Marching Toward the Somme*, a mask or persona through which individuals, when confronted by violence, come to terms with their ruptured identities. Indeed, the allegorical models of the past become the identities for the individuals. Heidegger's thoughts on modern, Western man serve as an ideal description of the characters: "Persona means the actor's mask through which his dramatic tale is sounded. Since man is the percipient who perceives what is, we can think of him as the persona, the mask, of Being."[173] Within the dramas of Friel and McGuinness, characters represent individuals whose lives, fractured by war, become simply a mask of historical drama through which they can experience existence. Their personas numb them from the reality of a very brutal present or relieve them of the burden of having to discriminate subtleties of thought and ideology. Like the characters from Montague's and Davie's poems, the figures in *Volunteers* and *Observe the Sons of Ulster* combine qualities of historic commemoration and a macabre existence in the present. It is a community very much reminiscent of Louis MacNeice's Northern Ireland

Over which country of cowled and haunted faces
The sun goes down with the banging of Orange drums
While the male kind murders each its woman
To whose prayer for oblivion answers no Madonna. (ll.21-24)

Mac Niece's "Belfast," with the sounds of prayers for numbness combined with the historic resonance of the lambeg drum indicting both communities under the archetypes of violence and brutality, could easily be a description of the historic landscapes offered by Friel and McGuinness and of any society trapped within violent cycles of traumatic repetition.

Likewise, Patrick Galvin's *We Do It for Love* offers a picture of a society trapped within a cycle of violent repetition and isolation. Many of his characters cling to tribal identifications. He portrays archetypes in one scene who stand side-by-side and alternate speeches. However, neither responds to the other; they simply mouth their positions on issues and they identities. For the Catholic/Republican side, a character calling himself Padraig Pearse says that he "loves Ireland,"[174] that he "gave" his "life for it."[175] He further adds that this "war began when the first English soldier step foot on Irish soil. It will go on until the last soldier has departed from these shores."[176] Pearse distrances himself and his community from the violence, displaces blame for the war and its conseuqeunces. He further justifies violence through a logical trap. In essence, he claims that violence will only end when no English soldiers are present. Therefore, his logic suggests, the English must be eliminated, even violently, for the violence to end. Pearse's counterpart is the "Man in the Street,"[177] a Protestant Everyman who declares himself the "Protestant Worker."[178] He displays a "Sterling Sub-machine gun,"[179] providing its details: "When loaded it weighs eight pounds. It fires 550 rounds per minute and it is accurate up to 150 yards."[180] Significantly, the man in the Street introduces himself through the gun. He never provides any other details regarding his identity. He then becomes his gun, unable to define himself except in these violent terms. Both he and Pearse exist then not as individuals but rather as archetypes of violent types.

Patrick Galvin later particularizes the conseuqnces of sectarian archetyping in the characters of a Protestant and a Catholic mother who also appear on stage at the same time, give alternating speeches, but fail to communicate with one another. They each alternate speeches, longing for contact. One says, "If only she'd say something."[181] The other responds, "If I knew what to say."[182] It is as if Galvin has them articulate an alternating interior monologue, revealing their like desires and intent but also revealing their deep divisions rooted in sectarian hatreds and suspicions. Mrs Ryan earlier reflects on her son's death, picturing him with his "mouth open,"[183] giving a "silent scream."[184] She believes that "[n]o one's listening."[185] Like her later speech in which she talks but does not get a response, her son's voice is mute. Sectarianism, by implication, then suggests an ability to speak but not to be heard. Mrs Castle, the name itself suggests isolation and entrapment, laments that her husband, called "Billy" like the English King William, cannot hear her, saying "you can't talk to Billy about politics. It's a game to him. I'm getting tired of games."[186] Politics dominates her husband's life and dominates their interactions. His hatred, his child-like games, isolate her from companionship and love. She has no voice that her husband can hear. Like Mrs. Ryan and her son, Mrs. Castle feels trapped within a society that cannot break free of prejudice and hatred. Ultimately, Mrs. Castle and Mrs. Ryan do communicate and sing out an indictment of sectarian tradition:

O to Hell with the Pope and King William
And the wars that we fought in Belfast
And to Hell with the Green and the Orange
As we rise to a nation at last.[187]

However, their voices fade with the scene into sounds of "police cars arriving, sirens, etc."[188] Galvin's ending suggests that, despite the women's personal revelation and song, that the circumstances of the war mute even cross-community, non-sectarian voices. The forces and powers of violence destroy even the beginnings of peace.

Within the masks of inherited myths, those masks taken from media archetypes, and those that obstruct social interaction, traumatized individuals come to terms with their violent environment but do not come to terms with violence in an effective manner. They never fully incorporate the structures of trauma into their true identities so as to overcome them. In the place of identity, individuals adopt a system of references, and, "in the end . . . [such] a world of perception cannot be organized in a valid way, cannot be constituted in a human way."[189] Brian Friel, speaking of the situation in the North, wrote that a climate of masks," is a dying climate-no longer quickened by its past, about to be plunged almost overnight into an alien future. The victims in this situation are the transitional generation. The old can retreat into and find immunity in the past. The young acquire some facility with new cultural implements. The in-between ages become lost, wandering around in a strange land." [190] In the North, the "strange land" becomes a culture of masks, a society consumed by "Idées Reçues," by a "knowledge [that] no longer requires application to reality."[191] Essentially, for the generation coming of age in the Troubles, "ideas are propagated and disseminated anonymously; they are repeated without attribution."[192] The "ideas" are masks of reality, a projection of the real taken for the real.

NOTES

[1] Fintan O'Toole, *Strongholds: New Art from Ireland,* (Liverpool: Tate Gallery, 1991), 19.

[2] Christopher Monte, *Beneath the Mask,* (Philadelphia: Harcourt Brace Publishers, 1995), 6.

[3] Ibid.

[4] Ibid.

[5] Julia Kristeva, *Powers of Horror,* trans. Leon Roudiez, (New York: Columbia University Press, 1982), 11.

[6] Bessel Van der Kolk, and Alexander Mc Farlane, "The Black Hole of Trauma," *Traumatic Stress: The Effects of Overwhelming Experience on Mind, Body, and Society,* ed. Bessel Van der Kolk, Alexander Mc Farlane, and Lars Weisaeth, (London: The Guilford Press, 1996), 9.

[7] Ibid., 9.

[8] Jean Baudrillard, *Selected Writings,* ed. Mark Poster, (Stanford: Stanford University Press, 1988), 171.

[9] Van der Kolk and McFarlane, "Black Hole," 9.

[10] Ibid.

[11] Martin Heidegger, *Being and Time,* trans. John Macquarrie and Edward Robinson, (New York: Harper and Row, 1962), 152.

[12] Van der Kolk and McFarlane, "Black Hole," 9.

[13] Ibid.

[14] Carl Jung, *Analytical Psychology,* (New York: Vintage Books, 1968), 153.

[15] Ibid.,154.

[16] Elin Diamond, *Unmaking Mimesis: Essays on Feminism and Theater*, (New York: Routledge, 1997), 4.

[17] Van der Kolk and McFarlane, "Black Hole," 9.

[18] Sigmund Freud, *General Psychological Theory*, trans. Joan Riviere, (New York: Collier, 1972), 170.

[19] Joseph Roach, "Culture and Performance in the Circum-Atlantic World," *Performitivity and Performance*, ed. by Andrew Parker and Eve Kosofsky Sedgewick, (New York: Routledge, 1995), 237.

[20] Christina Reid, *Did You Hear the One About the Irishman?* and *The Belle of Belfast City*, (London: Methuen, 1989), 67.

[21] Ibid., 71.

[22] Ibid.

[23] Ibid., 82.

[24] Ibid., 85.

[25] Ibid., 89.

[26] Jacques Lacan, *The Four Fundamental Concepts of Psycho-Analysis*, trans. Alan Sheridan, (New York: Norton, 1981), 45.

[27] Ibid.

[28] Reid, *Did You Hear?*, 85-86.

[29] Anne Devlin, *Ourselves Alone with A Woman Calling and The Long March*, (London: Faber and Faber, 1986), 41.

[30] Ibid., 16.

[31] Judith Butler, *Bodies that Matter: On the Discursive Limits of Sex*, (New York: Routledge, 1993), 204.

[32] Ibid., 55.

[33] Ibid., 56.

[34] Ibid., 69.

[35] Ibid., 70.

[36] Joan Dayan, *Haiti, History, and the Gods*, (Berkely: University of California Press, 1995), 4.

[37] Kristeva, *Powers of Horror*, 12.

[38] Eileen Fairweather, *Only the Rivers Run Free: Northern Ireland, the Woman's War*, (London: Pluto Press, 1984), 130.

[39] *Second Commission on the Status of Women*, (Dublin: Stationary Office, 1993), 44.

[40] Van der Kolk and McFarlane, "Black Hole," 9.

[41] Christina Reid, Letter to Author, 19 September 1995. Christina Reid asks that it be recorded that these were her thoughts at the time she wrote the letter. The letter does not necessarily reflect her current views.

[42] Devlin, *Ourselves Alone*, 39.

[43] Ibid., 81.

[44] Homi Bhabha, *The Location of Culture*, (New York: Routledge, 1994), 66.

[45] Reid, *Did You Hear*, 71.

[46] Ibid., 74.

[47] Kristeva, *Powers of Horror*, 65.

[48] Reid, Letter.

[49] Ed Cairns, *Caught in Crossfire: Children and the Northern Ireland Conflict*, (Belfast: Appletree Press, 1987), 71.

[50] *Violence in Ireland*, (Dublin: The Irish Council on Churches, 1976), 48.

[51] Roland Barthes, *S/Z*, trans. Richard Miller, (New York: Hill and Wang, 1974), 41.

[52] Baudrillard, *Selected Writings*, 167.
[53] Anthony Buckley, and Mary Catherine Kenney, *Negotiating Identity: Rhetoric, Metaphor,and Social Drama in Northern Ireland*, (Washington: Smithsonian Institution Press, 1995), 68.
[54] Arjun Appadurai, *Modernity at Large*, (Minneapolis: University of Minnesota Press, 1997), 7.
[55] Patrick White, *The Needs of Young People in Northern Ireland*, (Belfast: Youth Link, 1993), 3.
[56] Ibid.
[57] Ibid., 8.
[58] Van der Kolk and McFarlane, "Black Hole," 9.
[59] White, *Needs of Young People*, 8.
[60] Kenneth Branagh, *Public Enemy*, (London: Faber and Faber, 1988), 15.
[61] Ibid., 18.
[62] Ibid.
[63] Ibid., 43.
[64] Ibid. 16.
[65] Ibid.
[66] Ibid., 16.
[67] Ibid., 16.
[68] Ibid., 28.
[69] Ibid., 43.
[70] Ibid., 39.
[71] White, *Needs of Young People*, 8.
[72] Branagh, *Public Enemy*, 39.
[73] Ibid., 20.
[74] Ibid., 52.
[75] Ibid., 44.
[76] Ibid.
[77] Ibid., 19.
[78] White, *Needs of Young People*, 8.
[79] Branagh, *Public Enemy*, 9.
[80] Ibid., 18.
[81] Ibid., 9.
[82] Ibid., 10.
[83] Ibid.
[84] Ibid., 11.
[85] Ibid., 3.
[86] Ibid., 7.
[87] Ibid., 19.
[88] Ibid., 7.
[89] Ibid., 24.
[90] Ibid., 25.
[91] Ibid.
[92] Ibid., 29.
[93] Ibid.
[94] Ibid., 38.
[95] Buckley and Kenney, *Negotiating Identity*, 147.
[96] Appadurai, *Modernity*, 155.

[97] Van der Kolk and McFarlane, "Black Hole," 9.

[98] Branagh, *Public Enemy*, ix.

[99] Ibid., 2.

[100] Ibid., 9.

[101] Ibid., 4.

[102] Ibid., 48.

[103] Jung, *Analytical Psychology*,140.

[104] Ibid.

[105] Joan Harbison, *Children of the Troubles*, (Belfast: Stranmillis College, 1993), ix.

[106] Ibid.

[107] Ibid.

[108] Cairns, *Caught in the Crossfire*, 11.

[109] Ibid.

[110] Jung, *Analytical Psychology*, 145.

[111] Van der Kolk and McFarlane, "Black Hole," 9.

[112] Buckley and Kenney, *Negotiating Identity*, 12-13.

[113] Kristeva, *Powers of Horror*, 8.

[114] Christopher Murray, "Drama, 1690-1800," *The Field Day Anthology of Irish Writing*, vol. *I*, ed. Seamus Deane, (Derry: Field Day Theatre Company, 1991), 504.

[115] Brian Friel, *Volunteers*, (Boston: Faber and Faber, 1979), 21.

[116] Ibid.

[117] Joep Leerssen, *Mere Irish and Fior Ghael*, (Cork: Cork University Press, 1996), 78-79.

[118] Frank McGuinness, *Observe the Sons of Ulster Marching Toward the Somme*, (London: Faber and Faber, 1986), 18.

[119] Ibid., 14.

[120] Ibid., 17.

[121] Michael Etherton, *Contemporary Irish Dramatists*, (London: Macmillan Publishers Limited, 1989), 48.

[122] Murray, "Drama," 504.

[123] McGuinness, *Observe the Sons*, 18.

[124] Michael Cronin, *Translating Ireland*, (Cork: Cork University Press, 1996), 144.

[125] McGuinness, *Observe the Sons*, 50.

[126] Ibid., 52.

[127] Ibid., 48.

[128] Ibid., 30-31.

[129] Sigmund Freud, *The Standard Edition of the Complete Psychological Works of Sigmund Freud, vol. I-XXII*, (London: Hogarth Press, 1953-1974), XVI, 382.

[130] Leerssen, *Mere Irish*, 79.

[131] Kristeva, *Powers of Horror*, 9.

[132] Jacques Derrida, "Signature Event Context," *Margins of Philosophy*, trans. by Alan Bass, (Chicago: University of Chicago Press, 1982), 22.

[133] McGuinness, *Observe the Sons*, 9.

[134] Ibid., 47.

[135] Baudrillard, *Selected Writings*, 167.

[136] McGuinness, *Observe the Sons*, 9.

[137] Patrick Galvin, *Three Plays*, (Belfast: Threshold, 1976), 142.

[138] Ibid.

[139] Ibid., 129.
[140] Ibid., 133.
[141] Ibid., 149.
[142] Ibid., 150.
[143] Ibid.
[144] Ibid., 159.
[145] Ibid. ,182.
[146] Ibid.
[147] Van der Kolk and McFarlane, "Black Hole," 9.
[148] Roy Ellen, "Rates of Change: Weasel Words and the Indispensable in Anthropological Analysis," *When History Accelerates: Essays of Rapid Social Change, Complexity and Creativity*, ed. C.M. Hann, (London: Athlone, 1994), 69-70.
[149] Fran Brearton, "Dancing unto Death: Perceptions of the Somme, the *Titanic* and Ulster Protestantism," *The Irish Review*, 20 (Winter/Spring 1997): 101.
[150] John Langshaw Austin, *How to do Things with Words*, (Cambridge: Harvard University Press, 1962), 14.
[151] Richard Kearney, *Poetics of Modernity*, (Atlantic Highlands: Humanities Press, 1995), 71.
[152] Christopher Murray, *Twentieth Century Irish Drama*, (Manchester: Manchester University Press, 1997), 204.
[153] Brearton, "Dancing," 97.
[154] Ibid., 97-98.
[155] John Wilson Foster, "Imagining the Titanic," *Returning to Ourselves: Second Violume of Papers from the John Hewitt International Summer School*), ed. Eve Patten, (Belfast: Lagan Press, 1995), 333.
[156] Ellen, "Rates of Change," 69.
[157] McGuinness, *Observe the Sons*, 80.
[158] Benedict Anderson, *Imagined Communities: Reflections on the Origins and the Spread of Nationalism*, (London: Verso, 1991), 7.
[159] Ellen, "Rates of Change," 70.
[160] Friel, *Volunteers*, 16.
[161] Ibid., 44.
[162] Ellen., "Rates of Change," 70.
[163] Michael Longley, "Letter," *Irish Times*, 2 March 1985, 23.
[164] McGuinness, *Observe the Sons*, 10.
[165] John Wilson Foster, *Forces and Themes in Ulster Fiction*, (Totowa, New Jersey: Rowman and Littlefield, 1974), 9.
[166] Richard Kearney, *Myth and Motherland*, (Derry: Field Day, 1984), 62-63.
[167] Ibid., 63.
[168] Brearton, "Dancing," 101.
[169] Ibid., 98.
[170] McGuinness, *Observe the Sons*, 49.
[171] Ibid., 51.
[172] Jean Baudrillard, *Selected Writing*, ed. Mark Poster, (Stanford: Stanford University Press, 1988), 170-71.
[173] Martin Heidegger, *Being and Time*, trans. John Macquarrie and Edward Robinson, (New York: Harper and Row, 1962), 62.
[174] Galvin, *Three Plays*, 137.
[175] Ibid.

[176] Ibid.
[177] Ibid.
[178] Ibid.
[179] Ibid.
[180] Ibid.
[181] Ibid., 174.
[182] Ibid.
[183] Ibid., 155.
[184] Ibid.
[185] Ibid.
[186] Ibid., 160.
[187] Ibid., 179.
[188] Ibid.
[189] Lacan, *Findamental Concepts*, 52-53.
[190] Brian Friel, quoted in Richard Kearney, "Transitional Crisis," *The Honest Ulsterman*, (Winter 1986): 37.
[191] Edward Said, *Orientalism*, (New York: Random House, 1978), 116.
[192] Ibid.

5

"Carnival":
The Reconstruction of Identity

A mural that appeared on Belfast's Flax Street in 1994 details an image that would be familiar to many residents and visitors in the North of Ireland. A feminized image of Ireland sits alone and apparently abandoned by a stream in the Irish countryside. Such depictions are normally a call to arms in defense of the Irish Republican ideal, a summons to defend Ireland from invaders, or a call to restore the lady to her dispossessed lands. However, on this particular mural, the caption does not solicit support for the Provisional Irish Republican Army, nor does it summon the memory of past wrongs. Rather, the caption on this mural reads "Meon an phobail a thógail tríd an chultúr,"[1] (the people's spirit is raised through culture). Moreover, the female image of Ireland releases a dove from her hand. The mural summons associations of both conflict and the hope for peace by referencing the image of the aisling. The woman represented in the aisling, since her origins, consistently provided an imaginative stimulus to the disenfranchised Catholic majority and later the authors of the Celtic Twilight who found in her the answer to their imaginative longings for a mythical, feminized Ireland. In the North of Ireland, the image of a feminized Ireland provided a empowering metaphor for the disenfranchised Catholic minority. Specifically, the female personification of Ireland has long stood for both the recognition of past wrongs, including traumatic and violent rupture, and the hope for a restoration of an integral Irish identity. This particular depiction, however, suggests a non-violent alternative for peace and integration, a sense of wholeness. Consequently, the mural very obviously utilizes the images common to traumatic rupture and masks of violence and transforms them into an image of an identity that integrates components of the Troubles into a new self-conception fashioned in order to lay the seeds of recovery. Ultimately, the mural produces an effect similar to Antonio Benitez-Rojo's carnival.

For Benitez-Rojo, carnival functions as a forum to expose the masks of those in power, to reveal their motives for maintaining order. It also functions as a forum for insurgency. In both cases, it functions as a way to come to terms with violence.

It is an embrace of social engagement. However, ultimately, its performative aspects are "unifying" and represent a "sociocultural synthesis." The theatre of the Troubles that focuses on the restorative functions in a way that would be familiar to the practitioners of Benitez-Rojo's carnival and to observers of the Flax Street mural. Specifically, much of contemporary Irish drama "performs" the masks of oppression and the means for liberation from those masks. Consequently, the drama details the reconstruction of social relationships, the rebuilding of mythic and spiritual constructions, and an engagement with history without the limiting archetypes of violent rupture. Essentially, the drama details the struggle to center an integrated view of self in relation to society, to spirituality, and to history. The theatrical representations of violence detail a process within which the violent structures of traumatic rupture lose much of their virulence. Within this process, a new ethnicity comes into play in the North, and "ethnicity has emerged as the key issue as various 'marginal' practices . . . [that] are becoming de-marginalized at a time when 'centered' discourses of cultural authority and legitimation . . . are becoming increasingly de-centered and destabilized."[2] Essentially, the traumatic structures that dominated Northern society are giving way, making room for non-traumatic means of interaction. Within this context and the construction of the new ethnicity, marginalized systems of understanding emerge as primary methods of communication. What Iain Chambers writes of the West, is true for traumatic structures in the North:

For if the West is in decline there have also unmistakably emerged from its shadows others who speak its languages while simultaneously signalling their provenance elsewhere: both in but not completely out of the West. . . . These voices, along with those who have been historically defined as internal Other, called upon to represent the obscured and denied side of occidental reason . . . apparently flaunt a disturbing excess. In this context rendez-vous within the languages of the West there emerges a supplement that becomes irreducible to the imperious unity that its languages were once presumed to embody.[3]

Basically, the non-traumatic language of marginalized discourse increases in influence and power in the North and, like the mural on Flax Street, builds forums and means of expression onto the components of traumatized discourse ultimately to escape from trauma.

Significantly, the new discourse and new ethnicity, like other narratives of Irish history, does not destroy the past. In fact it is precisely

the *absence* of a sense of an ending which has characterized the national narratives of Irish history. This has less to do with the 'unfinished business's of a united Ireland than with the realization that there is no possibility of undoing history, of removing all the accretions of conquest - the English language, the inscriptions of the Protestant Ascendency on the landscape and material culture, and so on. For this reason, there is no prospect of restoring a pristine, pre-colonial identity: the lack of historical closure, therefore, is bound up with a similar incompleteness in the culture itself, so that instead of being based on narrow ideals of racial purity and exclusivism, identity is open-ended and heterogeneous. But the important point in all of this is that the retention of the residues of conquest does not necessarily mean subscribing to the values which originally governed them. . . . Even the sheer survival of cultural artifacts from one era to another may transform their meaning, so that the same building (or, perhaps, even the same statue) 're-located' in a new political era becomes, in a sense, a radically different structure.[4]

Luke Gibbons's observations could easily read as a description of plays that portray individuals from the North who successfully refashion conceptions of identity. Within these plays, the elements of traumatic rupture, including sectarian notions of history and historical change and sometimes divisive religious and cultural practices, find a new means of expression, altered and, indeed, transformed by individuals who create identities that are "open-ended and heterogeneous." Therefore, the "cultural artifacts" that once represented violent rupture now stand for recovery and positive change. The theoretical observations regarding positive change find a resonance in clinical discussions regarding structures necessary for recovery from post-traumatic stress disorder. Specifically, the

search for meaning is a critical aspect of traumatized people's efforts to master their helplessness and sense of vulnerability. . . . Concepts such as fragmentation of awareness and conditioning do not address the spiritual and philosophical beliefs that are central to individual identity and motivation. These beliefs are also sustained by the cultural context and social fabric, which bind individuals to their social groups. These beliefs can be damaged in many traumas. . . . Religion provides a historical lineage of human suffering and capacity for regeneration. Prayers, music, and icons provide a powerful sense of endurance, despite the repeated onslaughts of disaster and war; prayer and the identification with the suffering of others can also provide a way forward.[5]

The search for meaning represented in some examples of Northern drama enables characters traumatized by events to master their sense of vulnerability. Moreover, the drama also portrays the restoration of identity through spirituality, interpersonal involvement, and constructive engagement with history.

SPIRITUAL AND MYTHIC RECONSTRUCTION

In "Solstice" Gerald Dawe writes of the birth of his son, who arrived in "that bad winter/when I was like a man/walking in a circle no one else was near" (ll. 1-3). Further, nature and the crisis of violent history accentuate the speaker's personal feelings of isolation. "The lakes had frozen, . . . and the news was all discontent/of *Sell-Out* and blame for the dead/country-boy faces that already were/fading from church wall and gate" (ll.4, 6-9). However, with his child's birth, the speaker

. . . saw the ice outside fall
and imagined the fires burning
on the Hill of Tara ring
across the concealed earth
towards a silent hospital

and our standing still
all around you, Olwen,
transfixed by your birth
in such a bitter season. (ll.16-24)

The speaker comes to terms with the violence and sites of traumatic rupture that surround him, as a consequence of the birth of his son, converting his introspective and solipsistic circling into an image of rebirth and renewal. Moreover, the speaker transforms his private circle into a communal one, paying homage with friends and family to his child. In addition, his new circle finds a resonance in ancient Irish myth and legend, consciously referring to the solstice rites on Tara. Furthermore, the poet's careful use of assonance in the lines that portray his renewal reinforces the natural thaw and the spiritual rejuvenation he feels at the birth of his son. The speaker "saw" the ice "fall" and imagined the rites of "Tara" leaning "towards" the hospital where he and his friends are "standing." The vowel and consonant sounds create a subtle unity between the speaker's personal images of renewal, the rebirth of the natural world, and ancient spiritual rites of resurrection. The speaker reconstitutes his identity, through the birth of his child, developing a personal alternative to the violent forces of the Troubles.

The difficult process for developing alternative, reconstituted identities, within the framework of Vincent Woods's *At the Black Pig's Dyke* and Seamus Heaney's *The Cure at Troy*, involves components akin to Gerald Dawe's reflections and to clinical stratagems for recovery. Specifically, in terms of the "re-establishment of secure social and cultural contacts,"[6] the two plays establish rituals, based in part on received images and traditions but also based on personal variation and revisions to those traditions, designed to recognize the factors that rupture identity and perpetuate that rupture. In addition, Woods's and Heaney's theatre provides an alternative identity that incorporates traumatic structures into a fully reconstituted sense of self. Furthermore, in a process similar to the clinical matrix of recovery that stresses the "accumulation of restorative experiences,"[7] the plays explore a process through which individuals regain control and mastery of their environment by recalling and incorporating into their consciousness the ruptured memories that cause trauma. Essentially, within the plays, characters come to terms with violence and transform the ruptured components of identity into a newly fashioned identity by combining received mythic images and a personal spirituality.

Many of the characters in the plays make a distinction between the emotional repercussions of violence and the objective factors that ultimately inform identity. As a consequence, they reconstitute a personal spirituality that enables them to re-establish meaningful personal, historical, and mythic contacts. Essentially,

if we can succeed in discriminating between objective knowledge and emotional value-judgements, then the gulf that separates our age from antiquity is bridged over. . . . The importance of this realization should not be underestimated, for it teaches us that there is an identity of fundamental human conflicts which is independent of time and place, . . . an indissoluble link binds us to the men of antiquity[that represents] . . . the way of inner sympathy on the one hand and of intellectual comprehension on the other. By penetrating into the blocked subterranean passages of our own psyches we grasp the living meaning of classical civilization, and at the same time we establish a firm foothold outside our own culture from which alone it is possible to gain an objective understanding of its foundations[8].

Jung's program for "transformation," considered within the context of Northern Irish drama, reveals that the characters come to understand the foundations of their personal and community history by severing the link that trauma has created between themselves and the violent factors that inform their understanding of their society. Moreover, once the link is severed, individuals, like the speaker of Gerlad Dawe's "Solstice," can then achieve a sense of the "living meaning" of their own classical civilization. Specifically, they come to terms with Irish historical, mythological, and geographical images and places that help them recover from traumatic experiences by refashioning their identities to include socially and historically engaging imaginative constructions.

Restoration of Social Support

In order to protect themselves from further trauma, traumatized individuals must relinquish autonomous masks adopted as protective guards against vulnerability to violence and adapt a reconstituted social self. However, before "it can adopt a positive voice, freedom [from the paralyzing effects of trauma] requires an effort at disalienation. . . . It is through the effort to recapture the self and to scrutinize the self, it is through the lasting tension of their freedom that men will be able to create the ideal conditions of existence for a human world, . . . the quite simple attempt to touch the other, to feel the other, to explain the other to myself." [9] Basically, the newly forged link requires an act of will, a gesture of acceptance of one's personal and communal heritage. Moreover, the method of restoration differs from "cultural narratives" in that it involves a primacy of emotional interaction, rather than an intellectual acceptance, not only with familial and community networks but also with the past. A confidence within one's own culture opens up the potentiality of "Romance" which "seems to offer the possibility of sensing other historical rhythms, and of demonic or utopian transformations of a real now unshakably set in place," in turn setting in motion "the salvational perspective of romance to a reexpression of Utopian longings, a renewed mediation on the Utopian community, a reconquest . . . of some feeling for a salvational future." [10] Therefore, a confidence in and an empathetic understanding of one's own culture and background, a firmly grounded sense of historical identity allows an individual to approach other cultures without a sense of threat and menace. In the North of Ireland, attempts to forge such links occur within narratives, an ideal forum for performing joint and individual communal identities. For the individual, "the solution to the 'unity of diversity' question is fairly simple. Most people can, at will, construct a simple narrative that unites their particular worlds into a single, overarching, syntagmatic framework. . . . This enables that person to dramatize the notion that his different identities are compatible. He is, therefore, not several people, but only one. . . . Specific dramas can draw together several of an individual's multifarious partial identities into a single unified identity." [11]

In terms of inter-community relations, "in an area where there were remarkably good relations between Catholics and Protestants, individuals on both sides tended to tell the same oral history. The stories were told to uphold the virtues of being a good neighbor, to denigrate excessive devotion to making money, and in particular to emphasize the importance of maintaining good, friendly relationships across the sectarian divide." [12] In the collective experience, offered by the narrative, of understanding, indeed living through performance, each community's history extends an individual's emotional attachment with his/her environment, even if that environment is constituted, as in the North, by rivals.

In response to ruptures to identity created by traumatic events, Vincent Woods's *At the Black Pig's Dyke* and Seamus Heaney's *The Cure at Troy* ritualize a method for re-establishing social and cultural support. Through allegory, the playwrights present a process for integrating the traumatic event into a character's consciousness in order to come to terms with trauma and to refashion a fully-integrated identity. In clinical terms,

emotional attachment is probably the primary protection against being traumatized. People seek close emotional relationships with others in order to help them anticipate, meet, and integrate difficult life experiences. . . . In recognition of this need for affiliation as protection against trauma, it has become widely accepted that the central issue in acute crisis intervention is the provision and restoration of social support. [13]

In plays that present the restoration of social support, the process for overcoming traumatic disruption involves several parts. Initially, individuals must come to terms with the extent of the traumatic disruption and the extent of their emotional isolation. In terms of the North of Ireland, this part of the process involves recognizing the full impact of sectarian and colonial rupture. Subsequently, individuals exposed to trauma must put behind them flawed dynamics of protection, including masks of historical or cultural resonance that seem to disrupt traumatic threat. Within the context of Northern Ireland, the process includes structures that enabled the individual to find status or protection from violence; roles of martyr, Republican volunteer, and Orange loyalist are just a few examples. Next, individuals must articulate a framework for overcoming violence that contains within it elements with a non-sectarian cultural resonance. Finally, individuals must provide their own variation on the cultural framework, adapting it to their individual needs and to their particular traumatic reaction.

Ultimately, both playwrights produce an allegorical resolution through which they express recovery. The individual interpretation of the cultural framework, the articulation of difference, proves essential in the development of a type of hybrid identity that integrates not only traumatic elements into an individual's consciousness but also serves as a model for a fully integrated society. Essentially, the

representation of difference must not be hastily read as the reflection of *pre-given* ethnic or cultural traits set in the fixed tablet of tradition. The social articulation of difference, from the minority perspective, is a complex, ongoing negotiation that seeks to authorize cultural hybridities that emerge in moments of historical transformation. The 'right' to signify from the periphery of authorized power and privilege does not depend on the persistence of tradition; it is resourced by the power of tradition to be reinscribed through the conditions and contradictoriness that attend upon the lives of those who are 'in the minority.' The recognition that tradition bestows is a partial form of identification. In restaging the past it introduces other, incommensurable cultural temporalities into the invention of tradition.[14]

Basically, individual interpretation of cultural tradition insures that the tradition will not overwhelm an individual's identity or become a mask of identification with no internal, substantive resonance. The individual must improvise, using the cultural forms as a starting point, in order to re-establish ruptured cultural and social dynamics and identifiers.

In specific terms, the final image of *The Black Pig's Dyke* suggests a type of ritual healing of communal bonds. Elizabeth, whose character creates a narrative of the Strange Knight at the beginning of each act and just before the final curtain, describes a three-part process by which the land can be renewed after violence. The process involves a series of movements from harmony to strife. The first part includes the recognition that the land exists in a state of chaos as a consequence of violent disruption. "The Strange Knight remained in his castle. He watched from the ramparts and no one came. The land around him grew rancid from the decay of bodies in the ground."[15] The Knight realizes that his kingdom is "rancid" and that he is alone. His acts of violence that created the decaying bodies distance himself from communal involvement. Significantly, he initially seeks others from his "ramparts," from the defences of his castle. He comes to terms with the world inside his protective cocoon of violent conquest.

Subsequently, in the second part of the process, the Knight attempts to bring harmony back to the land. "He ordered a banquet but there was no food; a ball but there were no musicians; a duel but there was no one to fight. He posted orders that a beautiful woman be brought to him to sire an heir; all night he lay alone, naked, in his bed. And the Strange Knight grew lonely and came to be filled with sorrow."[16] The Knight requests four forms of ritual healing. Each begins with a ceremonial attempt to restore harmony to the land but ends with a further recognition of chaos. The first form, a banquet, includes components not only of a communal gathering but a type of spiritual communion as well, a ceremony in which food is digested to restore an equilibrium and vitality to the land. However, at this point within the Knight's tale, there is no sacred communion. The second type of healing involves a courtship ceremony. Through dance and ritualized movement, a type of mating ritual occurs on a large scale. However, in the Knight's tale, the music, a necessary component of the ritual, is unattainable. Next, the Knight orders a duel, a ceremonial form of sacrifice. However, once again the

Knight's desires are thwarted because there is no one to sacrifice. Ultimately, the Knight seeks to restore vitality to the land through a ritualized sexual encounter. An heir would serve as a metaphor for the vitality of the kingdom. However, once again, circumstance frustrates the Knight's plans. No one comes to consummate his ceremonial act of replenishment. Despite the Knight's recognition of the emptiness of his landscape and his efforts to restore vitality through a series of rituals, each attempt to replenish his kingdom finds frustration, representing an attempt to bring harmony to chaos but culminating in simply a recognition of further chaos.

Ultimately, in a process reminiscent of ancient sacred rituals, the Knight emerges from his castle.

He walked back along the road he had travelled till he came to the place where he'd met the woman with the riddle. He fell to the ground and begged to be forgiven. His tears fell like rain on the soil and the water soaked down, down into the heart of the dead woman. And out of her heart grew a flower-a blood-red poppy. And the Strange Knight plucked it and when he did it fell asunder. (*Elizabeth lets the poppy pedals in her hand drift to the ground.*) Petal after petal drifted to the ground and out of each sprang a dozen women with hooks and seeds and implements to sow and harvest. They yoked the Strange Knight to the ground and so began the endless task of restoring the land to life and the beginning of happiness. (*Elizabeth scatters the final petals of the poppy and stands still as the lights fade, very slowly, into darkness.*)[17]

The Strange Knight's tale is reminiscent of ancient rites. Specifically, in ancient ceremonies the ritual elements include "the centre of the campsite, which will become the hearth, the ceremonial meeting place, the threshing floor, and finally the agora . . . the dancing ground."[18] On the land where he committed his first crime, the Knight's tears and blood create the ritual components. On this land, a ceremonial dance occurs through which a harvest of sacrificial death emerges. His recognition of his isolation creates an empty center onto which his tears can flow. Likewise, in ancient rites, the dancers "leave the center empty, like the evening sky, and into this potent emptiness" the "dancing is directed, unself-conscious, mirrourless, questioning. The circle is charmed because it encloses emptiness. The emptiness is charged not only because" it was "constructed by joining hands and gazing inward, but also because it is what our dancing bodies address."[19] Within the Knight's story, the "women with hooks" engage in a dance, addressing the Knight's empty space to restore potency to the ravaged land. The Knight's ritualized empty center becomes a threshing floor that produces seeds to replenish the land and sacred food, the Knight's body. Moreover, as the ritual components come together in the Knight's final acts, they express on an individual level, the formulaic ceremonial cures he attempted earlier. The ceremonial dance finds expression in the women's movements. The Knight becomes the sacred communion, the ceremonial sacrifice. Initially, his tears and later his blood inseminate the earth producing a harvest that will renew the land. Ultimately, the Knight's individual interpretation enables the healing ritual to proceed. Indeed, in ancient ceremonies of healing, the participants in the rite "find that the secret of song and dance composition is the emergence of solo work from the ensemble."[20] Essentially, in the ancient rituals, individuals must offer their own creative interpretation, their own variation of received ceremony and ritual in order for the rite to prove successful. Indeed, the Knight becomes not simply the organizer or a participant in the rite of healing. Rather, he becomes a component in the ritual. Consequently, within the Knight's tale, ancient ceremonies, music, and ritualized dance become not simply masks behind which the rupture of traumatic experience can lie but components through which the land can be restored. Woods's play provides the ceremonial elements of confrontation of violence, the recognition of traumatic disruption and emptiness, and the allegorical healing of the land. His character of the Knight, then, finds not a sense of futility in death and destruction but a sense of purpose within ritual.

Earlier components of the Knight's story detail recognition of rupture and certain nuances of sectarian history particular to the North of Ireland, offering a vision of sectarian conflict that recognizes the animosity and violent rivalry between the two sides but also recognises the role the English play in accentuating the rivalry. Within a portion of the allegory, the Knight stands for the British:

The Strange Knight went on till he arrived at a fair where two men were haven' a dispute over a piece of land. He said he could settle it and offered a fine price to whichever of them would sell it to them. One man said he'd sell it that minute, the other said he wouldn't sell it for love or money. So the Strange Knight said to the second man: you're the owner, it's your land. . . . Then he shot the two of them and had the land for himself.[21]

Exploiting the tensions between the two parties, the Knight imposes a settlement on them, using his vision of justice to arbitrate the dispute. Ultimately, however, the Knight exploits the weakened condition of both sides to take the land for himself. Like the English in the North, whose troops imposed on both Protestant and Catholic communities decisions from a remote parliament, the Knight's arbitrary use of power exploits the rivalries between two factions to benefit himself. At this point in the Knight's story, there is no offer of reconciliation between factions. However, that the sectarian history of the North would find allegorical representation in the image of two parties exploited by an interloper suggests a common history for warring factions. Furthermore, it is in this imagining of a common past, that reconciliation may come to fruition. Indeed, "*Imagine* is the operational word for the liberationist who, far more than the nationalist, needs the sanction of previous authority if history is to be blown open. That sanction comes from history not as a chronological narrative but as symbolic pattern, in which certain utopian moments are extracted from its flow."[22] As Declan Kiberd argues, liberation from sectarian divisions finds expression in the "imagined" symbols of pluralism. In the Knight's tale, the created story of a common enemy simultaneous with the recognition of sectarian conflict creates a utopian moment that can be extracted from the violent past in order to offer the possibility for reconciliation or at least the imaginings of a common heritage. In the words of Seamus Deane, the

Knight's tale offers a counter to a Romanticised, sectarian history and "seeks to escape from it into a pluralism of the present."[23] The plural dream, as articulated by the Knight's tale, does not dismiss the sources and heritage of violence but rather explores the violence in which third parties have exploited the divisions in the North to the disadvantage of both Protestant and Catholic communities. Within the common history of exploitation, the possibility for negotiations toward a pluralistic and non-sectarian identity can begin.

In a further allegorical representation of sectarian history the Knight's tale details elements of common struggle against a king, recalling the co-operation between Protestants and Catholics in rebellions such as the 1798 rising:

The Strange Knight walked on again till he came to a castle. There was a rook perched on the rampart with blood on its beak. The Knight asked whose blood was it and the rook said: "It's the king's blood. The people have killed the King and his body is in pieces in the courtyard inside." So the Knight thanked the rook and went inside to the people. He told them they had done a wonderful thing and he wanted to be their leader. So they elected him their leader and that night held a great banquet where he set one half of them against the other; and they fought till there was no one left alive but the Strange Knight. . . . And he was happy then: to have evaded answering the riddle, to have the piece of land for himself and to have the castle without King or people to bother him.[24]

Once again, the allegory of the Knight details how a third party exploits the divisions within a community. However, within this portion of the tale, the Knight does more to create sectarian conflict that in his earlier sectarian allegory. Here, he literally disunifies the rebellious populace so he might better control them. English colonial history in Ireland is full of such reports of British interference in Irish affairs with the intention of disrupting inter-community relations in order to govern the island more easily. Once again, in the recognition of a common history of exploitation, the allegory offers the possibility of a unified, pluralistic society in the North. Indeed, the plural vision "need not always take the high road: where there are borders to be crossed, unapproved roads might prove more beneficial in the long run than those patrolled by global powers."[25] As Luke Gibbons argues, the "unapproved" roads of allegory and narrative, of symbolic imagination, without the inteference of outside powers might prove beneficial in short-circuiting the colonial divide. Within the recognition of the British role, in creating and accentuating colonial divisions, lie the seeds of a potential pluralistic vision for the North, uniting Protestant and Catholic parties in opposition to outside forces.

The Knight's tale also recognizes the various colonial divisions existing between the Republic and the North. It begins with the confrontation between the riddle woman and the Knight:

At that time there was a Strange Knight on the road. He met a woman with a riddle. How many people were in the world before the world was made? How many graves did it take to bury them? What way were they laid? - Facin' north, south, east or west? And did they rest or not from then till now? He said he'd answer any riddle in three parts but not in four.

As She rose her hook to kill him - but if she did he shot her first - through the heart with a golden bullet.[26]

Within the four parts of the riddle lie the symbols of the four provinces of Ireland. The geographic divisions stand for the Northern province of Ulster, the Southern province of Munster, the Eastern province of Leinster, and the Western province of Connaught. Further, within the riddle woman's questions, reference is made to ancient traditions in Ireland that recognize not only previous civilizations but alternative traditions to contemporary English customs. The allusion to the direction of the bodies recalls the ancient manner of burying the dead standing up and ready for battle. However, the Knight refuses to answer her questions because they are in four parts and he will only answer a riddle in three, recalling the partition of the four provinces. Essentially, the Knight creates a division in the riddle woman's questions where no division existed. The allegorical tale of the riddle woman's death functions in two ways. "By creatively reinterpreting the past, narrative can serve to release new and hitherto concealed possibilities of understanding one's history; and by critically scrutinising the past it can wrest tradition away from the conformism that is always threatening to overpower it."[27] By creatively recognizing that there are four parts to one riddle, the allegorical tale recognises that there are four parts to one Ireland. In addition, the tale releases the understanding that the Knight, an outsider, divides the riddle into separate parts and destroys the unifying principle behind the parts, the riddle woman. The Knight's tale then, in Kearney's words, wrests tradition from the conformism of a divided history. The tale recognises the ruptures created by sectarian and colonial history and attempts to reconcile them within its allegorical components.

A similar allegorical process occurs in Seamus Heaney's *The Cure at Troy*: A poetic expression recognizes and metaphorically heals components of cultural and social identity ruptured by violence. However, Heaney's play emphasizes not so much the factors that directly contribute to the destruction of identity but rather the masks of identity that certain characters adopt in order to come to terms with violence. The chorus in Heaney's play acknowledges the transitory and limited nature of masks of identity and posits an alternative that directly confronts all the implications of violence, attempting to incorporate them into a new identity capable of re-integrating traumatic elements into individual identity. Heaney's chorus creates a type of hermeneutic identity: "Hermeneutics is concerned with the permanent spirit of language . . . . Poetic and mythic symbols (for example) do not just express nostalgia for some forgotten world. They constitute a disclosure of unprecedented worlds, an opening onto other possible meanings which transcend the established limits of our actual world."[28] Within *The Cure at Troy*, Heaney's choric poetry discloses new possibilities for the re-establishment of secure social contacts outside the masks of ideological representation. The actual world of the North then is transformed from one in which the archetypes of history dominate individual consciousness, because of their seemingly invulnerable facades, to a world of possible reconciliation within the allegorical representation of unprecedented worlds of common memory, heritage, and suffering.

   Just as the process of the Knight's tale's rejuvenation of the land begins in the recognition of the damage to the landscape, Heaney's chorus begins the process of coming to terms with masks of violent identity by recognizing the nature of masks. The chorus observes "Gods and human beings [who are]/All throwing shapes, every one of them/[is]Convinced he's in the right, all of them glad/To repeat themselves and their every last mistake,/No matter what."[29] For the gods and men who "throw shapes," their "whole life [is] spent admiring themselves/For their own long-suffering."[30] Essentially, "they're fixated,/Shining with self-regard like polished stones."[31] For the gods and men, the adoption of masks of identity, of "shapes" of identity, enables them to create an image of themselves that is like a "polished stone," an image that removes all stain of blame from their consciousness and makes their vulnerable identities impenetrable behind the stone mask. Rather than come to terms with suffering, each comes to terms with an image of a long-suffering character, created in response to traumatic threat but unable to shield the individual from violence because the polished mask prevents the individual from coming to terms with anyone beyond himself.

   However, just as in the Knight's tale, a curative is offered through an allegorical representation. The chorus recognizes that it was "poetry" that "allowed the gods to speak. It was the voice/Of reality and justice."[32] Poetry offers a "real" alternative to the imagined identities rooted in "long-suffering" and solipsism. Poetry offers the possibility for communication, for communal interaction; it "allowed the gods to speak." Just as the Knight recognizes the necessary elements for rejuvenation but is at first incapable of realizing their individual potential, the chorus in *The Cure at Troy* recognizes ritual elements and procedures, advising the spectators to

. . . hope for a great sea-change
On the far side of revenge.
Believe that a further shore
Is reachable from here.
Believe in miracles
And cures and healing wells.
Call miracle self-healing:
The utter, self-revealing
Double-take of feeling.
If there's fire on the mountain
Or lightning and storm
And a god speaks from the sky
That means someone is hearing
The outcry and the birth-cry
Of new life at its term.[33]

Within the chorus's speech, just as in the Knight's survey of the landscape, there exists a recognition of the devastation of the land. However, in Heaney's play, the chorus goes beyond a simple recognition of chaos and penetrates into the causes for chaotic violence. The chorus challenges the individual to reach beyond "revenge" for "self-healing" that is a product of "self-revealing" acknowledgment of emotions. Therefore, within the traditional symbols of "healing wells" and "fire on the mountain," the chorus indicates there is communication-"someone is hearing." Within the revelation that self exists independent of the masks of identity, a curative of social discourse offers itself, a discourse that proves regenerative, a discourse of "new life" that recalls Gerald Dawe's "Solstice."

The clear product of this recognition supplies a poetic counterpart to the Knight's individual interpretation of the ceremonial elements. The chorus explicitly refers to the masks of violence and martyrdom in the North and penetrates into the common bond between communities, mutual suffering. Essentially, the masks of violent identity fall away to reveal genuine human emotion rather than avoidance, and a sense of community rather than solipsism. The chorus observes

Human beings suffer,
They torture one another,
They get hurt and get hard.
No poem or play or song
Can fully right a wrong
Inflicted and endured.
The innocent in goals
Beat on their bars together.
A hunger striker's father
Stands in the graveyard dumb.
The police widow in wails
Faints at the funeral home.
History says, *Don't hope*
On this side of the grave.
But then, once in a lifetime
The longed-for tidal wave
Of justice can rise up,
And hope and history rhyme.[34]

The chorus recognizes the masks consequent of traumatic disruption. Individuals "get hurt and get hard." They fail to recognize their individual identity behind their hard masks of "polished stone." Moreover, nothing, not even poetry can "fully" compensate for suffering and violence. However, within the "rhyme" of "hope and history," within the poetic expression of historical suffering and the possibilities for reconciliation, the chorus can "leave/Half-ready to believe/That a crippled trust might walk/And the half-true rhyme is love."[35] The promise for the "crippled trust" lies in the mutual suffering behind the masks of traumatic disruption. Both the family of the hunger striker and the dead policemen, martyrs from both communities, suffer. Their sufferings and its recognition and expression of commonality with violence through poetry equip the society, so the chorus suggests, to form a communal bond beyond pain and in "love." The "half-true rhyme" then is that both communities are united, despite the masks of violence that separate them, by a common history. If the violent and disruptive particulars can be acknowledged but then set aside, the remaining half truth of common suffering can supplant the divisive masks of identity that prevent communal interaction. Essentially, commonality through suffering is only half of the truth. The whole truth is a history of division. Just as the Knight's tale allegorically recognizes the rivalries of sectarian history and the divisions of colonial intervention, the chorus acknowledges the masks and histories of both communities. Similarly, just as the Knight's tale forms a bond in mutual victimization, the chorus forms a bond between the sides through a mutual recognition for the consequences of history in the suffering of both communities, uniting them into one community and metaphorically healing the cultural and social divisions consequent of traumatic disruption and skewed adaptation to violence.

Accumulation of Restorative Experiences

An additional method of coming to terms with trauma involves the establishment of feelings of control that culminate in a sense of mastery of day-to-day existence, establishing a sense of the real that exists beyond the dominion of traumatized reality. "Such a breach in 'reality' can therefore be fruitfully exposed and explored in order to deviate and unpack the languages that previously blocked our passage to the recognition of other realities."[36] Basically, the recognition and reinforcement of a non-traumatic daily life enables an individual to acknowledge the transitory and self-defeating qualities of the mask of violent interaction. The compensation involves an identity not reliant on the contingencies of a sometimes violent society because the newly-found identity is open to change and transformation. Indeed, the new identity must always change and adapt in order to ward off the possibility of traumatic re-experience. In the North of Ireland, the newly formed identities must acknowledge the fragmentary narrative affected by violence and chance and incorporate them into consciousness displacing the seemingly whole narratives of ideological history. In an obvious way, the new "ethical imagination . . . resists using narrative in a totalising or ideologizing manner . . . . It obviates the temptation of *grand narrative* by retrieving and projecting 'fragmentary narratives's whose very incompleteness serves as a critical reminder of their own *narrative origins*. Refusing to do violence to the past or the future by reducing history to some principle of triumphalist identity, ethical imagination keeps narrative sensitive to local and situational judgement. . . . Hermeneutic imagination is ethical, in short, when it keeps narrative perpetually mindful that it is *narrative*-- and, therefore, open to being other than it is." [37] Basically, the new identity must acknowledge differences between Catholic and Protestant, between Nationalist and Republican, between the RUC, the British government, and Protestant paramilitary groups. A new hermeneutic identity is not an artificial synthesis of diverse identities but rather a purging of threat and violence from difference. Further, it is necessarily marked by its ability to function within the norms and structures of ordinary life, outside the perpetual cycles of repeating stress and violence that are essential to maintain traumatic masks of identity. Basically, the new hermeneutic identities are equipped to handle stress by reacting to potentially threatening circumstances in ways that are designed to eliminate the sense of threat in those circumstances.

At the Black Pig's Dyke and *The Cure at Troy* also detail a process in which individuals regain control and mastery of their environment by recalling and incorporating into their consciousness the ruptured memories that cause trauma. The characters confront traumatic experiences and convert them from factors that destroy identity into conditions that inform a reconstituted identity. Within this process, mythic and personal memories combine to counteract the traumatic rupture. In clinical terms, "because the reliving and warding off of traumatic memories are the central psychological preoccupation of traumatized people, there is little room for new, gratifying experiences that might allow for reparation of past injuries to the self. Patients need to expose themselves actively to experiences that provide them with feelings of mastery and pleasure."[38] The reconstituted identities of Woods's and Heaney's plays base themselves in a framework similar to the clinical matrix. Essentially, characters achieve a sense of mastery and pleasure when they abandon the traumatic structures in favor of a personally reconstituted identity that incorporates the violence into their consciousness within a matrix that gives individuals a sense of control over the violence. Carl Jung defined such a process as

the *objectification of impersonal images*. It is an essential part of the process of individualization. Its goal is to detach consciousness from the object so that the individual no longer places the guarantee of his happiness, or of his life even, in factors outside himself, whether they be persons, ideas, or circumstances, but comes to realize that everything depends on whether he holds the treasure or not. If the possession of that gold is realized, then the centre of gravity is *in* the individual and no longer in an object on which he depends.[39]

Basically, the subjects of Jung's analysis and the characters in *At the Black Pig's Dyke* and *The Cure at Troy* must wrest control from "circumstances of life," such as traumatic violence in order to achieve a sense of contentment. A character is, essentially, "faced with the necessity of finding an individual method by which the impersonal images are given shape. . . . But if he is able to objectify the impersonal images and relate to them, he is in touch with that vital psychological function which from the dawn of consciousness has been taken care of by religion."[40] In order to repair the "individual psyche" that has been "severed" by traumatic rupture, the characters must "find an individual method" through which they can incorporate traumatic structures into their consciousnesses and gain control over them.

One such method occurs in *At the Black Pig's Dyke*'s mummers's musical and dance sequences, in which they come to terms with sectarian violence and, as a consequence, accumulate restorative emotional experiences that confront trauma and integrate it into their personalities, through music and dance, but do not avoid it or attempt to fashion an escape from it. Initially, however, Captain Mummer appeals to music as a diversion from violence, saying "pigs squeal in Ulster, echoed all 'round/Strike up the music to block out the sound."[41] Indeed, the most immediate musical sequence could be read as an escape. However, shortly thereafter, the mummers's performance imaginatively re-creates Sarah and Lizzie's death.

Captain Mummer picks up the lantern and holds it aloft with one hand; with the other hand he raps his stick on the ground, moving/swaying as if he were trying to shoulder open a door. The circle of mummers moves/sways to the same rhythm and on the fifth rap the straw wall bursts open and falls, the mummers scatter and the bodies of Lizzie Boles and Sarah fall to the ground with a scattering of red confetti.[42]

Within the play, the mummers create a space through which Lizzie and Sarah will eventually tell the story of their own lives and the factors surrounding their deaths. Ritually recreating the moment of the women's deaths, through the repetition of movement and sound, allows for a sense of control over the violent event and simultaneously allows for an emotional coming to terms with the act. Symbolically, the captain illuminates the scene; he sheds light on the deaths of the women by "pick[ing] up the lantern and hold[ing] it aloft." He confronts the stark reality of violence in his effort to "shoulder open a door." At the same time, he initiates a ritualistic recreation of the violence with his other hand. As he moves and sways, the "circle of mummers moves/sways to the same rhythm." Subsequently, the red confetti recreates the moment of death and casts the mummers as the cause of the women's death; the mummers let loose the blood. By taking the role of the assassins, Captain Mummer and his troupe take the sin of murder upon themselves, coming face to face not only with a horrific moment of sectarian violence but also ritually beginning a process through which they can purge themselves and their society of the most serious repercussions of the traumatic event by integrating it into their personalities. Subsequently, through music, the mummers ritualistically resurrect Lizzie and Sarah. Captain Mummer tells his men to "play the tune, play the tune that was her favourite. And make a good job of it for the last time."[43] The troupe responds by playing the

first verse of the Enniskillen Dragoons and [when they are playing] . . . the second verse [they are] . . . interrupted by the return of Tom Fool (minus mask) who rushes in stage left beating a badhran. . . . The musician plays another verse of the Enniskillen Dragoons. Tom Fool then begins a slow single-note beat on the badhran. The mummers pick up the straw wall, Lizzie Boles and Sarah rise up and stand still for a few beats, looking out at the audience. They exit through the small door as the mummers move upstage, hang the straw wall in two sections on the side-walls and stand facing the audience, backs to the walls. Tom Fool and Miss Funny stand stage left and when all the others are in place they march downstage-centre to the badhran beat.[44]

The drum beat with its ceremonial repetition and the "favourite" song" repeated one "last time" conjure Sarah and Lizzie from the dead. When they rise, they stare directly into the audience, summoning the audience into the ritual as witnesses to the circumstances and hatred surrounding the murders. The ceremonial elements of the ritual, even though they recall the traumatic event in clear and unambiguous terms, provide the basis for emotional recuperation. Indeed, the "paradox of the restoration of behaviour resides in the phenomenon of repetition itself: no action or sequence of actions may be performed exactly the same way twice; they must be reinvented or recreated at each appearance. In this improvisatory behavioral space, memory reveals itself as imagination."[45] Like the Knight's tale and the choric elements of Heaney's play, it is not simply in the recognition of the traumatic event but in the imaginative coming to terms with the event that recuperation occurs. Moreover, by pulling the audience into the play, Woods makes the spectators participate in the ritual. He imaginatively engages them so that they become not simply observers but a part of the performance. By breaking down the "fourth wall," he refuses to allow them to be passive but demands imaginative engagement and involvement. In this sense, the mummers and the audience become part of the ritual restoration and coming to terms with traumatic violence. The house has a stake in the production.

Throughout the play, Vincent Woods does stage moments of restorative rites, but not all of them engage the audience in terms of tragedy and suffering. In one scene, Woods uses humor to recognize and then resolve sectarian divisions.

Captain Mummer: The straw wren-it's a long time since I saw one of them. Do you know the story of the wren? *(Sarah shakes her head.)* Well, the way I heard it, it was the wren betrayed Saint Stephen and him hidin' on the Roman soldiers in a field of corn. The bird flew up and gave away his hiding place and ever after he was hunted and killed for a traitor. *(Some of the mummers have been nodding their heads in agreement; others shaking their heads in obvious disagreement. Of the latter Tom Fool and Miss Funny are the most vehement.)* That's my version of it-though I know some of ye heard different.
Tom Fool and Miss Funny: No, no, no, The way we heard it was. . .
Tom Fool: it was the wren that betrayed a regiment of Billy's men at the Battle of the Boyne. . .
Miss Funney They were creepin' up on a gantry of others that was asleep. . .
Tom Fool: And didn't the wren fly up and waken them.
. .
Miss Funny :They routed Billy's men and killed every last one of them. . .
Tom Fool: That's why the Orange men kill the wren the same as everybody else. . . .
Captain Mummer: Isn't that a good one? The same wee bird in a field of corn in the East and in a battlefield in this whelp of a country.[46]

The wren, a symbol of ritual sacrifice, becomes a tool for comic resolution. Captain Mummer identifies himself as a Catholic by recalling the tradition of St. Stephen and the wren. His story loosely conceals an allegory of colonial relations. Within the tale, Rome and Britain and the Irish and early Christians parallel one another. The wren stands as the informer. By ritualistically purging the wren from their society, those sympathetic to this version of the story symbolically purge themselves of not only colonial dominance but cultural impurities; the allegory takes on further significance later in the play as Hugh is killed for being an informer. The alternative version of the tale also isolates traitorous or impure components of a society and singles them out in the body of the wren for sacrifice: "the Orange men kill the wren the same as everybody else." However, rather than resolve the conflict between the two stories through sectarian confrontation, the captain humorously points to the similarities between the stories. Moreover, he takes on the role of the fool, assuming the guise of someone who believes both versions of the stories. The subsequent laughter, from the audience, symbolically kills the captain and resolves the sectarian differences. Essentially, the captain offers himself up as the object of ridicule in order to resolve the tension surrounding both versions of the stories, the alternative stories standing for the alternative traditions of both communities. Within his humorous representation of the verity of both traditions, the captain undermines the earnestness and claims of exclusiveness of both sides, offering a space for reconciliation. Subsequently, the laughter focuses the tension and subtle aggression on the figure of the captain, whom the audience marks as a fool by their inevitable reaction. Once again, Woods engages the audience in the rituals of the play, makes the spectators participants in the ceremonial restoration. The captain's act of insurgent humor finds a resonance with more serious restorative rituals. Essentially, the

borderline work of culture demands an encounter with 'newness's that is not part of the continuum of past and present. It creates a sense of the new as an insurgent act of cultural translation. Such art does not merely recall the past as social cause or aesthetic precedent; it renews the past, refiguring it as a contingent 'in-between' space, that innovates and interrupts the performance of the present. The 'past-present' becomes part of the necessity, not the nostalgia, of living.[47]

Basically, the captain straddles the borderline between the two traditions, comically legitimizing yet subtly undermining both. Subsequently, his act does not simply recall the past but rather renews the past with laughter focused on him as the figure of the fool who undermines both traditions but also brings them together and brings audience and actors together in the simultaneous act of laughter.

    Conversely in Sarah's and Lizzie's story the motif of sacrifice and informer takes on more horrific proportions in order to come to terms with a post-traumatic, reconstituted identity. Their narrative does not resolve confrontation through humor. Indeed, their stories do more to recognize the horror of traumatic rupture. Specifically, Lizzie, through her thoughts about her lover Hugh, comes to terms with the violent history of her family and focuses on the masks of violence and how they distort individual identity.

Sarah: (singing)
The Wren, The Wren, The King of all Birds
On Saint Stephen's night was caught in the furze.
Lizzie: You remember that?
Sarah: I remember it. Daddy singin' it to me. I
remember his eyes. (*louder/direct*) Hugh's eyes have
changed since Sean was killed. I don't know him any
more.[48]

Within their exchange, mother and daughter introduce the wren as a symbol of
sacrifice and associate that sacrifice with a father who was murdered and a lover
whom violence has changed. After the death of Sean, Hugh adopts a mask of the
violent Republican volunteer to achieve revenge, to combat a sense of helplessness
in the face of death, and to protect himself from emotional vulnerability. The mask
distorts Hugh's identity so much that his lover no longer recognizes him.

Sarah, later in the play, more clearly sees an association between Hugh and her
father, one subtlety hinted at in her reference to Hugh's eyes immediately after she
discusses her father's eyes.

I always imagined his eyes were the same as Daddy's. I had it in me head since I was a child
that father's eyes were brown. I remember sittin' on his knee and starin' at him-tryin' to
make him blink. And Hugh's eyes-though they were different-they were like his. When I
told him-it was a Sunday and we'd driven over to Leitrim, up to The Dawn of Hope. He got
annoyed first and then he laughed a bit and he told me how his grandfather had one blue eye
and one brown. . . . Brolly and Clements. Brown eye and blue. Oh, he told me it all. How
his grandfather with the two different coloured eyes was the child of May Brolly and
Clements - the man who drowned her brother. Can you imagine what it was like for that
woman? Dragged up to the Big House and left pregnant and then promised the lot-that he'd
follow her on and marry her if she'd go to America. Then nothing and nothing again till she
got word he was drowned on the lake and John, her own flesh and blood, drowned with
him.[49]

Significantly, Sarah's recollections and further association between Hugh and her
dead father recalls even earlier sectarian violence and death. Sarah goes even
further, linking Hugh not only to historical and personal instances of death and
sacrifice but also to mythic images of ritualistic violence: "Remember after we met
Hugh - and we went on that drive across over The Black Pig's Dyke. We looked
out over the lake where your ancestor was drowned by Clements and sat by the old
nunnery where we could see out to the Holy Island. Remember the place we went
to-with the view out over all the counties-The Dawn of Hope."[50] In her
recollections and associations, Sarah summons subtle and deliberate motifs of
sectarian violence and sacrifice. The theme of the wren merges with images of
Hugh, whose later death will eerily parallel the wren's. Both merge with an image
of her father, slaughtered on his farm, his innocent blood pouring onto the fields,

recalling the guilty Strange Knight's death. Subsequently, those images find resonance with class and religious distinctions and the violence those differences can bring. Ultimately, the image of Hugh, Sarah's father, and the sectarian strife in Ireland merges with geographical locations. The Black Pig's Dyke, both the ancient boundary of Ulster and the mythic location of the battle marking the end of the world, becomes the ultimate symbol for sectarian violence. However, the images culminate in a more optimistic location-The Dawn of Hope. Sarah comes through her myriad of associations, marking violence and sacrificial death, to a symbol of resurrection. Mysteriously, in her acknowledgment of death and the horror of violence, Sarah converts the negative memory of slaughtered ancestors and the transformation of her lover, from an image of her father to an image of the gunman, into the possibility of renewal. Within her reconstituted spiritual recollection of the past, of her lover, and of the mythic geography of her home, Sarah comes to terms with the possibilities for renewal and an end to violence. She, like the audience whose laughter creates an image of a sacrificial fool, converts the deaths and violence of her community and familial history into sacrificial acts that can renew her identity. Essentially, by acknowledging the complete extent of traumatic rupture, Sarah creates a personal mythology, with a resonance of local and familial history and local myth, which can reconstitute her self-conception despite and even as a consequence of violence. In her act, Sarah converts the traumatic event from one of rupture alone into one which can be used to renew identity, a process which finds a resonance in what Mbembe and Reitman call "the possibility for self constitution":

According to this formulation, we are not interested primarily in the problematics of resistance, emancipation, or autonomy. We distance ourselves from these questions in order to better apprehend, in today's context, the series of operations in and through which people weave their existence in incoherence, uncertainty, instability, and discontinuity; then, in experiencing the reversal of the material conditions of their societies, they recapture the possibility for self-constitution, thus instituting other 'words of truth.'[51]

Basically, Sarah comes to terms with the "incoherence, uncertainty, instability, and discontinuity" of sectarian violence and then reverses the "material conditions" of traumatic rupture, using myth and personal memory to "recapture the possibility for self-constitution."

Vincent Woods's multilayered dramatization of renewal and reconstitution finds a resonance with Seamus Heaney's translation of *The Cure at Troy* in an Irish context. Heaney's characters also, through a communion with a mythological past, come to terms with the personal traumatic ruptures of their lives, converting a scene of violent rupture into one that offers the possibility for renewal. Within the play, Neoptomemus escapes the mask of traitor and deceiver and is won over to his true self through an emotional bond with Philoctetes and through communion with Hercules. Initially, Neoptomemus was sent to trick Philoctetes into handing over the bow. Neoptomemus says "The bow/Is like a god itself. I feel this urge/To touch it./For its virtue/Venerate it."[52] Heaney uses short lines to signify Neoptomemus's internal struggle. Previously, his certainty was mirrored in the steadiness of his speech, characterized by a pentameter or hexameter, mostly iambic rhythm. However, the rhythm of these lines, although it begins in iambic hexameter quickly changes. Initially, Neoptomemus remains certain of his deception. However, as he sees the bow, and all that it implies, so freely offered, he becomes uncertain about his mask. His speech deteriorates into a series of excited spondees only to culminate in a more relaxed rhythm with the word "virtue" and then the word "venerate." The abrupt change in metre signifies a change in personality. Neoptomemus drops his mask and offers himself in devotional reverence leaving behind his lust for glory and coming to terms with his true character. Significantly, the bow is a symbol of death and skill. Like the straw wren, it serves as a marker for both sacrifice and renewal. Neoptomemus claims the divine object by accepting the renewal of his personality in his reverence for the instrument of death. He accepts that the instrument itself stands for much more than a useful weapon of war. He realizes that its meaning implies a communion with the gods, beyond the transience of human conflict. In his acceptance of the bow, Neoptomemus praises not its destructive potential but rather a whole "economy of kindness/Possible in the world; befriend a friend/And the chance of it's increased and multiplied."[53] Essentially, Neoptomemus sacrifices his old self, within his mask of deception, in favor of an emotional bond, through the bow, with his former enemy. The sight of the bow essentially kills his masked self and gives birth to his true self.

Neoptomemus abandons the ruptured personality, adopted in order to gain some recognition in war, and adopts a more integrated personality. Likewise, Hugh Brolly, from *At the Black Pig's Dyke,* drops his mask of revenge and war in favor of a more integrated personality; he allows emotion and pity to purge him of his mask. He begins with the intention to do violence:

What I've been doin' tonight I've been doin'-since they killed Sean. Delivery work. . . . Tonight was to be a pick-up in the yard like I always did. They promised me it'd be the last run. There was no sign of anyone when I drove in, so I went up to knock on the back door. I could hear them inside talkin'. (Pause) What I was bringin' over tonight-the stuff I was collectin'-it was to be used on Staurt's weddin' on Tuesday. They're bound to have known half the country would be there. . . . I didn't let on a thing, but collected the lot. I drove the back road like they said, but I stopped, south of the Dyke and I dumped the lot in the lough there-into the deepest spot at the Long Point. I stopped again, over this side-at the loneliest phone box I could find-and I rang the police. If anyone lifts a finger at that weddin' they're behind bars or dead.[54]

Like Neoptomemus, Hugh rejects his mask of violence and embraces emotional engagement with his former enemy. He abandons the instruments of war in the mythic symbol of the battle of the end of the world. He rejects the symbols of violence in favor of life. In doing so, he realizes that he marks himself for death. However, within his sacrifice, he embraces emotional interaction with a larger community, offering the possibility for at least a limited halt to sectarian violence. Both Hugh and Neoptomemus, within their masks of warriors were "confined within too narrow a spiritual horizon. Their life has not sufficient content, sufficient meaning. If they are enabled to develop into more spacious personalities, the neurosis generally disappears."[55] Each adopts the "more spacious personalities" that embrace emotional involvement and reject their masks.

Indeed like the "Carnivals" of Benitez-Rojo and the Earl of Shaftesbury, Vincent Woods's *At the Black Pig's Dyke* and Seamus Heaney's *The Cure at Troy* function as forums to expose the masks of those powers that have control of the lives of their characters. Specifically, through the accumulation of restorative experiences and through the establishment of secure social contacts, characters wrest control of their lives from the forces and powers of the Troubles that disrupt identity and personal, historical, and spiritual ties. Like the speaker in Gerald Dawe's "Solstice," many of the characters in Heaney's and Woods's plays draw from a mythological heritage to express a personal hope for communal renewal. Moreover, like the speaker of Robert Greacen's "A Wish for St. Patrick's Day," who calls on the saint to "Send your green fire into the frozen branch" (1.4), the characters from the plays summon the gods and saints of their ancient heritage to transform an environment and individuals ruptured by violence and traumatic threat.

RECONSTRUCTING SOCIAL RELATIONSHIPS

Carol Rumens in "Passing a Statue of Our Lady in Derry" creates a multifaceted image of the Catholic Virgin. In part, the statue of Mary is "tired" and "dressed" in "white stone" (1.1). The statue exists as a wounded reminder of childhood innocence robbed of its power in the face of violence. Indeed, the statue itself bears the wounds of its time in Derry. Moreover, its stone setting implies a calcified idol, wearing the trappings of purity but with none of the power and force necessary to rid the society of traumatic rupture. However, the poem later details an image of a restored and revitalized image of the Virgin. Carol Rumens discovers possibilities for power and hope, reinvigorating what had become a dead idol with the power to refashion not only her identity but the face of a society troubled by violence and terror.

Similarly, Stewart Parker's *Pentecost* and Anne Devlin's *After Easter* detail the efforts to refashion components of identity ruptured as a consequence of the Troubles. Specifically, in a process akin to the clinical classification of recovery from trauma through education, Greta, the protagonist of Devlin's play, reconstitutes the means of her interaction with a violent society, finding a vocation as a storyteller. Moreover, throughout the play, characters come to terms with words and symbols, discovering what culminates in an almost new mythology of communication. Indeed, "myth is a system of communication, in that it is a message. . . . Myth cannot possibly be an object, a concept, or an idea." Rather "it is a mode of signification, a form."[56] The new forms of communication fashioned by Greta and the members of her family build on traditions and concepts taken from components that in other guises contribute to the rupture of identity through violence and brutality. In essence, Greta's and the other characters's use of tradition re-makes the "refuse [of] the current consciousness of reality by invoking something else which precedes or exceeds it, which remains, as it were, sub-conscious or supra-conscious" and open to "paradigms which redeem us from the depressing facts of the present" and "bring history to a standstill and enable us to attend to ancestral voices," making individuals in contemporary society "contemporaries with the 'dead generations's of the past, transmuting the discontinuities of our empirical existence into the unbroken continuity of an imaginary essence."[57] Similarly, also within the play, by identifying feelings, characters recognize the limits of brutal forces within their community, either accentuated by the Troubles or catalyzed as a consequence of the violence. Subsequently, in the recognition of the limits of the seemingly dominating powers, the characters come to terms with an

Irish modernism, a form which . . . unites a sense of the providential yet seemingly accidental encounters of characters with aesthetic closure and projects those onto a radically different kind of space, a space no longer central, as in English life, but marked as marginal and ec-centric after the fashion of the colonised areas of the imperial system. That colonised space may then be expected to transform the modernist formal project radically, while still retaining a distant familial likeness to its imperial variants. This Third-World modernism slyly turned the imperial relationship inside out, appropriating the great imperial space . . . . to organise the space of the colonial city, and to turn its walks and paths into the closure of a form and of a grand cultural monument.[58]

Basically, the characters in *Pentecost* and *After Easter* adopt the forces of the dominant society and introduce uncertain elements of variation and improvisation, of artistic and spiritual vision into the forces. In the process, they liberate themselves from these forces and, as a consequence, construct identities that integrate trauma, colonial discourse, and the ruptured components of colonized identity into their consciousness. Moreover, they begin to transform their society from one organized around the structures of violence to one organized around the processes of recovery from violence.

Stabilization through Education

Education requires that individual victims of trauma begin to take control of their lives, wresting power away from official narratives and creating, instead, structures that allude to the past and conflict but that also refer to change and plurality. Essentially, patients must integrate the violent event(s) into their lives, take responsibility for their lives away from external contingency, and educate themselves regarding the way in which they can come to terms with violent recollections or even further trauma. The process is reminiscent of what Jung called "the objectification of impersonal images," which he saw as "an essential part of the process of individualization. Its goal is to detach consciousness from the object so that the individual no longer places the guarantee of his happiness, or of his life even, in factors outside himself, whether they be persons, ideas, or circumstances, but comes to realise that everything depends on whether he holds the treasure or not. If the possession of that gold is realised, then the centre of gravity is in the individual and no longer in an object on which he depends." [59] In terms of the North of Ireland, this "education" or "process of individualization" takes the form of individuals who wrest control of the violent events from the paramilitary groups and declare their desire that the violence come to an end. Specifically, "getting rid of . . . prejudicial attitudes requires a methodology of emotional healing. Without this healing, prejudices are retained, lasting attitude-change is incomplete, community building hampered and personal creativity and leadership stifled."[60] Basically, the methodology involves "cross-community work [that] emphasises prejudice reduction, mutual understanding, reconciliation, tolerance, acceptance of diversity, respect for one's own identity and the identity of the other. All this includes a critical awareness of history, politics, religion and cultural tradition."[61] Ultimately, by shedding light on the hostile appropriation of Northern inter-community relations by the colonial discourse of a series of conflicts, individuals can begin to place their traumatic personal and societal histories in a larger context and can, for the first time, begin to imagine that the violent events will come to an end.

In Anne Devlin's play the characters, particularly Greta, achieve control over the traumatic forces that rupture identity by educating themselves about the forces and about themselves. Ultimately, Greta articulates a refashioned identity, through narrative, that represents a hybrid tradition, incorporating now valued components of her identity that were de-valued as a consequence of trauma with traumatic elements. Greta and her family's struggle find a resonance in clinical evaluation of trauma victims.

Patients are often confused by their symptoms and believe that they are "going crazy." . . . Developing a cognitive frame that helps patients understand their intrusions and avoidance helps them gain some emotional distance from the experience, and begins to put the event into the larger context of their lives. They first need to get a sense of time: This experience had a beginning, now has progressed to the next phase, and eventually will come to an end in some way.[62]

Specifically, like the patients of Van der Kolk's study, the characters in *After Easter* do question their sanity; indeed, the play's opens with Greta in a sanatorium. Ultimately, though, Greta develops a "cognitive frame," in her case an identity as a traditional story-teller, which enables her to come to terms with trauma. Within this frame, Greta recognizes the prejudice and brutality endemic to not simply the situation in the North but to British/Irish relations in general. In addition, Greta comes to understand the limits of British control over an understanding of herself and her Irish identity by discerning weaknesses in traditional and seemingly impervious forces that arrayed themselves against her.

Specifically, *After Easter* acknowledges the prejudice and discrimination against

Catholics and the Irish in England but then counteracts those negative experiences through a positive portrayal of Irish identity. Essentially, Devlin's play comes to terms with and educates its characters through the recognition of the ruptured identities consequent of colonial dynamics and then empowers a disempowered cultural representation. Specifically, Greta tells her analyst that she does not "resent being Irish" but only "resents[s] it being pointed out" and "resent[s] being the only Irish person at every gathering."[63] Moreover, Helen, Greta's sister, observes "London isn't a good place to have an Irish accent right now. I find when I'm buying or selling an American accent gets me through the door. Whereas an Irish accent gets me followed round the store by a plain clothes security man."[64] In addition, Manus, Greta and Helen's brother, says that he does not "feel like a citizen of the world when" he's "treated like a Paddy and a Fenian git."[65] The anti-Irish bias extends to places that should be more sympathetic. Speaking of her experiences with English Catholics, Greta recalls that "once when I had an art teaching job, they used to call me the Irish Art Teacher. And the girls used to say in front of me-as if to offend me-as if I cared: Father So and So's a bog Irish priest."[66] In each of these cases, Irish external markers of identity, including accent and religion within a national context, become sources of shame and catalysts for ridicule or suspicion. Significantly, each case, with the exception of Manus's , also highlights how the Irish are made to feel out of place in mainland Britain. For all the rhetoric of the North being one nation with the other members of the United Kingdom, the Irish in England become marked as outcasts and as somehow inferior. Dealing with these stigmas, Greta finds herself in a mental institution and Helen masks her identity behind an American accent. However, the play does not only allow for shame regarding an Irish heritage. Rather, the play emphasises an Irish identity beyond that of victim. In a scene that references elements of previous (within the play) discrimination, Manus observes, "He robbed us, you know. My daddy. He brought us up like Protestants. . . . I'm talking about the music, the language, the culture. It was traditional, he said it was nationalist so we never learnt it. Now I spend all my time trying to get it back."[67] Manus distinguishes between notions of "nationalist" and "traditional," between politics and cultural inheritance. He embraces that latter while acknowledging but not validating the prejudicial association of Ireland with violence. Manus's father internalized the prejudices and hatreds of the dominant culture, so much so, that he sought to strip his life and his children's lives of any reminder of a stigmatized heritage. Manus comes to terms with his father's fears and renounces them, ultimately creating a ritual of traditional music: "Manus is playing the end of a reel. . . . A woman patient [a mental patient] in a pink quilted dressing gown does a slow dance, a reel, as he moves around her. She'd be very pretty and poetic if she wasn't roundly pregnant as well. Other patients in dressing gowns and night visitors to the hospital drift towards the fiddler and the girl."[68] Manus reclaims an Irish traditional heritage within earshot of his father's hospital bed, entertaining the patients in the ward. Importantly, one of those patients is a pregnant mental patient, recalling Greta's institutionalization. Essentially, Manus invigorates an outcast tradition and enfranchises a mental patient; he gives her a forum in which she is nearly "very pretty and poetic." Essentially, through his music and his words, Manus "educates" his family and the patients of the hospital about the positive potential of traditional, non-violent, Irish cultural markers. His act recalls Kuan-Hsing Chen's observations regarding "postmodernism and cultural studies" which both "emphasize *relative* continuity and rupture" and "both see 'history' as the (discursively articulated) records or archives of war between the dominant and the dominated of various kinds[69] Manus ruptures the negative bias against Irish tradition and nationality and embraces a continuity of creative tradition. He rejects an exclusively Catholic identification with traditional music telling a Protestant patient that traditional music is "not anti-English" but "Irish" and by telling him that he "can play the 'Ould Orange Flute.'"[70] Ultimately, Manus brings the "repressed voice" of the mental patient back within a context of artistic expression. In his actions, Manus reveals that the stigma associated with Irish indigenous traditions and the Irish people is a product of the "war" consequent of "dominant" British bias.

Manus's and his sisters's liberation through self-education continues when they return home. Once again, the play dramatizes the potentially brutal consequences of colonial rule and bias. Helen conveys her trauma to her brother after a British patrol stops him and subsequently pursues him into his home: "Frig it! Look I'm trembling. (Holds her hand in front of her.) That officer just gave us three plausible reasons for shooting you. You defied a road block; you might have been armed; it might have been an ambush. The sort of thing you read about in the newspapers all the time. No one would have batted an eyelid in England."[71] Significantly, Helen represents the incident as it would be represented in England, telling her brother that the absurdity of his murder by security forces would be transformed into a routine and non-absurd, even normal, occurrence. She assumes the perspective of the dominant culture. However, in doing so, she subtly undermines their power. Unlike her earlier representation and justification for her American accent, Helen does not simply resign herself to discrimination. Here, by representing Manus's potential death as an absurdity that would have been distorted in England, Helen puts the blame for the brutal rupture of identity, not on herself through the mask of an American accent, but on the dominant society, casting them as absurd. Moreover, Aiofe, another sister, represents the true tragedy of the potential loss as the loss of "our story."[72] Greta agrees, adding that "all we have to do is stay alive and tell the truth."[73] Aiofe and Greta place a primacy on narrative education as a curative to brutal rupture. In telling, the sisters seek to "bring the repressed voices of history back into the historical agenda."[74] Manus responds by sharing the truth he wishes to convey.

I want to paint on the walls of all the police stations and army barracks: 'Forget 1690! Forget history! Remember - the pursuit of happiness is a 'Right of Man!'. . . The fact that words are up there, it's a promise, a covenant of something. Otherwise they might get lost. Even if no one spoke them and they got painted over, it wouldn't matter, they'd come through again and again, they'd come through. So you have to do it-paint the words on the wall- . . . Write them up there before it's too late.[75]

Manus calls for a public statement to educate the community. He hopes to wrest linear history and absolute devotion to historical heritage from the discourse of the North, rupturing its hold on the consciousness of the inhabitants. Moreover, in its place, he proposes to posit the concept of devotion not to a historical ideal but to a personal and, ultimately, communal "plurality of origins and that of trajectories of movements" not in the "unitary" representation of "dominant"[76] history. Moreover, in the telling, Manus establishes a "covenant" with his society. Literally, his appeal is an ethical appeal, a plea for the way his society should be. Furthermore, "ethical doing . . . needs poetical making in order to be effectively communicated and cultivated."[77] Manus and his sisters privilege an "inter-subjective community," a society which relies not on an exclusivity of traditions nor on calcified historical ideals, like "1690," but on inter-reliance and emotional sanction, the "pursuit of happiness."

Ultimately, Greta, as protagonist, most clearly states the need for education and articulation to overcome the ruptures consequent of traumatic disruption. However, in her stories of the dispossessed, both Irish and East African, she does not initially value language. Addressing the corpse of her father she tells the story of a man who

left Mayo in '56, . . . and his clock stopped. Only he didn't know that it had. He'd been promoted on the railways, and he had to make a report at the end of every day. Just a brief note. A sort of memo of the numbers of trains and times and if anything unusual had been reported to him. But he couldn't write-and he thought if he told them they would sack him. So he copies the reports of all the other memos for previous years. As long as nothing unusual occurs he can go on copying. But he's afraid of being found out. So I'm teaching him to write.[78]

The man from the Irish West remains locked within a time and place decontextualized from contemporary English society in which he finds himself. He records the movements of trains and the circumstances of railroad life from another time; his records imitate letters from other records and have nothing to do with the current railroad movements. He engages in the "substituting [of] signs of the real for the real itself."[79] Significantly, he, as sign maker, functions as part of a railroad, representing industry and commerce. The implication is that both signs and industry marshall not meaning but a dissimulation of meaning and the dissimulation of individual interpretation. Likewise, Greta speaks of "a Hindu child" who

came to me. He came to England from Nairobi when he was nine. He was sitting in the classroom on his first day of school and he copied the name of the person sitting next to him because he hadn't learned to write. And for a long time no one noticed that he'd been writing someone else's name, and it wasn't the name he was called at home. He didn't know what his own name looked like written down either. Somewhere along the line the link between sounds and words had been broken-lost.[80]

For the young boy, identity itself is wiped away and in its place a word with an uncertain referent becomes his appellation. Significantly, the railroad man and the schoolboy come from societies marginalized in England. As outsiders they highlight the fissures in British masks of meaning. They are reminders of what James Clifford, in his essay "Travelling Cultures," calls the "disconcertingly hybrid 'native'" whom Clifford describes as being "met at the ends of the earth."[81] In Devlin's stories, however, these individuals, who are "strangely familiar, and different precisely in that unprocessed familiarity,"[82] come from the ends of the earth and into the centers of British commerce and education. Once there, their voices, within a world of signs that have no referential meaning, articulate the uncertain foundations of contemporary British society. In the words of Fredric Jameson, who like Clifford also describes English uncertainty consequent of interaction in "far away places," meaning is lost after the realization that

a significant structural segment of the economic system as a whole is now located elsewhere, beyond the metropolis, outside of the daily life and existential experience of the home country, in colonies over the water whose own life experience and life world-very different from that of the imperial power-remains unknown and unmanageable for the subjects of the imperial power, whatever social class they may belong to; it can never be fully reconstructed; no enlargement of the personal experience, no intensity of self-examination, no scientific deductions on the basis of internal evidence can ever be enough to include this radical otherness of colonial life, colonial suffering and exploitation, let alone the structural connections between that and this, between absent space and daily life in the metropolis, can no longer be grasped immanently, no longer has its meaning, its deeper reason for being within itself.[83]

For the English in Devlin's story, the "disconcertingly hybrid 'native'" comes to the "metropolis" and once there exists as a constant reminder of the "absent space" within the metropolis.

In these faces of "the man from Mayo and the Hindu child,"[84] Greta recognizes herself as she says, "I am the same. I too am a copier. I do it out of fear. It was then I realized that we weren't the only ones: the man from Mayo, the Hindu child and me. I listened to people speaking and I hear that there are no individuals, only scattered phrases and competing ideas which people utter to bewilder effect all the time."[85] Positioned in such a way, on the periphery of society, marginalized and stigmatized because of her Irish ancestry and birth, Greta recognizes the emptiness of the society that labels her. The British "commonsensically . . . understand experience to be the uncontestable stable ground of being and knowing, what we conceptualize and speak *from*."[86] However, Greta understands that "experience comes to consciousness *through* discourse," like the tracings of the boy and the Mayo man,

making it impossible to attach to a secure interiority or 'self.' The linguistic sign is . . . infinitely citational, movable from any given context, thus incapable of stable referentiality. To believe that subjecthood is produced by experience which can then be narrativized as identity is to be infected, so this argument goes, with the delusions of 'presence,' the fantasy that one is fully present (transparent) to oneself, free of the divisions of the signifier and unconscious desire.[87]

Greta's stories articulate the false, commonsense articulations of British society, exposing the illusions of presence. However, Greta's indictment of discourse does not fully extend to a refutation of the purposefulness of all language. In the play's final scene, she articulates, performs, a narrative representation of her own story. Greta is at home, rocking a baby, telling it a story. The traditional empty chair is placed near the storyteller:

After Easter we came to the place. It was snowing in the forest and very cold in the fifth month. My mother and I were hunting. But because of the cold we couldn't feel anything or find anything to eat. So we sat down by the stream. I looked up and saw it suddenly, a stag, antlered and black, profiled against the sky. It stood on a ridge. This stag was from the cold north. It leapt off the ridge and down into the stream. It leapt through hundreds of yards to reach us. And arrived gigantic in the stream. My mother was afraid, but I saw that it was only hungry. I took some berries from my bag and fed the stag from the palm of my hand. The stag's face was frozen and I had to be careful because it wanted to kiss me, and if I had let it, I would have died of cold. But gradually it ate, its face was transformed and it began to take on human features. And then the thaw set in-I could hear the stream running, and the snow began to melt. I could hear all the waters of the forest ruching and it filled my years with a tremendous sound. (Pause.) So I got on the stag's back and flew with it to the top of the world. And he took me to the place where the rivers come from, where you come from . . . and he took me to the place where the rivers come from, where you come from . . . and this is my story.[88]

Within the traditional role of the storyteller Greta positions herself away from the contradictions and oppressive voices of British society. She values her culture, giving substance to a formerly de-valued articulation. Within the story, she also references her Catholic heritage, veiling its symbols within a narrative that takes place "after Easter." Her articulation frames itself as a hybrid, a fusion of her traditional and religious inheritance. Moreover, Greta further values her gender, creating a society of female hunters and fusing within her hybrid tale aspects of classical myth. Essentially, Greta's articulation, unlike the British society encountered by the man from Mayo and the boy from East Africa, does not vest its authority in exclusion and bias. Greta's tale does not repudiate diverse elements of her consciousness; it embraces them, creating a fusion of myths and traditions. Empowered by her alternative discourse, Greta feeds the threatening, masculine creature and thaws its features into a semblance of human form. She then mounts the stag, embracing a living method of travel, as opposed to the railroad and the mechanized means of transportation identified with the British in the play. In her travels, rather than meeting "disconcerting natives" and reminders of uncertainty, she discovers her origins, the source of her life. In her narrative, rather than written articulation, orality and spoken words represent not truth in and of themselves, not the recording of objective facts but the impression of sentiment and expressionistic truth. There is no "gap" between sign and signifier because the sign stands for many things simultaneously.

Greta articulates an optimistic view of creative imagination similar in its symbols and designs to James Joyce's river of origins which articulates meaning within a colonial metropolis: "Soft morning, city! Lsp! I am leafy speaking. Lpf! Folty and folty all the nights have falled on to long my hair. Not a sound, falling. Lispn! No wind no word. Only a leaf, just a leaf and then leaves. The woods are fond always. As were we their babes in. . . . It is for me golden wending."[89] Like Greta, Anna Livia in these lines articulates not one referent but many to arrive at truth. The words are hybrids of meaning, representing Irish and English (at least) articulations. "Folty" puns faulty and suggests the leaves, punning pages of a book, falling from their original, faulty meaning into the river. However, "folty" also puns the Irish words "folt," meaning both long hair and foliage, and "fáilte,"[90] meaning welcome. The many interpretations of seemingly faulty representation form a "golden wending," a train of flowers or even of hair for Anna Livia. For her, the multiple puns represent a marriage of meanings, a hybrid tradition invulnerable to "gaps" between sign and signifier because, like Greta's narrative, they have no single, true meaning. Anna Livia's and Greta's articulations are a type of "performance art" in that they are

extraordinary in precisely this articulation of social/personal experience; its historicization, however, is not carried out discoursively but *imagined exoterically* in a force field of conflicting temporalities marked by the detritus of consumer culture. Using dialectical images to bring past and present into collusion, these feminist artists turn performance time into a now-time of insight and transformation.[91]

Diamond, in her observations, does not specifically refer to Anna Livia or Greta, but Diamond's observation find a resonance in their articulations. Both Anna Livia and Greta find themselves uttering esoteric and even obscure, imagined alternatives to precise discourse. Recognizing the inherent faults and weaknesses of "consumer culture," including the rail road and the education system, she creates a collage of past meanings, transforming non-referent symbols into a performance of hybrid insights.

Stewart Parker's *Pentecost* also represents a validation and valuing of a clearly marginalized experience through the production of a "cognitive frame" that recognizes the ruptures of identity, acknowledges a marginalizing experience that created the rupture, and produces a narrative that integrates the pain of isolation/marginalization with shared experience. Parker achieves the ultimate identification and valuing of emotions by staging the relationship between Marion, a Catholic antiques dealer who purchased a old house in a Protestant neighborhood, and Lily, the ghost of the former owner of the house, herself a Presbyrterian housewife. The play's staging provides an allegorical frame for their relationship:

Everything is real except the proportions. The rooms are narrow, but the walls climb up and disappear into the shadows above the stage. The kitchen in particular is cluttered, almost suffocated, with the furnishings and bric-a-brac of the first half of the century, all the original fixtures and fittings still being in place. . . . [I]t has all clearly been the object of a desperate, lifelong struggle for cleanliness, tidiness, orderliness—godliness.[92]

The suffocated feel of the kitchen, with its outdated "fournishings" and "fittings" suggests boundaries, limits, and exclusion. Certainly, the fixtures and excessories of the house have outlasted their usefulness and now take the life out of an audience as a consequence of their suffocating impression. In addition, the signs of a "desperate, lifelong struggle" indicate an awareness of those boundaries and limits and of their destructive potential. Moreover, the desperate nature of the struggle suggests an inability or an unwillingness to come to terms with a more permanent or fruitful resolution to an outdated way of life. Ultimately, however, the unreal aspect of the proportions, with the disappearing walls argues for an unconscious resolution, beyond the bounds of the ordinary or of ordinary experience. Essentially, Parker's play dramatizes a subconscious process of healing and valuation, creating a conscious narrative that moves beyond sectarian divisions and personal grief.

Dramatizing the suffocating feel of the setting, Parker creates a clear association between sectarian hatred, marital fidelity, and children. Lily's ghost, justifying her life to Marion, relays a familiar discourse of spousal pride and loyalty. Lily declares that it was her husband who discovered the house and made it his "life."[93] The house becomes a symbol of their love, of her husband's industry and initiative, and of his abiding loyalty and duty. Indeed, her sentiments are admirable. However, the superficial nature of her dialogue indicates a limited understanding of the underlying issues. At times, her language seems pre-packaged, re-affirming marital stereotypes of the hard-working husband and his loyal, supportive wife. At other times, her language is notably void of sentiment. Lily tells Marion that she (Lily) and her husband in "one week, married" and "moved"[94] into the house. She adds that her husband was a "good man" who would have been a "loving father" even though "Good Lord didn't"[95] send them a baby. Audiences hear Lily's life struggles and her potentially sorrowful experiences; she and her husband had no children. However, an audience does not hear how her experiences affected her. Lily's pronouncements are short and abrupt and without loving remembrances. It is as if she lays labels on her experiences, as a type of intellectual shorthand absent emotional meaning. Moreover, Lily also echoes the clichés of sectarianism when she tells Marion that "Fenian savages"[96] ruined her house. Ultimately, Lily uses an anti-Catholic stereotype by asking Marion if there are "not enough runty litters running the streets, whelped by your kind."[97] Catholics, within the stereotype are not people but animals, who are dirty and who cannot exercise control over their violent and sexual impulses. Lily's use of stereotypes, clichés, and pre-packaged prejudice and bias reveal her anger, her desire to create boundaries and limits. In the association of these three ideas-children, Catholics, and marital loyalty-Lily reveals the intellectual structures that limit her experience, that create boundaries between herself and others, that create an exclusive view of her world. Subsequent scenes in the play reveal the reasons for Lily's unconscious associations.

Specifically, Marion discovers Lily's diary, her attempt at conscious articulation of her painful experiences. It relates how she fell in love with a British airman, while her husband was away. The clichés and stereotypes that describe her relationship with her husband pale in comparison to the original language and images that she uses to describe the affair. She writes that he had "fair" skin and that he "didn't like the sand." She goes on to describe the landscape in very poetic terms. Specifically, she recalls the setting sun "hanging out of the sky like a big swollen blond orange" and recalls the water "glistening with the redness of it and the sky and the hills on fire with it."[98] An audience knows intimate physical details about the airman, that make him a person and not the cliché of the supportive man, that is Lily's husband. Moreover, Lily reveals details about herself, in her revelation of epiphanic joy. She reveals her sense of oneness with nature, her sense of joy and rapture within the relationship. She reveals a capacity for love and not simply endurance, loyalty, and prejudice. Indeed, the diary represents a step in self-actualization and healing. It is a private valuing of personal experience, a recognition of pain and rupture. Indeed, as Marion rightly guesses, Lily wrote it because she had to communicate her ideas and her feelings to someone.[99] However, it is not fully healing because of the limited nature of the discourse. Lily hid the diary.[100]

Nonetheless, the diary represents an important step forward because it makes conscious Lily's pain and also makes conscious her unconscious or repressed experiences. The diary represents a record of genuine emotion, preserved although forgotten. Marion articulates, by reading the diary, Lily's emotions, bringing them once again into the conscious realm. More specifically, the diary reveals that her non-emotional declarations of loyalty to her husband mask a marriage absent love, a marriage of penance, an effort to go to her "grave respectable."[101] She, by repressing her emotions, her regrets, "atoned."[102] Moreover, the diary suggests a cause for Lily's anti-Catholic prejudice. Earlier, she had linked her negative stereotypes to both her love for her husband and to Catholic families's large numbers of children. By putting up a wall of prejudice against Catholics, within the context of her husband's efforts to keep the house safe from "Fenian savages," she both expresses loyalty to him and disdain for those who try to destroy her home. In addition, Lily became pregnant with the airman's child; she gave up the child anonymously. By hating Catholics, specifically because of their number of children, Lily links herself to them. In her expressions of hate for Catholics, Lily reveals a self-hatred. The diary, then, read by a Catholic women, becomes an important record of both repression and the genuine experience of emotion. Marion relays Lily's story to her friends and associates, integrating Lily's experience into the "modern" relationships of the play. She creates an empathy between Lily and the other characters in the play. Marion describes Lily during a German raid on Belfast: "She lay down on the dark on her own now, and pictured him, up there, burning a hole through the sky, a dark angel, and her ears roared now with the rage of a wholesale slaughter, pounding the ground under her and the air all round her, Armageddon, random and blind, pulverizing her whole body until she once more came and came again, and she composed herself to die there."[103] Marion's story captures the imaginations of those around her, dissolving Lily's silent suffering into an empathetic bond with a new generation, also suffering a city in flames. Marion's images of self-punishment, mixed with sexual fulfillment accurately depict Lily's state of mind and heart in the years after her affair ended. Marion then, a Catholic woman, the object of Lily's hatred and prejudice becomes a voice through which Lily's vitality is felt again. Indeed, the sexual images suggest that a new creative force empowers both Marion and Lily, a creativity bred of their communication; indeed, the story is not taken verbatim from Lily's diary. The violence of the images also suggests that Lily's pain was indeed real. Like the stage walls that "disappear," Marion's relation of Lily's narrative dissolves the walls of sectarian hatred, prejudice, and cliché that separated Lily from the society of her time, demarginalizing a formerly marginalized experience.

Just as the *Pentecost*'s text and setting play out a healing, restorative process by recognizing divisions and overcoming them through the production of a narrative, the play's original production in Derry City in the North of Ireland would have carried out a similar process. By performing sectarian conflict and resolution in a city torn by sectarianism, an alternative, healing discourse achieves validation, and offers a society suffering violence a means of overcoming violence.

Identification of Feelings

Another part of the treatment of traumatized people includes helping victims come to terms with violence by integrating, through words and images, the traumatic event into the emotional and intellectual matrix of their lives. The verbalizing and imaging process buttresses people against the repercussions of trauma. Indeed, "such images offer a way of imposing an imaginary coherence on the experience of dispersal and fragmentation"[104] associated with psychological rupture. In Northern Ireland, both formal and informal "verbalizing" and "ritualizing" forums increasingly gained strength throughout the Troubles. From the work of the Quaker Peace Project, which brought together young people from both communities to interact through staged improvisations that gave voice to fears and hatreds as well as possibilities for reconciliation, to the work of playwrights like Margaretta D'Arcy, Marie Jones, and Martin Lynch who organize community theatre groups that provide an outlet for the frustrations and possibilities of life in contemporary Northern Ireland, creative forums offer an emotional sanction for traumatic experience and help give voice to internalized anxiety and lay the foundations for growing beyond violence. Within this work lies the assumption that, indeed, "Ireland's binary politics have consistently misrepresented its cultural plurality."[105] An examination of the literature produced by Ulster people suggests that, "instead of brooding on Celtic and Orange dawns, its inhabitants might accept this province-in-two-contexts as a cultural corridor. Unionists want to block the corridor at one end, republicans at the other. Culture, like common sense, insists it can't be done. Ulster Irishness and Ulster Britishness are bound to each other and to Britain and Ireland. And the republic will have to come cleaner about its own *de facto* connections with Britain. Only by promoting circulation within and through Ulster will the place ever be part of a healthy system."[106] Creativity, including "literature" and theatre, demonstrates the limits of trauma and violence, creates a place that is immune from the threat of force, and offers a method for coming to terms with trauma, giving individuals a sense of possibility for overcoming violence.

In Anne Devlin's *After Easter*, the play's protagonist comes to terms with her emotional identity ruptured as a consequence of exposure to traumatic events. Within the play, many of her revelations are private and have no overt application or seeming association with the Troubles. However, after identifying her feelings, after achieving a sense of self-control over her emotions, she proceeds to seek out circumstances within the Troubles or associated with sectarian violence to express her personal spiritual vision developed as a consequence of her private revelations. Moreover, the factors that inform her spiritual visions are informed by those same factors that operate simultaneously with sectarian violence in Anne Devlin's earlier works, notably *Ourselves Alone*. Specifically, Devlin's play addresses issues associated with physical and sexual abuse or religious and feminist issues. Furthermore, Greta, the play's protagonist, undergoes a process akin to clinical evaluations of trauma victims in recovery. In a process referred to as "verbalizing," a "critical element in the treatment of traumatized people is to help them find words for emotional states. Naming feelings gives patients a sense of mastery and mental flexibility that facilitates comparison with other emotions and other situations."[107] By naming her feelings, by articulating her personal spiritual insights, Greta feels empowered enough to reach out to Northern society at large and offer potential solutions to sectarian violence. Within Greta's personal revelations, "[m]yths which day has forgotten continue to be told by night, and powerful figures which consciousness has reduced to banality and ridiculous triviality are recognized again by poets and prophetically revived."[108] Greta reaches into her deep cultural, religious inheritance reaffirming marginalized and trivialized factors that inform her consciousness, including women and Celtic tradition. In doing so, she reaches out to "the thoughtful person" in gestures that may be considered insane but that represent a composite of Northern Catholic cultural memory.

In *After Easter* Greta gives voice to her emotional experiences by articulating of her visions. By confessing her spiritual insights to her cousin, Elish, a Catholic nun, Greta sanctions both her personal interpretation of her faith and a bond with a community of women devoted to spirituality. Initially, Greta articulates her experiences only with great trouble: "I can't say this-I'm sorry, I'm finding this very difficult."[109] Previously, she had attempted to explain her actions, to intellectualize them. However, with Elish, Greta, after her initial difficulty in giving her visions form, decides instead to describe images and not initially to attempt to interpret them for her cousin. The substance of the visions suggests a Catholic spirituality fused with a sense of artistic vocation, troubled by threatening masculine figures. The first vision she describes, actually her third visionary experience, occurs on Pentecost. Greta tells Elish that a

flame appeared in the curtain facing my bed. It was growing bright-I was not sleeping or dreaming. I wanted to switch on the light beside me, . . . So I looked away for a second to find the switch, and when I looked back, the flame had disappeared. . . . I lay for several hours with the light on just gazing at the place where the flame had been then I got up around seven and opened the curtains. I went down to the kitchen and made a cup of tea. I needed to hear some human voices. . . . So I turned on the radio--there was singing, and then a man's voice said: 'Let us pray on this Pentecost Sunday . . .' I am not a religious person. My father is an atheist and my husband is a Marxist. And I had ceased to be a Catholic so long ago I had no idea when Pentecost was.[110]

Within her vision, Greta finds a resonance, of non-temporal origin, with a Catholic feast of vocation. As a consequence of the Holy Spirit's descent, the Church teaches, the apostles were infused with the wisdom and courage to begin their ministries. For Greta, the initial vision does not carry with it a sense of specific vocation. However, some important elements can be discerned. Specifically, her vision runs counter to the ideals of her father and husband. Moreover, her experience finds a resonance in the Catholic sacrament of confirmation, in which a candidate reaffirms the promises made on his or her behalf by his or her parents and godparents at baptism. Essentially, Greta's vision acts as her confirmation, of her growing into a mature awareness that the "Marxist" and "atheist" articulations of her husband and father fail to encompass the totality of her experience. In addition, she experiences a preternatural sacrament, an outward sign, with a resonance of her mother's and cousin's faith, designed to give insight into if not a sense of vocational direction at least a calling away from the beliefs framed for her by her father and husband.

Notably, Elish asks Greta if she was "alone at that time."[111] Greta reveals that she "was unhappy. My husband didn't want children and I did."[112] Elish's question contrasts sharply with the play's initial scene, in which Greta interacts with a male therapist whose questions challenge Greta's intellectual self-conceptions, rather than ask Greta about her emotional reactions. The exchange with the therapist reads like the transcript of an interrogation. Campbell asks Greta, "Do you still think you're the Virgin Mary," "When asked why you refused to return to your house, you said, 'It's a Protestant house,'" and "When asked about your relationship within your mother, you said, 'Venus is my mother' "[113]; the doctor's questions continue on these same lines. Significantly, the final two questions are not really questions at all. Although they begin with the word "when," they are statements clearly designed to confront and not to explore the emotional repercussions of her experiences. Alternatively, Elish asks an open ended question about Greta's emotional state. Significantly, Greta answers that her husband does not want children. Greta's husband dictates her reproductive future, closing out the possibility that Greta could realize a personal dream. Clearly, Greta's experience of a vocational calling that leads her away from her husband and father finds a resonance with her internal need to escape her husband's control. Greta's first spiritual vision occurred "in November." For three days, she "couldn't sleep."

Greta: This made me very tired and I became delirious enough to believe that the sleeping bag in on the floor of my room was the womb and I had gone back into it to be born again. . . . I was aware during the experience of being in the womb on my birthday, my twenty-fourth birthday, that I could see out of two separate windows each with a different view. I felt very far down inside my body. As I looked around the room, I saw an old man in the corner watching me. And I said to myself, I knew it. I knew that old man was there. I have felt watched all my life.
Elish: It was the devil you saw.
Greta: I knew that immediately. He looked like an old priest.
(Elish makes a movement.)
He was dressed like a priest in a long black soutane. He had a pointed beard. I must have been weak and small because I was looking around what I took to be the edge of a chair, a wing chair, or perhaps it was a pram hood. At any rate, the old priest loomed over me and placed a pillow on my face. I tried to cry out but he was smothering me. I was being silenced. And it was this I had to struggle against. I struggled against this smothering blackness until a voice said in my ear-a kind warm voice: 'Turn round. You have to turn around.' So I did, I turned myself around and found I could breathe again and ahead of me I could see this oh most beautiful globe, a sphere lit up in space far below me, and I found myself floating falling towards it. And the same voice, the one that told me to turn around, said 'Enjoy your fall through space and time.' So I knew I was born that night. Or I was reliving my birth.[114]

Greta's vision of rejuvenation/animation contains elements common to her final revelation. Specifically, a male figure restricts her means of expression. In the other event, her husband prevents her from having children. In this event, a priest-like figure, the devil, smothers her and forces himself on top of her, an image of rape. She escapes this figure to be born again, to rise out of smothering oblivion. Significantly, her vision also has a resonance with the Celtic feast of Samhain, which occurs at the same time of year. On this feast "sacrifices were certainly offered"[115] and Greta's death can be read as a type of sacrifice in the sense that her vision of smothering/sexual interaction also recalls the Celtic, Samhain "union of the tribal god and the nature goddess who nourished the territory." Their union focuses on "the renewal of the fecundity of the earth and its inhabitants."[116] Greta, in this sense, sacrifices one life for the renewal of another life. She is both mother and daughter and, indeed, "felt very far down inside" her "body." By coming through her interaction with the priest/devil figure, Greta counteracts a version of male power and domination, not only over herself, a renewal that manifests itself in this scene, but also over her society, a renewal that reveals itself later in the play.

In Greta's other vision like themes manifest themselves; her second experience occurs on "February 2," the feast of the "Purification." Greta and her husband

had some people in to dinner and I was relighting the candles on the table, which had burnt down and gone out. As I moved the candle to the fireplace and reached into the fire and then transferred the lit candles to the stand-the flame leapt. It lit up my hair, which at that time was long and I suddenly found myself surrounded by a curtain of flame. . . . A strange cry came out of my mouth-when the fire caught-it was almost as startling as the fire itself.[117]

When asked to describe the sound of her cry, Greta recreates it "making a beautiful sound, echoing the nuns's singing."[118]   Greta's spiritual experience links itself through Catholic feasts to ancient Celtic rites celebrating the feminine and rebirth. Symbolically, Greta becomes a "burnt offering," a sacrifice for rebirth and healing. Significantly, her unconscious self sacrifice comes on the feast commemorating two things. Primarily, in the contemporary Catholic church, the feast celebrates the presentation of the infant Jesus at the Temple in Jerusalem, a ceremony in which, marking the birth of their first son, Jesus's parents offer a sacrifice of thanksgiving to the Hebrew God. Greta's sacrifice, within the context of this tradition, transfers the sacrificial standard onto herself. In addition, the feast commemorates Mary's "purification." Traditionally, Mary had to bathe forty days after giving birth, not because she was considered unclean but rather as a final step in a ritual purification process. Within Hebrew teaching, a woman was made sacred as a consequence of child birth; the purification ceremony simply functions as an outward sign, a sacrament, of physical purity mirroring the woman's spiritual purity. Further, that Elish would stress the feast's commemoration of Marian devotion suggests a subtle emphasis on female spirituality. In the modern Church, the day is universally called the "Presentation," and, although it is not unusual for older feast names to linger in the Catholic community in Ireland, it is significant that so modern a nun who wears a "tracksuit" and a "hairband"[119] and no habit and veil would use the older appellation. It is also certainly significant then that Greta's sacrificial experience occurs within the context of her husband's aversion to children. Even though the couple will eventually have children, and one of Greta's concerns involves her husband's efforts to take them from her because of her institutionalization, Greta's sacrificial offering and experience links itself not just to physical fertility. Indeed, as a consequence of the feast's associations with ancient pre-Christian, particularly Celtic spirituality, Greta becomes of symbol of societal renewal. Specifically, February 1 commemorates the feast of Saint Brigid, an apocryphal Catholic figure associated with the ancient Celtic goddess of the same name. On this feast, processions of candles traditionally honor the saint. However, the procession of lights has its origins in the Celtic seasonal feast of Imbolc, which honored Brigid, "a wise woman, daughter of Dagda" and "a potent fertility goddess with perhaps specially emphasized attributes of learning and healing."[120]   Moreover, in Christianized Celtic terms, the season also commemorated the sacred rebirth of the earth, finding an echo in the ancient Hebrew rituals. Significantly, hybrid Christian/Celtic commemorations of Christmas include a feast of female sacredness and sacrifice, traditions that culminate on February 1st. On the feast of the Epiphany, called Nollaig na mBan, or women's Christmas, ceremonial candles are lit and then blown out to be re-lit at Imbloc, Brigid's day, and the eve of the Purification. Moreover, Nollaig na mBan further honors a female transubstantiation. Traditionally,

Oíche na Trí Rithe

Deintear fíon den uisce
Síoda den triopall
Agus ór den ghrean.
[On Three King's Night/Water is drawn from wine/silk
is drawn from rushes/ and gold is drawn from sand.]

The words emphasize the earth's healing rebirth in addition to stressing a tripartite structure of transubstantiation that includes wine, milk, and gold.

The three parts recall both Greta's series of three visions, the Catholic masculine Trinity, and also the three Brigids. "Another particular aspect of the Celtic deities, male and female, is that of triplism. This matter has been explored a good deal. It is not a tendency to trinitarian concepts, or of the union of three distinct supernatural beings. It is, in fact, an expression of the extreme potency of any one deity."[121] Greta's power comes from her blessing, consequent of her three visions. Elish tells her that "you have been given a holy order, you are chosen, you have been spoken to directly but you are also chosen by evil as well. Nothing stands alone."[122]

Acting on her instinct toward vocation, Greta reaches out to a North of Ireland society devastated by war. Specifically, during her brother's confrontation with a soldier demanding to inspect a box, "Greta intervenes. She takes the box from his hands and opens it; it contains three white veils. She drops the box and holds the veils in her hands. . . . Greta remains holding the veils in her arms. The soldiers remain with their guns fixed on the people in the yard. The first soldier is looking with curiosity and amusement at the scene."[123] Greta exposes the harmless contents of the box to the soldiers. She disarms a potentially threatening situation, dispelling emotions of fear and hatred with her simple act. Moreover, her act carries with it a spiritual resonance. The communion veils symbolize not only a Christian communion with the divine but a pre-Christian renewal of the earth in Spring. By giving form, through her gesture, to her brother's innocence, Greta creates an atmosphere of "curiosity and amusement" out of a potentially life-threatening situation. Moreover, Greta, earlier,

went to Clonard Monastery and took a chalice from the side alter during a Low Mass, and walked out with it, before anybody realized what was happening. . . . Then she took a bus to the city centre still holding the chalice. It was full of communion wafers-which she began distributing-
Aoife: To the people in the bus queues.
Helen: Yes. All over the town. To anyone who would
take them off her.[124]

Greta consciously associates her act with the political situation in the North, calling for integrated schools as a method to increase trust and a communion of peace in the North. She, in this sense, functions as a type of priest, ministering spiritual healing to all people. Moreover, she attempts to change the substance of the situation in the North to one of mutual trust and respect from that of hatred and suspicion. Greta's act is misinterpreted in the press, however, as a declaration for female priests. Nonetheless, even in misinterpretation, Greta communicates something of her internal vision to the populace. Indeed, "poetics transgresses the narrow limits of the cognitive."[125] Greta's acts extend beyond the narrow limits of the recognizable and produce intellectual and emotional repercussions that she cannot anticipate.

Her personal vocation and her emotional understanding of her visions may not overtly lead to a reform of the situation in the North, nor do her experiences and actions help her regain a sense of control over her reactions to trauma. Her defusing of the potentially explosive situation with her brother becomes an object of laughter and bemusement. Her distribution of communion wafers is misunderstood. However, Greta's situation is not without its rewards because, like Mbembe's "worlds of truth,"

we are not interested primarily in the problematics of resistance, emancipation, or autonomy. We distance ourselves from these questions in order to better apprehend, in today's context, the series of operations in and through which people weave their existence in incoherence, uncertainty, instability, and discontinuity; then, in experiencing the reversal of the material conditions of their societies, they recapture the possibility for self-constitution, thus instituting other 'worlds of truth.'[126]

Essentially, after communicating her spirituality to her cousin, Greta intervenes within the conflict in the North, arming herself with spiritual symbols to counteract the threat of violence. However, that she does not significantly alter the situation in the North does not mean that she fails. Essentially, because she names, articulates, her spiritual visions to her cousin and because she offers gestures of hope and transformation, even if they are not immediately successful, Greta does find success because she "reverses the material condition" of herself within society. She articulates her emotional response to traumatic threat and weaves that response into her community. She "recapture[s] the possibility for self-constitution" and for "other worlds of truth" in the North.

Finally Greta's visions find expression within a spirituality rooted in her Catholic faith, her desire for motherhood, and her more submissive role within her family. Greta's vocation does not exactly express itself within traditional feminist liberationist terms. However, through her visions, Greta embraces and values alternative forms of discourse and communication. Specifically,

if there is *agency*, it is to be found paradoxically, in the possibilities opened up in and by that constrained appropriation of the regulatory law, by the materialization of that law, the compulsory appropriation and identification with those normative demands. The forming, bearing, circulation, signification of that sexed body will not be a set of actions performed in compliance with the law, the citational accumulation and dissimulation of the law that produces material effects, the lived necessity of those effects as well as the lived contestation of that necessity.[127]

Paradoxically, Greta regains control of the dynamics of her world and comes to terms with the possibility of self control by articulating and acting out her emotional responses to her environment. She operates within certain norms or "regulatory" frameworks of expression, but she revises the forms she cites and appropriates them for a counter discourse rooted not in restriction and prohibition, not in the dominance of male figures of priest, husband, father, and soldier, but in her own emotional framework and bond with her cousin and her sisters. Through personal recognition and valuation of her emotional state, Greta offers a model of renewal for the North.

Like Greta's process of emotional validation, Marion, from Stewart Parker's *Pentecost*, begins her path to recovery by recognizing and naming her feelings. Unlike Greta, Marion does not articulate any supernatural visions. Rather, Marion's validated emotional experiences are her normal everyday needs and concerns. She confidently asserts, "I need a house."[128] Heruse of the personal pronoun "I" indicates self-confidence and self-assurance. Her short sentences suggest unambiguous articulation. Shortly thereafter, she argues that such confident and clear pronouncements are not consistent with her "normal" range of behaviors: the "pure" gestures and the "free-spirited"[129] actions. Her use of the words "free" and "pure" reveals not only the unambiguous nature of her decision but also her sense that what she's done is right and completely consistent with her consciousness. Moreover, she liberates her sentiments from the constraints others have put on them. Later in the play, Marion tells her ex-husband that she is indeed comfortable with "Feeling. Passion."[130] Once again, her articulations are short and confident. Previously, when she would "stubb" her toe or "smash" something, or "swore," her husband tried to send her to the "psychiatrist."[131] Her husband alienated her from her impulses and emotions. Marion begins the play, and begins her process of emotional validation by recognizing them and naming them with a sense of self-confidence and liberating purity.

Subsequently, Marion reaches out and comforts those around her. Significantly, each time she expresses compassion toward her associates, she actually validates part of herself and her experience. Marion welcomes her friend Ruth into her house; Ruth bears the recent wounds of her husband's violence. Marion repeatedly tells Ruth that she is "safe now."[132] The repetition of the word "safe" with its soft "s" sound further reinforces Marion's gestures of comfort. Ruth is physically beaten by her husband. Marion was emotionally restricted by her former partner. In her comforting gestures toward Ruth, Marion comforts and heals the part of herself that was wounded by her husband. Moreover, because Ruth's husband works for the security forces, and takes part in the violent repression of Catholics, Marion allegorically heals the wounds of sectarian oppression and violence. More significant still, Marion makes a remarkable gesture of validation across sectarian lines. She wants to put Lily's house on the "National Trust."[133] Her efforts would equate Lily's struggles with the esates on "Coole" and "Castleward."[134] Specifically, Marion wonders why Lily's home should have less value than an aristocrats home. After all, Lily's "home speaks for a far greater community of experience"[135] than an aristocrat's home. Marion not only makes a connection across sectarian boundaries, her impulse towards validating Lily's life, as a working-class woman in Belfast, also validates Marion's world. She too comes from a working-class community. Essentially then, Marion's gestures outward validate a range of her own experiences.

Importantly, Marion recognizes both the value and the limits of her variety of vicarious empathetic gestures; she, ultimately, understands that she must directly validate her experience. She understands that the National Trust was the wrong "impulse," a "mistaken idea" that would have "condemn[ed]" Lily to a state of indefinite suspension.[136] Marion understands that recovery cannot base itself on a freezing of the past, no matter how well intentioned. She understands that the "basics" of Lily's life, combined with her (Marion's), personal vision, and brought together with the life-generating forces of "air and light" will foster growth and development. Validation was a necessary step, even vicarious validation, but Marion understands she must move on, asserting herself. To that end, Marion expels her ex-husband from her life telling him "we're all quits."[137] Marion unites her private revelations and new confidence to the divine gift of the Holy Spirit at Pentecost. She expels her husband from her life, directly validating her experiences of limitation and pain within her marriage. Essentially, she realizes that she must come to terms directly with her past and with the wounds present in her society in order to heal both. Like Greta, whose actions begin a healing ritual within herself that spreads outward, Marion begins a process for herself and within herself that eventually grows beyond herself.

Marion and Greta, like the poet/speaker of Carol Rumen's "Passing a Statue of Our Lady in Derry," discover new and vital components of identity within seemingly wounded or even dead and destructive traditions, forces, and "myths." The reconstituted components of identity invigorate the characters in Stewart Parker's *Pentecost* and in Anne Devlin's *After Easter*, helping them come to terms with the violence and brutality endemic to Northern society plagued by the Troubles. Essentially, the characters create "cultural narratives [that] represent a dialogue of sorts (however conflictive) between various modern Irish minds and the traditions from which they derive, and which they often seek to transform or transcend."[138] The plays, consequently, stand as

a re-interpretation of its own history, an attempt to retell the story of the past as it relates to the present, an act of "understanding otherwise" the motivating subworld of symbols which informs our consciousness of the world . . . where the text of imagination interweaves with the context of history . . . a mode of narrative imagination prepared to demystify the ideological abuses of myth while re-inventing new possibilities of experience . . . a narrative re-writing of the old [essentially becoming] a culture [that] invents its future by re-inventing its past.[139]

The characters write a new history, without disregarding the disruptive components of the past, that incorporates images and emotions associated with trauma into newly fashioned structures that reinvent the characters's past, that re-read the past from the perspective of a newly-fashioned identity that integrates and invigorates.

ESCAPING HISTORY

In "Graveyards" Sam Burnside writes of two choices. One means focusing on the dead relics of the past, cleaning them up and using them as a "safe" path. The stones, in this sense, stand for the archetypes of history that overwhelm and destroy individual conceptions of self and relation to contemporary society. It is no accident then that the speaker finds himself rummaging alone through the stones in the graveyard with only the dead for company. Any interaction with the living, by implication, is informed by the violent ghosts of the past. However, Burnside also writes of another alternative. Specifically, he speaks of "children and lovers" who "delight to kick them [the stones markers of the dead] aside" (1.9). The young, getting on with the business of living, disregard the archetypes of the past. They do find themselves in the graveyard, on the site of memorials to old traditions, but rather than allow those traditions to "sap" the vitality from their lives, they opt to disregard their traumatic inheritance for interaction and social, non-violent discourse.

In Frank McGuinness's *Carthaginians* and in Christina Reid's *My Name? Shall I Tell You My Name?*, characters, like the lovers and children from Burnside's poem, transform traumatic memories and responses and re-structure relationships disrupted as a consequence of trauma. In each play, the authors represent characters who build on the ruptured fragments of memory and experience to reconstruct lives that integrate traumatic structures into newly fashioned components of identity. Significantly, the characters do not simply disregard the violent past, for

a task of reinvention cannot be fulfilled by a wholesale abolition of tradition or a schismatic war against the past. The iconoclastic impulse to demythologise culture-however indispensable-also has its limits. The projection of the new needs to be accompanied by a narrative rewriting of the old. It is a mistake to oppose in an absolute fashion the utopian horizons of tradition. For a culture invents its future by reinventing its past.[140]

In *Carthaginians* and *My Name?*, characters do not abolish their past. Rather, they re-invent it so that its traumatic structures actually serve to revitalize the present. Such a process, consequently, "may not mark the end of the 'real' but perhaps inaugurates the termination of the epistemological pretensions that once elevated western 'realism.'"[141] For the characters in Reid's and McGuinness's plays, the "pretensions" of realism manifest themselves in the violent and brutal traditions and the history of their society. The Northern Ireland that begins these plays is one in which the Troubles overwhelm and consume individual identity. The Northern Ireland that ends each play manifests its hope for a termination of tragedy in the "reconfiguration, rewritings and re-routings" that lead individual characters to overcome traumatic structures and to develop a fully integrated consciousness capable of coming to terms with violent contingencies.

De-Conditioning of Traumatic Memories and Responses

An additional method for individuals to come to terms with a posttrauma identity is for the trauma victims to purge themselves of their masks of protection and violence by integrating their personality into the masks, transforming them from external components to fully incorporated elements of identity. Within a community, such a process "offer[s] the possibility of redeeming symbols from the ideological abuses of doctrinal prejudice, racist nationalism, class oppression, or totalitarian domination."[142] Essentially, trauma discrepant information becomes an "hermeneutics of affirmation" that "focuses not on the origin (*arche*) behind such symbols but on the end (*utopos*) in front of them-that is, on the horizon of aspiration opened up by symbols. In this way, it is possible to rescue social symbolizations from the distorting strategies of reactionary domination."[143] In societies like Northern Ireland, a focus on "utopos" offers the possibilities of a new "cultural identity" that is a matter of "becoming" as well as "being." It belongs to the future as much as to the past. It is not something that already exists, transcending place, time, history, and culture. Cultural identities come from somewhere, have histories. But, like everything which is historical, they undergo constant transformation. Far from being eternally fixed in some essentialised past, they are subject to continuous "play" of history, culture and power. [144]Within the North, practical changes will have to be made and are being made to define Catholic and Protestant, and even Nationalist and Unionist, identity in terms other than opposition, suspicion, hatred, and violence. Specifically, "Sinn Féin has increasingly taken pains to present itself as socially responsible. . . . Sinn Féin has come to disapprove of the impromptu riots that are associated with demonstrations and the building of bonfires."[145] Furthermore, Unionism/Loyalism is also trying to distance itself from violence. "There has been much talk lately of emphasising the folk-festival aspect of the Twelfth, restoring the carnival atmosphere of 'the old days before the Troubles.'"[146] New identities focus, as Kearney, Hall, Buckley, and Patterson suggests they must, not on recovering the inspirations of the past in July or August rituals but on maintaining a respect for those rituals but also adopting them to new contingencies, and most certainly contingencies of reconciliation and understanding.

In *Carthaginians* and *My Name? Shall I Tell You My Name?* the characters de-condition traumatic associations of memory and response by incorporating traumatic elements into a method of dealing with self and society that provides for a means for overcoming trauma. In essence, the characters involve themselves in a constant refashioning of identity in order to adapt their reactions from those associated with violence and trauma to new self-conceptions. Within these frameworks, the characters do not just shield themselves from traumatic violence, they purge traumatic threat from their lives. In clinical terms, in "order for the person to form a new, nontraumatic structure, trauma discrepant information must be provided. The critical issue is to expose the patient to an experience that contains elements that are sufficiently similar to the trauma to activate it, and at the same time contains aspects that are incompatible enough to change it."[147] The characters build their identities using the materials associated with traumatic rupture. However, rather than allow those elements to calcify and to form the basis for psychological response, the characters alter the traumatic conditions, allowing for positive associations with the factors that recall trauma. In order to understand the characters's refashioned identities, it is necessary to understand the nature of identity in general. "Perhaps instead of thinking of identity as an already accomplished fact, which the new cultural practices then represent, we should think, instead, of identity as a 'production,' which is never complete, always in progress, and always constituted within, not outside, representation."[148] The characters's identities are constantly changing, in order to allow for the de-conditioning of traumatic responses buried deep in their subconscious. However, because the newly-fashioned identities exist within representation, the characters's self-conception never masks trauma. Rather, the production of identity allows for a vigourous counter to traumatic response.

Within Frank McGuinness's *Cathaginians*, the characters come to terms with the traumatic and sudden notion of death by enacting a ritual through which they allegorically overcome death and, subsequently, can come to terms with their lives. Essentially, they decondition themselves so that death no longer has complete hold over their imaginations and existence. Specifically, in an exchange between Dido and Greta, Dido reveals that she believes in the supernatural possibilities of flowers.

Dido: This was a rose, Greta. Isn't it beautiful?
Greta: It's dead. I prefer them living. Why do you not?
Dido: Flowers are more gentle when they're dead.
Greta: Gentle?
Dido: Aye. They have more power in them. More magic. You can work spells with dead flowers, did you know that?[149]

Significantly, Dido believes in the power of dead flowers, believes that some positive force can unleash itself through death. Because the unexpected confrontation with death lies at the heart of her traumatic experience, Dido's spirituality in association with dead flowers indicates that her mind is either consciously or unconsciously inventing a ritual to come to terms with the unexpected contingencies of death. Her effort finds a resonance with more traditional ritual. Specifically, "in order to reach a new plane of existence in the initiation ritual, one must normally undergo "sufferings," an encounter with death, through which death is overcome: in sacrifice, in the act of killing, the will to live rises triumphant over the fallen victim. After this, a real death seems no more than a repetition, anticipated long ago."[150] Dido, in her musings on flowers, reveals that her mind manufactures a mechanism through which she can ritualistically come through death, can conquer and overcome death. Indeed, she later reveals an experience connected with flowers that confirms her spirituality. In conversation with her friends, she discloses a semi-ritualistic meeting with a stranger bearing flowers:

Dido: The happiest day of my life is a secret.
Sarah: What happened?
Dido: All right, I'll tell you. I was that happy I
thought I was dreaming. I probably was, for there
was a man involved. He was foreign and he was
pissed but he was beautiful. I met him when I was
wandering the docks.
Meala: Was he a sailor?
Dido: Likely. I didn't ask. He came up to me
carrying red roses and he gave them to me. He said
his name was John. He said he was from the Lebanon.
Meala: What was he doing in Derry?
Dido: Wandering through, like myself. When he gave
me the flowers I was sure I'd scored and then he put
his hand to my face and I thought, Yippie, but he
just knelt down on the ground like this. (*kneels*) He
said, 'Listen, listen to the earth. The earth can
speak. It says, Cease your violent hand. I who
gave birth to you will bring death to you. Cease
your violent hand. That is my dream. I pray my
dream comes true.' I said. 'I pray your dreams
comes true as well, but failing that I'll settle for
Derry City winning the European Cup.' He smiled and
called me Dido. I'd never met him or any like him
before. It was like as if he knew me. I turned on
my heel and ran like hell.[151]

Dido's "happiest day" contains many elements of ceremonial death and rebirth under the guise of an amusing if peculiar exchange. The ritual motifs of Dido's interaction with the man from the Lebanon include sexuality, courtly devotional gestures, and a metaphysical connection with the earth. Dido's stranger seems to step out from the mystical "orient," a place "since antiquity . . . of romance, exotic beings, haunting memories and landscapes, remarkable experiences."[152] Her "remarkable experience" involves the promise of romance and sexual licence. Indeed, when he touches her she thinks she has "scored." She encounters the promise of being freed from the sometimes prudish restrictions of her Derry upbringing. His contact liberates her from her upbringing. Moreover, he kneels before her, elevating her to the level of mystical romance as well. He, further, offers her flowers pulling her into the ritual. However, rather than an exotic sexual experience, her offers her a prayer for peace and reconciliation. Essentially, Dido momentarily leaves the world of Derry, dies to the Derry of her reality, and discovers a ceremonial prayer of peace and rebirth, delivered by an exotic messenger. She, feeling understood yet vulnerable, runs away from the man. She returns to the Derry of her reality.

However, in one of the final scenes of the play Dido tells her companions of a very real experience of dying to the Derry of traumatic association and rising to the possibility of a new Derry:

What happened? Everything happened, nothing happened, whatever you want to believe, I suppose. What do I believe? I believe it is time to leave Derry. Love it and leave it. Now or never. Why am I talking to myself in a graveyard? Because nobody in Derry talks to themselves. Everybody in the world talks to themselves. What's the world? Shipquay Street and Ferryquay Street and Rossville Street and William Street and the Strand and great James Street. While I walk the earth, I walk through you the streets of Derry, If I meet one who knows you and they ask, how's Dido? Surviving. How's Derry? Surviving.[153]

In Dido's final vision, the message of the Oriental sailor comes to fruition. Dido declares her intention of leaving Derry City behind her and of going out into the world. However, her world involves the sidewalks and streets of Derry. She declares them the "earth," using the same vocabulary as the Lebanese man uses in his plea for peace. Basically, Dido deconditions her traumatic association between Derry and sudden and unexpected death by ritualizing confrontations with death and then using those rituals as a means to come to terms with her home.

Another character from McGuinness's play uses ritual to come to terms with his traumatic memories. By constructing a pyramid from plastic garbage bags, Paul deconditions his memories's associations between the bags and death, using the bags to represent the possibility of new life and to give himself a sense of power and control over death. In the play's early scenes, Paul vests mystical power into his ritual act of construction, recalling

St. Malachy. He saw the end of the world. He prophesied it. He saw the waters rise over Derry. He saw the Foyle and Swilly meet, and that will be Derry gone. He saw it, but will he stop it? No. He sees the state of this town, but so do I see it. And I will search every dump in this town for rubbish. I'm building a pyramid. When the dead rise, I'll walk into the pyramid with them and walk away from this town and the state it's in. And if I find St Malachy hiding in this city, I'll kill him, I'll kill him, I'll knock his teeth down his throat.[154]

Essentially, Paul's declaration vests power over Derry's troubled history in a Catholic prophet who foresaw destruction and remains impotent in the face of violence. Paul's fantasy destroys the impotent seer and vests active prophetic powers within himself. Moreover, the refuse that functions as the building blocks of the pyramid is vested with a mystical power that can overcome death and give new life. Later in the play, Greta penetrates into the heart of Paul's ritual. When "Greta starts to rip the plastic bag apart,"[155] Paul tells her to

Stop it. Stop it. Stop it. (*grabs the plastic bag off Greta*) The plastic bags. They threw them over the dead. Bury them decently. Put them in the ground. Carrying the dead like a pile of rubbish through Derry on Bloody Sunday. Don't tear the plastic bags. Don't defile their coffin. Don't, please, don't. Don't let them die. Don't let them go mad. If they die, I'll go mad. I have to keep carrying them. That's where I keep them. Give them back to me.[156]

Essentially, Paul uses the markers of death to reconstruct life. He deconditions his traumatic memories by associating the power of life with the signs of death. In doing so, Paul wrests control over traumatic violence from forces beyond his control and vests that power within himself. Certainly, Paul's efforts also represent an individual with severe emotional and psychological problems. However, the associations with the bags nevertheless help him to come to terms with violence. Essentially, Paul's mind manufactures a rational response from irrational materials in order to decondition his traumatic associations. Ultimately, Paul will come to terms with the reality of violence. At the end of the play, he asks,

Do you remember their names? The dead of Bloody
Sunday?
Silence.
Bernard Mc Guigan, forty-one years, Iniscairn Gardens, Derry. Patrick Doherty, thirty-two years, Hamilton Street, Derry. Michael Kelly, seventeen, from Dunmore Gardens, Derry. William Mc Kinney, twenty-seven, from Westway, Derry. James Wray, twenty-three, Druncliffe Avenue, Derry. Hugh Gilmore, seventeen years old, Garvan Place, Derry. Jack Duddy, who was seventeen, Central Drive, Derry. William Nash, nineteen, Dunree Gardens, Derry. Michael McDaid, twenty-one, Tyrconell Street, Derry. Gerald Donaghy, seventeen, Meenan Square, Derry. John Young, seventeen, Westway, Derry. Kevin Mc Elinney, seventeen, Philip Street, Derry. Gerald Mc Kinney, Knockdara House, Waterside, Derry.[157]

Early in the play, however, Paul's delusion helps him to cope with the overwhleming reality of traumatic threat. Within his fantasy, the elements of reality are present. Death is still associated with trash. Paul does not mask the essentials of violence in an effort to shield himself from reality. Conversely, Paul subtly alters reality in an effort to come to terms with reality. His temporary delusion allows him to develop a mechanism through which he can ultimately articulate the names of the dead, simultaneously facing the reality and giving them life through memory and ceremonial incantation. Essentially, he fulfills, by reciting the names, the substantive promise of his delusional pyramid.

Christina Reid's play also details the de-conditioning of traumatic memories. In particular, *My Name? Shall I Tell You My Name?* explores a process of liberation from the fragmented and destructive associations of the protagonist's Protestant, Derry home. Indeed, in order to overcome traumatic associations with their Northern Irish home, the characters in Reid's play must understand that the

terms that we use to name ourselves carry their strings of echoes and inscriptions. Each represents an original misnaming and the simultaneous constant striving of the dispossessed for full representation. Each therefore must be used provisionally; each must be subject to new analyses, new questions and new understandings if we are to unlock some of the narrow terms of the discourses in which we are inscribed. In other words, at each arrival at a definition, we begin a new analysis, a new departure, a new interrogation of meaning, new contradictions.[158]

Within the play, Andrea recognises the original mis-naming, or rupture, that characterizeses certain aspects of Northern Protestant identity. Subsequently, she fashions an individual alternative to that discourse. In particular, Andrea and even, to a certain extent, Andy, Andrea's grandfather, ultimately break out from the colonial and the post-colonial discourse that so influenced their conception of community and wholeness. No longer do the characters assume the methods of oppression and dominance in their interactions with one another. Initially, Andrea perceives the truth about her grandfather, the truth that he assumed the prejudices of the colonizer society and destroyed his friendship with Edward Reilly. "He was the only other survivor with my grandfather. His greatest friend. . . . before the war. They were together in the middle of the photograph. After the war, he cut Edward Reilly out, and stuck the photo together again. They had their arms around each other's shoulders, so to get rid of Edward Reilly he had to cut himself out too."[159] She realizes that Reilly and her grandfather were friends. However, when Andy cut out the image from the picture, because of his hatred of socialism adopted as a means to demonstrate his patriotism, he also cut a part of himself away, literally mutilated himself in his gesture of repulsion. Andrea, in addition to recognition, takes positive steps to escape the cycle of limitation, of fragmentation, perpetuated by the discourse of isolation. She leaves the Sloan home, the Derry enclave in an alien England, in favor of an integrated community at university: "Dear Granda, I've moved out of Freda Sloan's to a room nearer the University. It cost[s] too much in tube fares. They're all students in this house, and we help each other with the work and share books and things, so that saves a bit more again. Tell mammy I'll write a long letter soon."[160] Andrea's gesture literally separates her from Orangism and allegorically embraces the cosmopolitan world of a near-socialist commune. Indeed, a group of students living together and sharing resources sounds suspiciously like the socialism advocated by Northern activists like Edward Reilly. While in the student residence, Andrea demonstrates a true concept of community apart from the prejudices that characterise colonialist discourse. She comes to love an individual because of his human characteristics, her judgement unclouded by notions of racial distinction.

Andrea stirs. Wakens. Looks at Hanif. Smiles. Is about to slip out of bed quietly without waking him, when he pulls her back. Laughter. Kisses. Very clear that they are both very much in love. In the distance the sounds of the military bands increase, then die away again.[161]

The military band plays for Remembrance Day, and Andrea ignores it, allegorically rejecting the jingoistic patriotism of her grandfather and the "marching season" tradition of her Ulster protestant heritage in favour of a relationship not propped up by ritual demonstrations but rather sustained by intimacy and giving communication. Ultimately, Andrea can come to terms with her grandfather's prejudices and forgive him. In the play's opening scene, she remembers him with pity and fondness. "'I learned you to talk and I learned you to walk,' he used to say. 'Your oul granda showed you how to make your way in the world.' I wonder who he talks to now. To himself. To the wall. To the memories locked away in the old tin box. I wonder does he ever think of me."[162]   Andy is not a hated representative of a dying, fragmented world. Rather, he is a pitiful old man, consumed in loneliness and irrevocably damaged by the biases of the colonizer society that he has adopted to service his view of community, a community that leaves him with the symbols of association but with no real communication. Eventually, Andrea can imaginatively strive to communicate with him, can desire contact not for the stability of home and affected custom but because she loves him. "I miss you. I need you. I need to make my peace with you. I love you in a way that I've never loved anyone else. I love you, even though I have grown to loathe everything you believe in. How can I make you understand that, when I don't understand it myself?"[163] Even Andy can verbalize the same type of love, although it is not as emotionally expressive as is his grandaughter's sentiment. "I wonder did she ever get to design a set for a play. I suppose she draws different pictures now, but she drew me before she drew anything else. And that's somethin' nobody and nuthin' can take away from me."[164] He does not remember Andrea as a communist or as a traitor to Ulster patriotism nor as a racial other because of her relationship to Hanif. Rather, he sees her as a granddaughter and an individual who possesses artistic qualities. No longer is she a caricature but a figure of affection ever so distant and seemingly remote. In the end, even though Andrea imagines a method of contact, utilizing the metaphor of war:

They say that one Christmas Day, during the First World War, a group of British and German soldiers called a halt to the fighting and declared a truce, Just for an hour. There must be an hour, a place, where he and I can meet. A piece of Common Ground. A no-mans Land. If it's possible for strangers, then it's possible for us. Or maybe it's easier to declare a truce with someone when you don't bear their name, or their face.[165]

The concept of military and colonial involvement separates them. Her grandfather remains imprisoned within the metaphor. She can only imagine contact with him through it. However, Andrea remains liberated from a self-imposed fragmented sense of community. There is rupture between grandfather and grandaughter, but the genesis of that rupture, in colonial biases imposed on and adopted by a subject people, even a settler community, no longer captivates Andrea's imagination. She has broken the cycle of repression and deconditioned her traumatic response to her environment.

Re-Structuring of Traumatic Personal Schemes

In clinical terms, the "re-structuring of traumatic personal schemes" involves the

adaptive resolution to a stressful experience [that] consists of a modification of one's view of self and others that permits continued attention to the exigencies of daily life. In order to deal successfully with distressing events, it is necessary not to generalize from that experience to the totality of existence, but to view it merely as one terrible incident that has taken place at a particular place at a particular time.[166]

In order to overcome a traumatic event, victims of trauma must also discover new means of interaction beyond the traumatized mask. They must adapt and continue to adapt to circumstance that could resurrect their traumatic experiences and inform their coming to terms with the world. Significantly, the new matrix, once established, should enable the individual to systematically and intellectually purge from identity, if not violence, traumatized reaction to violence, with all its attendant symptoms: fear, hatred, vulnerability, anger, brutality. In terms of the violence endemic to the North of Ireland, "adaptive resolution" manifests itself in terms of a "cultural narrative." Such a narrative is inherently cross-community and cross-cultural. It "represent[s] a dialogue of sorts (however conflictive) between various modern Irish minds and the traditions from which they derive, and which they often seek to transform or transcend."[167] Importantly, a "cultural narrative" does not represent the yielding of one culture to another. Protestant tradition need not acquiesce to Catholic tradition, nor must it adapt to a "Celtic core." Likewise, Catholic tradition need not relinquish its heritage in favor of a neutral, de-Celticized form. On the contrary, a "cultural narrative" embraces history and historical divergence. Further, a "belief in a pluralist society is growing," a society that wants to make a "genuine effort to incorporate all traditions, including that of northern unionism, into the national life."[168]

Basically, every "cultural narrative . . . is in some sense a reinterpretation of its own history, an attempt to retell the story of the past as it relates to the present, an act of 'understanding otherwise' the motivating subworld of symbols which informs our consciousness of the world. Narrative is where the text of imagination interweaves with the context of history." [169] Moreover, such a "narrative" would, indeed, relate a history of conflict. The "cultural narrative" would trace out a genealogy of violence, to discover the causes of current conflict. What emerges is something Foucault called "a multiplicity of genealogical researches, a painstaking rediscovery of struggles together with the rude memories of their conflicts." In addition, "these genealogies . . . are the combined product of an erudite knowledge and a popular knowledge."[170]

The characters tap into non-traditional forms of history, including the narrative and performative, and necessarily so, for it is these adaptable forms which allow for a non-traumatic matrix of new cultural identity not only to emerge but also to change as change becomes necessary to avoid further conflict. In Christina Reid's *My Name? Shall I Tell You My Name?* and Frank McGuinness's *Carthaginians*, the characters come to terms with the implications of traumatic events and, in that process, begin to wrest their lives from the control of the trauma. For Meala, in *Carthaginians*, control means divesting herself of the masks and delusions that shield her from acknowledging her daughter's death and the tragedy of Bloody Sunday. For Andrea, control involves coming to terms with her grandfather's and society's biases and prejudices and recognizing the pain that compels people to adopt bigoted views and the pain they cause. Ultimately, she overcomes the influence of these traumatic forces by embracing the humanity behind the masks of hatred and violence. Andrea offers what Richard Kearney calls a "hermeneutic imagination" as an alternative to an "ideological imagination."[171] Basically, Andrea and Meala discard the false consciousness of ideology and delusion and embrace the meaning behind the falsehood. Andrea comes to terms with her grandfather as a wounded individual, and Meala comes to terms with the reality of her daughter's death. Moreover, both Andrea and Meala embrace, in a manner similar to Kearney's and Ricoeur's "hermeneutics of affirmation," genuine "symbols" for or modes of "liberation."

In a series of scenes, Andrea rejects the destructive and fragmented historical symbols and their methods of affirming the vitality of the past in the present in favor of a personal method designed to sanction the past but without regard for her grandfather's legacy of death. The adult grandaughter, speaking in the initial stages of the play, accepts the legacy of her grandfather, not as warrior hero, but on very individual terms. "I was born on his sixty-ninth birthday. His last grandchild. His only granddaughter. To please him, my mother called me Andrea."[172] She carries on his name, was born on his birthday, is his living and vital legacy, as opposed to his inanimate bequest of medals and songs of death. Further, after she removes herself from the Sloan residence she can come to personal terms with the First World War: "Dear granda, Thanks for the book token. I brought an anthology of war poetry. We're doing an improvised play about war through the eyes of the writers. No, I won't get to see the big Armistice Day Parade in London. I've an awful lot of essays to write and I'll have time for nothing else this weekend. I'll be thinking of you in the Derry parade."[173] Instead of going as a passive observer to the parade in memory of the War, Andrea creates her own celebration, personalizes the memory of her grandfather, articulates it in her voice rather than rely on the practiced rituals of mass-produced lamentation. In time, Andrea is also able to confront directly the fragmented historical symbols and perceives a clear contrast to the human inheritance of sharing her grandfather's day of birth and name in a ritual heritage of death and pain.

Andrea drawing the statue of Edward Carson that stands in front of Stormont (the former N. Ireland parliament) the statue has one arm outstretched, two fingered victory sign.
Andrea: Edward Carson. The English lawyer whose rhetoric rallied the Ulster Protestants to fight the Home Rule Bill.
Joan: The English lawyer who prosecuted Oscar Wilde.
Andrea: They called themselves Carson's Army.
Andrea's Voice Over: My granda cut his thumb with his army knife, and signed The Ulster Covenant with his own blood.[174]

The scene draws Carson, re-presences him, manipulates his image to transform it from that of hero to him who prosecuted Oscar Wilde and stood for the biases of empire against artistic representation. Andrea then makes an association between Carson's attack on Wilde and Carson's force of will, recalling how her grandfather bloodied himself for the cause just as Andrea would be bloodied decades later, allegorically connecting the legacy of hatred within the colonizer community with that of the colonized community. In signing the Covenant, her grandfather does not affirm his individual identity and fashion a personal vision of the past as Andrea does in her play. Rather, the grandfather yields his will to a ritual of death and fragmentation that subverts his individuality to communal identity as a member of Carson's Army. In a further exploration of the alternative to an individualized continuity, Andrea relates the details of Wee Billy's funeral:

Wee Billy Matchett did drop dead eventually. One Twelfth of July when he was beating the big drum before the start of the Orange Parade. His funeral was nearly as big as the parade itself. The Lambeg Drum was set on the ground alongside the open grave. And Billy's ten year old son solemnly hit it three times as soil was sprinkled on the coffin. My grandfather patted the child on the head and said, "You carry the name, and one day you'll be man enough to carry the drum." God's good, and death goes on.[175]

Andrea changes the traditional prayer by substituting "death" for "life," demonstrating that the fragmented world of Wee Billy as expressed through the drum. It begins to articulate the boy's suffering not in a child's accents but in the rigidly life consuming tones of affected and over-emphasized ritual oppression-the incessant beat of the lambeg drum. Subsequently, recognition becomes transformation. Andrea re-approaches the more traditional expressions of her grandfather's ritual and personalizes them. She recalls

Samuel Thompson, Hugh Montgomery, Frederick Wilson, James Elliott, John Cunningham, Edward Marshall. . . . I was quite grown-up before I realised that it was a litany of the glorious dead. Just a handful of the five and a half thousand Ulstermen who died on the first day of The Battle of the Somme. July the First. 1916. By the end of the battle, the total number of dead- British, French and German- was one point two million. One point two million . . . .
Joan: Twenty fives miles of death. The greatest
slaughter in the history of The British Army.[176]

By recognising the humanity of the dead in the reality of mass blood letting, Andrea and Joan adopt Andy's litany to oppose imperialism not to perpetuate it. Later, Andrea recites the same litany, holding a candle for each soldier, as she is taken into custody by the police and in so doing she integrates the War dead into her life. She adopts the memory of the sacrifice in the same way that the soldiers at the Somme were roused to courage and action by the memory of the Ulster past and its glorious dead. However, there is a significant difference between the two expressions. On Greenham Common, the summoning is not a ritual of death fascination that perpetuates death but a ritual that seeks to embrace the humanity of the individuals. Each candle represents the life giving substance of those men in the present not just in memory. In addition, Andrea uses the litany for a peaceful confrontation designed to stop conflict not to perpetuate it. She celebrates what these men were and are, not what they've become in the memories of Ulster ritual, not what Ulster ritual has made them into, fashioned them into. Finally, upon her arrest, Andrea fights in the way her grandfather taught her by telling her name, not through the medium of patriotic rhetoric but by simple identification realizing the values of personal rather than communal inheritance. She writes Andrew telling him that she "didn't cry in court. But I didn't make any heroic speeches either. I just told them my name, and refused to promise to be a good little girl and keep the peace. So I'm a guest of her majesty for the next three weeks."[177] In this act of defiance, as in all her acts of re-fashioning her relationship with the continuity of time, Andrea witnesses to her searching for alternatives to the traditional forms of historic instruction, and acknowledges and represents the harmful and fragmented elements of conventional views of the past in her effort to personalize her inheritance, to make it whole and vital rather than segmented and dead.

Throughout the play, Andrea achieves moments of what some colonial and post-colonial scholars call "Liberation." In essence, she achieves a genuine communion with some apprehension and power within herself that recognizes the deleterious effects of colonialist and post-colonialist discourse and attempts to establish an individual method of coping with and possibly overcoming them. Christina Reid tells a reader that "in general, her self-assurance is low, but her drawing is confident, strong, clear."[178] Certainly, Andrea is most truly alive when painting, when expressing her individual artistry. Her vitality in these moments serves as a clear contrast to Andy's ebullience when he recites affected and non-specific poetry for the dead or when he takes the cane as a symbol of his identification with the aristocracy. Essentially, he accepts that these symbols are more vital than he is, not realizing how shallow and ultimately fragmented is the association between himself and his aspirations. In describing her work, Reid shows Andrea "drawing very fast." Seemingly possessed by a frenzy of creativity, she sketches the subject of the generic poem in Belfast's city hall and one of her grandfather's most virluent aspirations -communion with the glorious dead. She describes the painting to Joan:

He's wearing shorts. The officer is wearing shorts. A boy scout leading men in long trousers into battle. Fritz is being taken prisoner. . . top of the painting . . . more to the left . . . and another German soldier lies dying . . . not there . . . bottom left. An Ulsterman walks away from the dying man . . . he carries a bayonet . . . blood covered . . . he looks . . . nothing . . . . . blank. His eyes are wide open, but he looks blind.[179]

Andrea sees the individual face of the soldiers, sees their death, the incongruity of tropical uniforms in a European theatre allegorically recognizing the ridiculousness of aristocratic leadership that puts boys over men, turns officers into children. Her images represent the de-humanizing elements of war by demonstrating the monsters men create of themselves when they make themselves subject to violence and violent rhetoric. When it comes time to label her work, Andrea reflects

During the night, I thought I'd sign these drawings "the Ballad of Holloway Gaol". But that would be giving myself an honour I don't deserve. I've never been a hero. I've never been a campaigner, like you [Joan]. I was brought up in a city with soldiers on the streets, and armed policemen, and I never thought about it. I don't remember Derry without barbed wire, checkpoints. The war was always there, a part of everyday life. Going shopping and getting frisked by Security Forces in Security Zones. I didn't go the Greenham to protest about a lethal Security Zone. Nothing as noble as that. I was at home, on my own, feeling sorry for myself, and Miriam called and she said, 'Come to Greenham with me. Bring your sketch pad. Record it for history.' I went because I had nothing better to do. I hated it. Campfires and mud. I've always liked my home comforts.[180]

Andrea rejects a title that would have aligned her work to that of Wilde and the tradition of prison literature, an alignment that would have clearly been in keeping with her rejection of Carson. She could have stood in alliance with Wilde against the oppressive discourse of the colonizer. However, she opts not to stand with anyone, but only with herself. She says that her boredom motivated her to protest. However, she precedes that statement by recounting the images of the Northern War on her home streets suggesting that she protests that war, expresses outrage against the horrors of Unionist discourse in her individual act of protest. Truly, she does not resist and fight out of heroism but, rather, out of a firm knowledge of the oppressive nature of conflict and its inevitable de-humanizing effects. In the end, she is again bloodied, this time humiliated in a strip search during her period. "Andrea and Miriam are stripped searched. Miriam angry/contemptuous. Andrea crying silently. A small trickle of blood running down Andrea's leg. Andy's voice joins the music, singing the two lines of *Billy Boys*."[181] Here, unlike her grandfather, Andrea does achieve full association with the oppressive elements of the colonizer, with the society of Sir John and the prison staff, and with the colonized, her grandfather's singing celebratory verses and her bloodied humilation converting the potential for life into death and shame. In this final scene of the play, Andrea achieves the essence of "Liberation"-a full perception and full understanding of the destructive elements of both colonialism and post-colonialism. Without such a recognition, individuals like Andy and the Orangemen continue to associate themselves with fragmented and illusory constructs. For Andrea, "Liberation" is an effort to recognize and understand the broken traditions as broken and to fashion a coherent revelation that does not deliver her from pain but frees her from slavery and trust in the fragmented conceptions of painful discourse:

I miss you. I need you. I need to make my peace with you. I love you in a way that I've never loved anyone else. I love you, even though I have grown to loathe everything you believe in. How can I make you understand that, when I don't understand it myself? . . . Loyalty. Patriotism. Them or us. You daren't question what all that has done to you, because once you question even a small part of it, you end up questioning it all. And to do that would be to negate your whole life. Everything you've lived and survived by. Do you ever cry when there is no-one there to see? Or are you afraid you might never stop? I wonder if you're ever afraid. I wonder what you're doing now. I wonder if you ever think of me.[182]

Andrea establishes a connection with her grandfather by re-structuring her personal means of interaction with him. She does not allow his resentment of her or his prejudices to govern her interaction with his memory and with society. She, conversely, manufactures new methods for interaction apart from a wholly traumatic response.

In *Carthaginians*, Meala too restructures her relationship with a family member. However, in Meala's case, she re-establishes a connection with the reality of her daughter's death. Initially, Meala adopts a mask of maternal care for her dead daughter: "Meala spreads cloths upon a grave."[183] In addition, Meala holds conversation with her daughter and denies the daughter's death:

Meala has returned to the grave she had been
dressing and speaks to it.
Meala: You don't know the value of money, you know
that? I can't keep up with you. All you think
about is style. Isn't that right?
Silence.
Greta: What age would she have been?
Meala: You mean what age she is?
Silence.
I'm saving for her birthday. (*whispers*) A leather
jacket. I'm buying it for her. (*raises her voice*)
But we'll see. We'll just have to see. We'll just
have to see. Who knows?
Meala sings.
'Happy birthday to you, happy birthday to you, happy
birth . . ."
Silence.
She's not dead, you know. She's not. That's why I
saw what all three of us saw. That's why it's going
to happen. It has to, hasn't it.[184]

Essentially, Meala, unlike Paul who constructs a fantasy that contains realistic
elements of his trauma, masks her pain behind a delusion that denies any element
of traumatic rupture. She even denies the reality of Bloody Sunday: "Nothing
changed. Nothing happened that day. Nobody died. I should know, I was at the
hospital. If there had been anyone dead I would have seen them, and I saw no one
dead. (*Jumps to her feet*) I saw no one dead. I saw no one dead. You're telling lies.
You've driven away the dead. I hope you're satisfied. I hope your satisfied with
your lies. (*She exits.*)"[185] Ultimately though, Meala accepts the reality of her
daughter's death:

Meala: She's dead, isn't she?
Silence.
My wee girl's dead. They're running mad through the
streets of Derry and my daughter's dead. Do you not
understand that?
Dido: Understand what. Meala?
Silence.[186]

In confronting the reality of her daughter's loss, Meala equips herself to face the
world of reality, to cast off her delusion. The realization is a painful one:

I went for a walk. Through Derry. Everybody was
crying. What was wrong with them? All shouting. I
couldn't hear what. Was it at me? I wasn't

listening to them.
Dido:What were you listening to?
Meala: They said, 'She's dead. I'm afraid she's
dead. We can get you home safely in an ambulance.
There's a lot of bother stirring in the town.' I
said, 'what do you mean she's dead? There's a dead
thing in there and that thing is cancer, that thing
is not my daughter. My daughter's at home. I
better get back to her. I don't know what I'm doing
out.' The town's gone mad today hasn't it?
Dido: She's dead, Meala. Your daughter's dead.
Meala: No, doctor, you're wrong. My daughter is
alive. My daughter is not that thing. I'm going
home.
Dido: I'll go with you.
Meala: Nonsense. I'm perfectly capable of walking home. At my age I should know my way
around Derry. I've walked through it often enough. William Street and Shipquay Street and
Ferryquay Street and the Strand and Rossville Street and great James Street. I'm walking
home through my own city. Everybody's running and everybody's crying. What's wrong?
Why cry? Two dead, I hear that in William Street. I'm walking through Derry and they're
saying in Shipquay Street there's five dead. I am walking to my home in my house in the
street I was born in and I've forgotten where I live. I am in Ferryquay Street and I hear
there's nine dead outside the Rossville flats. They've opened fire and shot them dead. I'm
not dead. Where are there dead in Derry? Let me look on the dead. Jesus, the dead. The
innocent dead. There's thirteen dead in Derry. Where am I? What day is it? Sunday. Why
is the sun bleeding? It's pouring blood. I want a priest. Give me a priest. Where am I? In
Great James Street. It's full of chemists. I need a tonic for my nerves. For my head. For my
heart. Pain in my heart. Breaking heart. I've lost one. I've lost them all. They had no hair.
She had fire. She opened fire on herself. When she wasn't looking she caught cancer. It
burned her. She was thirteen. It was Sunday. I have to go to Mass. I have to go to Mass. I
have to go to Mass. Dido, take me to Mass, Dido.[187]

However, Meala's painful realization contains elements that ensure her recovery.
Specifically, she acknowledges the event and articulates the full implications of her
daughter's loss. She strips her mask and sees the truth. Furthermore, in her
confrontation with truth, she finds a resonance for her pain in the suffering of her
environment. She sees an image of the "sun bleeding." The image allows her to
come to terms with her inner sense of suffering, to legitimize it. Finally, she asks
for religious comfort, rejecting the notion that her problems are "in her head." She
acknowledges that a "tonic," of pain-masking curative will not sustain her. Within
her desire to "go to Mass," Meala expresses a longing for spiritual comfort, for a
willingness to not only come to terms with her grief but also to overcome it, to
begin to put the incident in the past and to struggle to purge its influence over her
life. Essentially, Meala's emotional outpouring of understanding represents a
"productive" act of poiesis. "*If poiesis* is indeed that which shows and brings forth
what is meaningful in action, it remains answerable to action."[188]   Basically,
Meala's act does not mirror her delusion that Bloody Sunday and her daughter's
death never happened. Meala produces, in her declaration, an image of her hidden

pain, an image of the depths of her trauma. As a consequence, she seeks a type of action to act as "guarantor" for her permanent acknowledgment of trauma and her effort to overcome her traumatic experience. The spiritual cure, rather than simply a tonic, ensures that she will take action to integrate the trauma into her life. Meala, like the other characters of *Carthaginians* and *My Name? Shall I Tell You My Name?* interacts with history. In terms of Sam Burnside's motif, they wander through a graveyard. For the characters of McGuinness's play, their memory ground is literally a graveyard where the dead of Bloody Sunday are buried. For Andrea and her grandfather, the graveyard is the memory of the dead of World War I and the living but inanimate traditions of Protestant hegemony. However, the characters from both plays, like the children and lovers from Burnside's poem, eventually alter their interactions with the past, de-conditioning their traumatic responses and altering interpersonal relations informed by violence. In essence, they undertake an act of historitization, and the "crux of 'historitization is change: . . . Spectators observe the potential movement in class relations, discover the limitations and strengths of their own perceptions, and begin to change their lives. . . . Historicization is . . . *a way of seeing*, and the enemy of re-usurpation and appropriation." Basically, the characters revisit the past, change it, incorporate it into their consciousness in such a way as to wrest traumatic control from their individual self-conceptions. They inaugurate "a new way of seeing" which involves the rejection of traumatic elements that inform their interaction with the past and opt, instead, for a reconstituted identity capable of coming to terms with daily and even sometimes violent contingencies.

   Indeed, not only in an attempt to escape from the violent archetypes of history but also in the effort to reconstruct social relationships and mythic structures, certain aspects of Northern Irish drama detail an imaginative restructuring of ruptured components of identity. Clearly, "the imagination, especially when collective, can become the fuel for action. It is the imagination, in its collective forms, that creates ideas of neighbourhood and nationhood, of moral economies and unjust rule, of higher wages and foreign labor prospects. The imagination is today a staging ground for action, and not only for escape." Drama and much creative production including the mural of a feminized Ireland on Flax Street, creates mechanisms that generate "an integrated account, a theoretically satisfying model that does genuinely incorporate historical events and processual change, both internally and externally induced." The result of these reconstructions of identity involves an acceptance of history and the Troubles but also entails growing beyond them.

NOTES

[1] Bill Rolston, *Drawing Support 2: Murals of War and Peace*, (Belfast: Beyond the Pale, 1995), 55.

[2] Isaac Julien, and Kobena Mercer, "De Margin and De Centre," *Staurt Hall: Critical Dialogues in Cultural Studies*, ed. by Davis Morley and Kuan-Hsing Chen, (New York: Routledge, 1996), 451.

[3] Iain Chambers, "Waiting on the End of the World." *Staurt Hall: Critical Dialogues in Cultural Studies*. Ed. by David Morley and Kuan-Hsing Chen. New York: Routledge, 1996. 207.

[4] Luke Gibbons, *Transformations in Irish Culture*, (Cork: Cork University Press, 1996), 179.

[5] Stuart Turner, Alexander Mc Farlane, and Bessel Van der Kolk, "The Therapeutic Environment and New Explorations in the Treatment of Posttraumatic Stress Disorder," *Traumatic Stress: The Effects of Overwhelming Experience on Mind, Body, and Society*, ed. Bessel Van der Kolk, Alexander Mc Farlane, and Lars Weisaeth, (London: The Guilford Press, 1996), 551.

[6] Bessel Van der Kolk, Alexander Mc Farlane, and Onto Van der Hart, "A General Approach to the Treatment of Posttraumatic Stress Disorder," *Traumatic Stress: The Effects of Overwhelming Experience on Mind, Body, and Society*, ed. Bessel Van der Kolk, Alexander Mc Farlane, and Lars Weisaeth, (London: The Guilford Press, 1996), 432.

[7] Ibid.

[8] Carl Jung, *Symbols of Transformation*, trans. by R.F.C. Hull, (Princeton: Princeton University Press, 1990), 4-5.

[9] Frantz Fanon, *Black Skin, White Masks*, trans. by Charles Lam Markmann (New York: Grove Press, 1967), 23.

[10] Fredric Jameson, *The Political Unconscious: Narrative as a Socially Symbolic Act*, (New York: Cornell University Press, 1981), 104-05.

[11] Anthony Buckley and Mary Catherine Kenney, *Negotiating Identity: Rhetoric, Metaphor, and Social Drama in Northern Ireland*, (Washington: Smithsonian Institution Press, 1995), 202-03.

[12] Ibid, 208.

[13] Van der Kolk, McFarlane, and Van der Hart, "General Approach,"432-433.

[14] Homi Bhabha, *The Location of Culture*, (New York: Routledge, 1994), 2.

[15] Vincent Woods, *At the Black Pig's Dyke*, (unpublished typescript, 1994), 80.

[16] Ibid.

[17] Ibid.

[18] Dudley Young, *Origins of the Sacred*, (New York: St. Martin's Press, 1991), 97.

[19] Ibid., 98.

[20] Ibid,. 97.

[21] Woods, *At the Black Pig's Dyke*, 2.

[22] Declan Kiberd, *Inventing Ireland*, (London: Jonathan Cape, 1995), 293.

[23] Seamus Deane, "Heroic Styles: The Tradition of an Idea," *Ireland's Field Day*, (Derry: Field Day Theatre Company, 1985), 45.

[24] Woods, *At the Black Pig's Dyke*, 44.

[25] Gibbons, *Transformations*, 180.

26 Woods, *At the Black Pig's Dyke*, 2.

27 Richard Kearney, *Poetics of Modernity*, (Atlantic Highlands: Humanities Press, 1995), 40.

28 Paul Ricoeur,"The Symbol as Bearer of Possible Worlds," *The Crane Bag of Irish Studies* (1982), 17.

29 Seamus Heaney, *The Cure at Troy*, (London: Faber and Faber, 1990), 1.

30 Ibid.

31 Ibid.

32 Ibid.

33 Ibid., 77-78.

34 Ibid.

35 Ibid.

36 Chambers, "Waiting," 203.

37 Kearney, *Poetics*, 208-09.

38 Van der Kolk, McFarlane, and Vander Hart, "General Approach," 433.

39 Carl Jung, *Analytical Psychology*, (New York: Vintage Books, 1968), 186.

40 Ibid., 187.

41 Woods, *At the Black Pig's Dyke*, 10.

42 Ibid., 15.

43 Ibid., 17.

44 Ibid.

45 Joseph Roach,"Culture and Performance in the Circum-Atlantic World," *Performitivity and Performance*, ed. by Andrew Parker and Eve Kosofsky Sedgewick, (New York: Routledge, 1995), 46.

46 Woods, *At the Black Pig's Dyke*, 58-59.

47 Bhabha, *Location*, 7.

48 Woods, *At the Black Pig's Dyke*, 51.

49 Ibid., 66-67.

50 Ibid., 75.

51 Achille Mbembe and Janet Roitman, "Figures of the Subject in Times of Crisis," *The Geography of Identity*, ed. Patricia Yaeger, (Ann Arbor: University of Michigan Press, 1996), 153.

52 Heaney, *Cure*, 36.

53 Ibid., 36-37.

54 Woods, *At the Black Pig's Dyke*, 73-74.

55 Carl Jung, *Memories, Dreams, Reflections*, (New York: Vintage Books, 1989), 140.

56 Roland Barthes, *Mythologies*, (New York: Hill and Wang, 1997), 109.

57 Richard Kearney, *Myth and Motherland*, (Derry: Field Day, 1984), 61-62.

58 Fredric Jameson, *Modernism and Imperialism*, (Derry: Field Day Theatre Company, 1988), 20.

59 Jung, *Analytical Psychology*, 106.

60 William Pegg, *Prejudice Reduction: A Workshop Approach*, (Coleraine: Centre for the Study of Conflict at the University of Ulster, 1992), 5.

[61] Johnston McMaster, *The Churches and Cross Community Work with Young People*, (Belfast: Youth Link, 1993), 3.

[62] Van der Kolk, McFarlane, and Vander Hart, "General Approach," 426.

[63] Anne Devlin, *After Easter*, (London: Faber and Faber, 1994), 4.

[64] Ibid., 9.

[65] Ibid., 39.

[66] Ibid., 13.

[67] Ibid., 39.

[68] Ibid., 37.

[69] Kuan Hsing Chen, "Post-Marxism: Between/Beyond Critical Postmodernism and Cultural Studies," *Staurt Hall: Critical Dialogues in Cultural Studies*, ed. by David Morley and Kuan-Hsing Chen, (New York: Routledge, 1996), 311.

[70] Devlin, *After Easter*, 38.

[71] Ibid., 54.

[72] Ibid.

[73] Ibid., 53.

[74] Chen, "Post-Marxism," 311.

[75] Devlin, *After Easter*, 54.

[76] Chen, "Post-Marxism," 311.

[77] Richard Kearney, *Poetics of Modernity*, (Atlantic Highlands: Humanities Press, 1995), 15.

[78] Devlin, *After Easter*, 59.

[79] Jean Baudrillard, *Selected Writings*, ed. by Mark Poster, (Stanford: Stanford University Press, 1988), 167.

[80] Devlin, *After Easter*, 59.

[81] James Clifford, "Traveling Cultures," *Cultural Studies*, ed. by Lawrence Grossberg, Cary Nelson, and Paula Treichler, (New York: Routledge, 1992), 97.

[82] Ibid.

[83] Fredric Jameson, *Modernism and Imperialism*, (Derry: Field Day Theatre Company, 1988), 11.

[84] Devlin, *After Easter*, 59.

[85] Ibid.

[86] Elin Diamond, *Unmaking Mimesis: Essays on Feminism and Theater*, (New York: Routledge, 1997), 148.

[87] Ibid.

[88] Devlin, *After Easter*, 75.

[89] James Joyce, *Finnegans Wake*, (London: Faber and Faber, 1943), 620.

[90] Brendan O Hehir, *A Gaelic Lexicon for Finnegans Wake*, (Berkeley: University of California Press, 1967), 325.

[91] Diamond, *Unmaking*, 148-149.

[92] Stewart Parker, *Three Plays for Ireland*, (London: Oberon Books, 1989), 156.

[93] Ibid., 156.

[94] Ibid.

[95] Ibid., 180.

[96] Ibid., 157.

[97] Ibid., 180.
[98] Ibid., 194.
[99] Ibid., 195.
[100] Ibid.
[101] Ibid., 196.
[102] Ibid.
[103] Ibid., 202.
[104] Staurt Hall, "Cultural Identity and Diaspora," *Identity: Community, Culture, Difference.* ed. Jonathan Rutherford, (London: Lawrence and Wishart, 1990), 224.
[105] Edna Longley, "Opening Up: a New Pluralism," *Troubled Times:* Fortnight *Magazine and the Troubles in Northern Ireland, 1970-91*, ed. by Robert Bell, Robert Johnstone, and Robin Wilson. (Belfast: Blackstaff Press, 1991), 141.
[106] Ibid., 144.
[107] Van der Kolk. McFarlane, and Van der Hart, "General Approach," 427.
[108] Jung, *Analytical Psychology*, 282.
[109] Devlin, *After Easter*, 24.
[110] Ibid.
[111] Ibid.
[112] Ibid.
[113] Ibid., 2.
[114] Ibid., 25-26.
[115] T.G.E. Powell, *The Celts*, (London: Thames and Hudson, 1989), 146.
[116] Ibid.
[117] Devlin , *After Easter*, 24.
[118] Ibid.
[119] Ibid., 21.
[120] Powell, *Celts*, 148.
[121] Ibid., 155.
[122] Devlin, *After Easter*, 29.
[123] Ibid., 59.
[124] Ibid., 46-47.
[125] Kearney, *Poetics*, xiii.
[126] Mbembe and Roitman, "Figures," 155.
[127] Judith Butler, *Bodies that Matter: On the Discursive Limits of Sex*, (New York: Routledge, 1993), 12.
[128] Parker, *Three Plays*, 152.
[129] Ibid.
[130] Ibid., 192.
[131] Ibid.
[132] Ibid., 159.
[133] Ibid., 177.
[134] Ibid.
[135] Ibid., 178.
[136] Ibid., 202.
[137] Ibid., 193.
[138] Richard Kearney, "The Transitional Crisis in Irish Culture," *The Honest Ulsterman*, 92 (Winter 1986): 31.
[139] Ibid., 38.

[140] Ibid.

[141] Chambers, "Waiting," 207.

[142] Kearney, *Poetics*, 75.

[143] Ibid., 74.

[144] Hall, "Cultural Identity," 225.

[145] Buckley and Kenney, *Negotiating Identity*, 92.

[146] Glenn Patterson, "29/12," *Troubled Times:* Fortnight *Magazine and the Troubles in Northern Ireland, 1970-91*, ed. by Robert Bell, Robert Johnstone, and Robin Wilson, (Belfast: Blackstaff Press, 1991), 146.

[147] Van der Kolk, McFarlane, and Vander Hart, "General Approach,". 430.

[148] Hall, "Cultural Identity," 222.

[149] Frank McGuinness, *Carthaginians*, (with *Bag Lady*), (London: Faber and Faber, 1988), 308.

[150] Walter Burkert, *Homo Necans*, (Berkeley: University of California Press, 1983), 296.

[151] McGuinness, *Carthaginians*, 326.

[152] Edward Said, *Orientalism*, (New York: Random House, 1978), 1.

[153] McGuinness, *Carthaginians*, 379.

[154] Ibid., 308.

[155] Ibid., 368.

[156] Ibid.

[157] Ibid., 378.

[158] Carole Boyce Davies, *Black Women, Writing and Identity: Migrations of the Subject*, (New York: Routledge, 1994), 5.

[159] Christina Reid, *Plays: 1*, (London: Methuen Drama, 1997), 36.

[160] Ibid., 76.

[161] Ibid., 80.

[162] Ibid., 5.

[163] Ibid., 115.

[164] Ibid., 116.

[165] Ibid., 117.

[166] Van der Kolk, McFarlane, and Vander Hart, "General Approach," 431-432.

[167] Kearney, *Poetics*, 31.

[168] Garrett Fitzgerald, "Steps towards Reconciliation," *Troubled Times:* Fortnight *Magazine and the Troubles in Northern Ireland, 1970-91*, ed. by Robert Bell, Robert Johnstone, and Robin Wilson, (Belfast: Blackstaff Press, 1991), 22.

[169] Kearney, "Transitional," 31.

[170] Michel Foucault, *Power/Knowledge: Selected Interviews and Other Writings, 1972-1977*, ed. by Colin Gordon, trans. by Colin Gordon, Leo Marshall, John Mepham, and Kate Soper, (New York Pantheon Books, 1980), 83.

[171] Kearney, *Poetics*, 74.

[172] Reid, *Plays*, 9.

[173] Ibid., 78.

[174] Ibid., 83.

[175] Ibid., 30.

[176] Ibid., 18.

[177] Ibid., 113.

[178] Ibid., 3.
[179] Ibid., 21.
[180] Ibid., 106.
[181] Ibid., 112.
[182] Ibid., 115.
[183] McGuinness, *Carthaginians*, 297.
[184] Ibid, 300-301.
[185] Ibid., 346.
[186] Ibid., 351.
[187] Diamond, *Unmaking*, 49.
[188] Arjun Appadurai, *Modernity at Large*, (Minneapolis: University of Minnesota Press, 1997), 7.
[189] C.M. Hann, "Fast Forward: The Great Transformation Globalised," *When History Accelerates: Essays of Rapid Social Change, Complexity and Creativity*, ed. C.M. Hann, (London: Athlone, 1994), 5.

6

"Coicead":
The Fifth Province

In her December 1990 acceptance speech, Mary Robinson spoke of her hope for uniting the people of Ireland, North and South. She reminded her audience that the

old Irish term for province is *coicead*, meaning a "fifth" and yet, as everyone knows, there are only four geographical provinces on this island. So where is the fifth? . . . It is a place within each one of us, that place that is open to the other, that swinging door which allows us to venture out and others to venture in . . . tradition has it that this fifth province acted as a second centre, a necessary balance. If I am a symbol of anything, I would like to be the symbol of this reconciling and healing fifth province.[1]

Robinson's remarks carry a resonance with many critical designations for new structures and formations that emerge in formerly marginalized cultures and experiences. Some critics call these structures the "third space," which is understood to be a

place of resistance, not defined by poverty, deprivation and toil, but a history that is acknowledged, that has a determining effect on personal and political identity. This place is neither the old margin nor the copying of the centre, but a third space where new subjectives, new politics and new identities are articulated. My new location has the resources of the centre but remains outside to disrupt and resist, continually threatening the centre with the contradictions of its margins.[2]

Within the third space, a process akin to healing after traumatic rupture takes place. Specifically, components of identity are healed, just as Robinson suggests, by the imaginative incorporation of those ruptured elements into the individual consciousness. The process of assimilation validates the wounded and discarded components of the sub-conscious and integrates them into new structures and means of coming to terms with the world that involves the "integration of body, mind, spirit, and culture,"[3] which allows individuals to grow beyond their marginalized or traumatized inheritance. The process is often difficult. However, it offers the opportunity for true growth and, ultimately, for recovery as well, as many writers and artists have demonstrated.

The creative production consequent of such a process enables writers to sample styles and meanings formerly devalued, including experimental dramatic forms or even Irish-language structures, giving rise to what Declan Kiberd call the "second Renaissance"[4] in contemporary Irish writing. However, as this study of Northern Irish drama within the context of the Troubles indicates, the fifth province, or carnival, can only come into being after careful consideration of the full effects of violent rupture. Contemporary literature from the North and, indeed, from all the Thirty-Two counties does focus on the intricacies of trauma and individual and societal responses to violence.

Specifically, Christina Reid's play, *Today and Yesterday in Northern Ireland*, explores the Troubles through the metaphor of old films and serials. Catholics in the North are implicitly paralleled, in a child's imagination, with black-hatted bandits in weekly Western adventures. Using a child's perspective, the older narrator reflects on her youthful aversion to these characters and on her adult awareness that the "bad guys" were simply defending their land. Similarly, the older narrator revises her childhood impression of the film *King Kong*. As a young girl, Christina, the narrator, adored the American soldiers and their heroic exploits against the giant monster. However, as she grew older, the narrator concedes, she grew to pity the giant ape and, ultimately, not only to sympathize with his plight but to empathize with his predicament as a misunderstood and alienated creature victimized by a militaristic society.

Indeed, the film can be seen, especially within the context of Reid's drama, as a means of understanding the disruptions in Northern society as a consequence of the Troubles. Like the giant ape, Catholics and Protestants alike are victims of violence. The Troubles rupture both societies' conceptions of identity and uproot old support structures, just as the ape was uprooted and taken from the support structures of his environment. Moreover, the film can be seen as a metaphor for the underlying dynamics that precipitated violence. Protestant notions of hegemony, coupled with British military power exploit the Catholic populace in just the same way that the hunters and soldiers exploit and then destroy King Kong. Certainly, within this context, the racialization and simianization of the Irish take on interesting implications. Specifically, "*King Kong* . . . has been read as the tragic story of a heroic beast and/or the fate of a black man."[5] Moreover, the film brings into focus "the debates on class and culture, hegemony and subjectivity"[6] that not only characterize critical explorations of Northern literature and society but wider-ranging discussions of race and empire.

Dublin-born artist Pauline Cummins gives form to a similar traumatic experience in her sculptures and video titled *Unearthed* (1989/90) explores the trauma consequent of discovering identities ruptured and destroyed by violence. Figures in black gloves with white paint on their bodies and faces make an effort to come to terms with themselves and their society. In grotesque and distorted movements, they struggle to express emotion but also not to be overwhelmed by emotion. Further, disembodied clay heads portray mutilated and racially ambiguous individuals, pained and motionless, apparently unable to confront the oppressive structures in the world around them. Her work, studied in the context of Christina Reid's radio play and Northern Irish drama exploring the rupture in the basic components of identity suggests that Irish society on both sides of the border finds itself struggling through a process akin to traumatic rupture.

Likewise, much of contemporary Irish literature and art explores themes similar to Northern Irish drama's depiction of individuals who assume societal archetypes as marks of identification. Specifically, Jack Pakenham, an artist born in Dublin but living and working in Belfast, portrays vaguely human figures, who resemble marionettes, in his *Picking the Masks* (1986). In a small room, men reach into a box containing masks. The faces painted on the masks detail anger, horror, hatred, and rage. The non-masked faces of the men stare blank eyed and emotionless inside a room whose only notable feature is a wall with either a window or a painted scene that reveals a city street tilted and its buildings, including a church, twisted into grotesque shapes that combine smooth facades and pastel colors with streaks of black paint and sharp and abrupt edges. The implications of Pakenham's work suggest a society so immersed in violence that its members, numbed by trauma, must turn to pre-packaged emotional masks in order to experience life. Like the buildings in the background of the featureless room, the masks offer in part comfortable and easy solutions. Like the pastel colors and smooth surfaces, the masks allow for an uncomplicated and simple way to come to terms with image and identification. However, the masks also in part have deleterious consequences. Like the buildings' grotesque shapes and the black streaks of paint on the pastel surface, the masks distort and disrupt human interaction with the environment. Emotion and a heathy interaction with the society, which would facilitate recovery from trauma, become subsumed in the effort to don the masks.

Similarly, Mairead O'Connor, one of the Armagh women, writes in a blank-verse sonnet, titled "The Troubles," of the distortion of the human and the loss of sanity:

The falling comes as greylight turns to black
and in that space the shapes of shadows turn
and make the smells and sounds of walls consumed
in waste and blood of months of days a scene
not real yet animate, and I see flies
with human faces, hair like women's hair,
their eyes like stone are cold and black, and in
that darkened place I hear the sound of wings,
a sound like horses screaming. Smells of piss
and sulfur fill the air, and I am more
a corpse than human thing, am pale as ash,
have felt no rain for many days nor seen
the sun, can only hear the distant sounds
of brutal thunder and a violent hail.[7]

As a consequence of her participation in the Republican movement and a series of prison protests, the speaker begins to lose her sense of identity, finding in herself not "human" elements but the emptiness of a "corpse." In her fellow prisoners, she discovers insect masks in the place of the human, and once friendly eyes turned "cold and black." Even the form of the poem, a blank-verse sonnet, suggests the idea of imprisonment, of restriction within meter and form without the aural sense of release provided by rhyme. A later poem, taken from the same sequence as "The Troubles," and titled "Release," speaks in free verse and occasionally rhyming lines of the recovery from violence in the recognition and recovery of emotion. However, in this, the first of three similar sonnets, the poet discerns only the masks of sentiment and of genuine human contact.

As sociologists and literary critics observe, the two factions in Northern society do indeed adopt masks of behavior to the detriment of their members, limiting their direct emotional engagement with their environment and, consequently, limiting their ability to overcome violence. Specifically, "habitual patterns of social interaction, reinforced by social control . . . maintain social boundaries. It is these that have caused division in society. And it is the social division that has created a need for distinctive cultural markers [masks] so that people can tell which person is on which side."[8] For most Catholics, who have adopted their "distinctive cultural markers," the "common nationalist view of tradition [is] as something which has come to a conclusion. Its exponents fancy that they are the final point of history and the past a foil to their narcissism."[9] For the Unionist who adopts masks of cultural identity, "the contemporary northern protestant's sense of history is markedly similar to that of the catholic nationalist."[10] Moreover, "what is at stake in all these forms of history is not historical truth. [On the contrary] . . . [F]acts are put into historically useful frames, each partially structured by the siege metaphor but each defining a different historical conclusion."[11] Essentially, the Nationalists and the Unionists who define themselves through the masks of cultural identification, turn to these ready-made support structures in response to the threat of violence. However, rather than offer the "truth" of history or identity, the masks offer, as they did for Mairead O'Connor and the figures in Pakenham's painting, not emotional engagement or identity but frustration and distortion.

However, as Mary Robinson's acceptance speech indicates, some in Ireland do move beyond the masks of identity to structure a sense of self and nation that goes beyond geographic and sectarian boundaries. Specifically, Jonathan Bardon, in his recent history of Ulster, begins with a reference to the landscape and proceeds to relate the common heritage of the North, a heritage certainly marked by conflict but also marked by the changing series of cultures that inhabited the land:

Just south of Coleraine a great ridge of basalt lies in the path of the Bann, after a serene passage from Lough Beg past Portglenone and Kilrea, the river is funnelled between bluffs to cascade in rapids and through weirs and sluices into a long estuary leading north-west to the Atlantic. The waters draining off nearly half the surface of Ulster pass through here, for Lough Neagh has only one outlet: at Toome where the Bann bursts through eel traps. . . . Here, where the Bann meets the tide, are reminders of Ulster's history: locks and sluices of nineteenth-century enterprise; quays from which Ulster Presbyterians set out to face the perils of an Atlantic voyage in the eighteenth century; fish weirs close to where sixty-two tons of salmon were netted in one day in 1632; the Cutts, where in 1611 men employed by the London Companies tried to hew a navigable passage upstream; the ruins of Castle Roe, where, a century before, the Tyrone O'Neills guarded their fishing from the O'Cahans to the west and the MacQuillans and MacDonnells in the Route; overgrown rubble of a stone castle a little upstream at Fish Loughan and hastily erected defences at Mount Sandel, from where the Normans kept a precarious hold over their manors of Twescard in the thirteenth century; and Mount Sandel fort impressively commanding the river, once perhaps the *dún* of a forgotten Gaelic king. The Norman ringwork on top of this Gaelic fort shows that here is a place where successive peoples and cultures meet, clashed and blended.[12]

Bardon's history consciously begins not by forgetting the past and its conflicts and divisions but by specifically acknowledging the multifarious communities that have comprised Northern and Irish history. He surveys not only native Irish traditions, the "*dún* of a forgotten Gaelic king" but also the "Norman ringwork" that tops off the ancient Irish fort. Significantly, Bardon also details Presbyterian contributions to a Northern heritage, ending his opening description of Ulster's sacred and political as well as literal geography by declaring, rather boldly in a culture where armed factions insist on exclusive access to an Irish past, that the landscapes of Ulster are "a place where successive peoples and cultures meet, clashed and blended."

Seamus Heaney also reflects on many influences that comprise the experience of identity in the North. He tells a story that demonstrates the actual narrative plurality of Northern culture writing that he

came across in the Dineen's Irish dictionary, a word with the letters *Doir* in brackets after it, a word which was thereby defined as being peculiar to the Irish spoken at one time in my own English-speaking County Derry. The word was 'lachtar,' meaning a flock of young chickens. Suddenly I was alive to the fact of loss. . . . The word had survived in our district as a common and, as far as I had known until then, an English word, but now I realised that it lived upon our tongues like a capillary stretching back to a time when Irish was the *lingua franca* of the whole place. Suddenly the resentful nationalism of my Catholic minority experience was fused with a concept of identity that was enlarging and releasing and would eventually help me to relate my literary education with the heritage of my home ground.[13]

Heaney goes on to sanction a uniquely narrative history, stressing its relation to the facts of historical record. He observes that

ancestry and loyalty are not everything. The myths of identity are only one domain of reality. The facts of lived experience are equally important, though, oddly enough, sometimes they are harder to establish. But a few years ago, long after finding links in 'lachtar' with an Irish-speaking Ulster, I remembered with equal affection a different word, one without any particular historical or cultural charge, a 20th century word, technological, without affiliation, as unattached on the South Downs as in South Derry, but also a word associated with the brooding world of chickens. This was 'incubator', and as I write it, its neuter syllables are alive with warmth and cheepings and musty smells, for the incubator was part of the idiom of chicken farming too. It summons the whole secret world of the child in the outhouse, the world of wonder and tenderness, And these deeply lodged intimacies, this phenomenological conditioning of the personal life, is as crucial to the salvation of our human souls as the conditionings we undergo from our myths of identity. And it is the educator's and the artist's special task to reveal to himself and to others the vitality of this inner personal world, and to testify to its fundamental value. The life that the word incubator lives in me has little to do with historical affections and group bonding; it lives in the ground of pre-reflective being and if I were to prepare my own sampler to remind myself of the complex recognitions we are all capable of and which we should all live up to, I could do worse than embroider it and its enigmatic cousin 'lachtar' on the pallid but durable texture of some old remnant of linen.[14]

Significantly, such individual, inter-community, and historical narrative functions as a "performance" that

highlights a distinction between social memory and history as different forms of cultural transmission across time: memory requires collective participation, whether at theatrical events, shamatic rituals, or Olympic opening ceremonies; history entails the critical (and apparently solitary) interpretation of written records. . . . The persistence of collective memory through restored behavior, however, represents an alternative and potentially contestatory form of knowledge-bodily knowledge, habit, custom.[15]

In the collective experience of understanding, offered by the narrative, indeed living through performance, each community's history extends an individual's emotional attachment with his or her environment, even if that environment is constituted, as in the North, by rivals. Essentially, "the growing co-extension of our soul [whatever one chooses to call the soul, even if that term does not imply a spiritual resonance] and the world, through the consciousness of our relationship with all things, is not simply a matter of logic or idealization, but is part of an organic process."[16] Such an "organic process" allows an individual to anticipate, meet, and integrate difficult life experiences.

Studying Deirdre O'Connell's "No Fire in the North/No Sun in the South" series that served as a starting point for this study one comes to understand through her metaphor of the "Hinterland," the title of her 1996 exhibition at the Orchard Gallery in Derry, that what is happening in Northern Irish artistic production is not a rejection or a forgetting of the past but rather an acceptance of the totality, however unpleasant, of each individual's multifarious heritage, a heritage that includes but is not limited to Ireland. Specifically, in order to demonstrate the human, the individual access to the inspiration of ancient forms, Deirdre O'Connell has created drawings. Taken together, their use of rich and vibrant colors suggests a tradition animate and alive. One, a drawing titled "Firmament," contains a light blue dome separated from an ultramarine sky scattered with stars. The two figures, of dome and sky, recall the creation from Genesis. The stars invoke the individual response to the myths of industry but also recall mosques in Islamic Spain with six-pointed stars letting light fall to the floor of the place of worship. Here, the stars have five points, implying improvisation and adaptation, a subtle interpretation of the ancient model. Further, the interaction with the ancient forms is complete. Human inspiration lies inside the temple, has an access the forces of empire could not achieve by riot or force of will. Another painting very clearly represents an open observatory. The grey interior light illuminates an indigo exterior and looks onto a starless sky. It is as if the light of the stars has been pulled into the structure suggesting a full integration of the ancient objects of inspiration and suggesting that this new power can stand against the darkness, the waste. Considered as a whole, Deirdre O'Connell's work, ranging from her early charcoal and pastels of the "No Fire in the Hearth/No Sun in the South" exhibition to her more recent drawings and sculptures, speaks coherently and consistently of the tension between the mythic and the random, between that which carries a resonance of historical and spiritual continuity and that which finds itself discarded and forgotten. Specifically, the idea of the hinterland literally involves the concept of an area of earth that is hidden from view influencing and feeding the more immediate landscape. The images contained in her work conjure impressions of burial and waste that suggest repressed memories and forgotten sentiments. However, they all convey information concerning the cultural subconscious not just of modern Ireland but of the modern world. Indeed, Deirdre O'Connell's work, whether her imaginative geography is catalysed by Islam, Ireland, or Europe, suggests that, for well or ill, this is what we have to confront. This is our inheritance. This is the product and also the image of our ancestors and, therefore, however unpleasant, the image of ourselves. In order to move forward in any meaningful way, a society must make the repressed manifest-in order to understand its past, in order to understand its potential, in order to understand itself. Perhaps, this is Mary Robinson's meaning when she calls on the people of Ireland to embrace "the symbol of this reconciling and healing fifth province."

Significantly, the metaphors employed to come to an understanding not only of writing and other artistic production emerging from Ireland but from many formerly marginalized places need to be understood only in the broadest terms:

Whether we speak of "The Fifth Province," "l'ecriture feminine," or "The Third Space," we are using a highly metaphoric language to suggest a different kind of space which is an alternative to the existing power structures. This is one of the functions of modern art and cultural theory, and there are instances when such concepts have effects in the "real" world: feminism is a good example. It would be foolish to imply that these names for alternative spaces are one and the same, or that these transcend time and place.[17]

As Irish artists come to terms with the apparent end to sanctioned sectarian violence, metaphors like the fifth province and Benitez-Rojo's carnival are helpful means of understanding the multifarious influences and forms of creativity. However, the structures offered by these metaphors must not limit either artistic production nor a critical understanding of art and literature. Indeed, the true benefit of Benitez-Rojo's carnival and Mary Robinson's fifth province lies in these metaphors's capacity to encompass the potentialities of Irish artistic production but not to restrict it within specific theoretical models.

NOTES

[1] *The Fifth Province-Some Contemporary Art from Ireland*, (Toronto: The Ireland Fund of Canada, 1991), 1.

[2] Frances Angela, "Confinement," *Identity: Community, Culture, Difference*, ed. Jonathan Rutherford, (London: Lawrence and Wishart, 1990), 73.

[3] Marten deVries, "Trauma in Cultural Perspective," *Traumatic Stree: The Effects of Overwhelming Experience on Mind, Body, and Society*, ed. By Bessel Van der Kolk, Alexander McFarlane, and Lars Weisaeth, (London: Guilford Press, 1996), 403.

[4] Declan Kiberd, *Inventing Ireland*, (London: Jonathan Cape, 1995), 618.

[5] Isaac Julien and Kobena Mercer, "De Margin and De Centre," *Staurt Hall: Critical Dialogues in Cultural Studies*, ed. by Davis Morley and Kuan-Hsing Chen, (New York: Routledge, 1996), 460.

[6] Ibid., 461.

[7] Mairead O'Connor, "Armagh," *Cuirt Journal*, 4 (1996).

[8] Anthony Buckley and Mary Catherine Kenney, *Negotiating Identity: Rhetoric, Metaphor,and Social Drama in Northern Ireland*, (Washington: Smithsonian Institution Press, 1995), 9.

[9] Kiberd, Inventing Ireland, 294.

[10] Terence Brown, *The Whole Protestant Community: The Making of an Historic Myth*, (Derry: Field Day, 1985), 8.

[11] Buckley and Kenney, *Negotiating Identity*, 50-51.

[12] Jonathan Bardon, *A History of Ulster*, (Belfast: Blackstaff Press, 1993), 1.

[13] Seamus Heaney, "Forked Tongues," *Troubled Times:* Fortnight *Magazine and the Troubles in Northern Ireland, 1970-91*, ed. by Robert Bell, Robert Johnstone, and Robin Wilson, (Belfast: Blackstaff Press, 1991), 114.

[14] Ibid., 116.

[15] Joseph Roach, "Culture and Performance in the Circum-Atlantic World," *Performitivity and Performance*, ed. by Andrew Parker and Eve Kosofsky Sedgewick, (New York: Routledge, 1995), 47.

[16] Pierre Teilhard de Chardin, S.J. , *The Phenomenon of Man* . (New York: Harper Colophon Books, 1975), 17.

[17] Joan Fowler, "Another Country: Differences and Identifications," *The Fifth Province--Some Contemporary Art from Ireland*, (Toronto: The Ireland Fund of Canada, 1991), 31.

Bibliography

Anderson, Benedict. *Imagined Communities: Reflections on the Origins and the Spread of Nationalism.* London: Verso, 1991.

Angela, Frances. "Confinement." *Identity: Community, Culture, Difference.* edited by Jonathan Rutherford. London: Lawrence and Wishart, 1990. 72-87.

Appadurai, Arjun. *Modernity at Large.* Minneapolis: University of Minnesota Press, 1997.

Austin, John Langshaw. *How to Do Things with Words.* Cambridge: Harvard University Press, 1962.

Bardon, Jonathan. *A History of Ulster.* Belfast: Blackstaff Press, 1993.

Barthes, Roland. *Mythologies.* New York: Hill and Wang, 1997.

---. *S/Z.* Translated by Richard Miller. New York: Hill and Wang, 1974.

Baudrillard, Jean *Selected Writings.* edited by Mark Poster. Stanford: Stanford University, 1988.

Bell, J. Bowyer. *The Troubles: A Generation of Violence, 1967-1992.* Dublin: Gill and Macmillan, 1993.

Bell, Sam Hanna. *The Theatre in Ulster.* Dublin: Gill and Macmillan, 1972.

Benítez-Rojo, Antonio. *The Repeating Island: The Caribbean and the Postmodern Perspective.* Translated by James Maraniss. Durham: Duke University Press, 1996.

Benjamin, Walter. *Illuminations.* New York: Schocken Books, 1969.

Bhabha, Homi. *The Location of Culture.* New York: Routledge, 1994.

Blaney, Roger. *Presbyterians and the Irish Language.* Belfast: Ulster Historical Foundation, 1996.

Boland, Eavan. *Selected Poems.* London: Carcanet Press, 1989.

Bourke, Angela. "Language, Stories, Healing." *Gender and Sexuality in Modern Ireland.* edited by Anthony Bradley and Maryann Gialanella Valiulis. Amherst: University of Massachusetts Press, 1997. 299-314.

Boyce Davies, Carole. *Black Women, Writing and Identity: Migrations of the Subject.* New York: Routledge, 1994.

Boyle, Kevin, Tom Hadden, and Dermot Walsh. "Abuse and Failure in Security Policies." *Troubled Times:* Fortnight *Magazine and the Troubles in Northern Ireland, 1970-91.* edited by Robert Bell, Robert Johnstone, and Robin Wilson. Belfast: Blackstaff Press, 1991. 52-56.

Branagh, Kenneth. *Public Enemy.* London: Faber and Faber, 1988.

Brearton, Fran. "Dancing unto Death: Perceptions of the Somme, the *Titanic* and Ulster Protestantism." *The Irish Review.* 20 (Winter/Spring 1997): 89-103.

Brown, Terence. *The Whole Protestant Community: The Making of an Historic Myth.* Derry: Field Day, 1985.

Buckley, Anthony and Mary Catherine Kenney. *Negotiating Identity: Rhetoric, Metaphor, and Social Drama in Northern Ireland*. Washington: Smithsonian Institution Press, 1995.

---. "Uses of History Amongst Ulster Protestants." *The Poet's Place: Ulster Literature and Society*. Edited by Gerald Dawe and John Wilson Foster. Belfast: Institute of Irish Studies, 1991. 259-272.

Burkert, Walter. *Homo Necans*. Berkeley and Los Angeles: University of California Press, 1983.

Burnside, Sam. *Walking in Marches*. Galway: Salmon, 1990.

Butler, Judith. *Bodies that Matter: On the Discursive Limits of Sex*. New York: Routledge, 1993.

Byrne, Ophelia. *The Stage in Ulster from the Eighteenth Century*. Belfast: Linen Hall Library, 1997.

Cairns, Ed. *Caught in Crossfire: Children and the Northern Ireland Conflict*. Belfast: Appletree Press, 1987.

---. "Social Identity and Inter-Group Conflict in Northern Ireland: A Developmental Perspective. *Growing Up in Northern Ireland*. Edited by Joan Harbison. Belfast: Stranmillis College, 1989. 115-130.

Caruth, Cathy. *Unclaimed Experience: Trauma, Narrative and History*. Baltimore: Johns Hopkins University Press, 1996.

Chambers, Iain. "Waiting on the End of the World." *Staurt Hall: Critical Dialogues in Cultural Studies*. Edited by David Morley and Kuan-Hsing Chen. New York: Routledge, 1996. 201-211.

Chen, Kuan Hsing. "Post-marxism: between/beyond critical postmodernism and cultural studies. *Staurt Hall: Critical Dialogues in Cultural Studies*. Edited by David Morley and Kuan-Hsing Chen. New York: Routledge, 1996. 309-325.

Clifford, James. "Traveling Cultures."*Cultural Studies*. Edited by Lawrence Grossberg Cary Nelson, and Paula Treichler. (New York: Routledge, 1992). 96-116.

Cronin, Michael. *Translating Ireland*. Cork: Cork University Press, 1996.

Culbertson, Roberta. "Embodied Memory, Transcendence, and Telling: Recounting Trauma, Re-establishing the Self." *New Literary History* 26 (1995): 169-195.

Davie, Donald. "Belfast on a Sunday Afternoon." *A Rage for Order: Poetry of the Northern Ireland Troubles*. Edited by Frank Ormsby. Belfast: Blackstaff Press, 1992. 31.

Dawe, Gerald. *The Lundys Letter*. Loughcrew, Oldcastle: Gallery Press, 1985.

Dayan, Joan. *Haiti, History, and the Gods*. Berkely: University of California Press, 1995.

Deane, Seamus."Heroic Styles: The Tradition of an Idea." *Ireland's Field Day*. (Derry: Field Day Theatre Company, 1985): 45-59.

Derrida, Jacques. "Signature Event Context." *Margins of Philosophy*. Translated by Alan Bass. Chicago: University of Chicago Press, 1982.

Devlin, Anne. *After Easter*. London: Faber and Faber, 1994.

---. *Ourselves Alone with A Woman Calling and The Long March*. London: Faber and Faber, 1986.

de Vries, Marten. "Trauma in Cultural Perspective." *Traumatic Stress: The Effects of Overwhelming Experience on Mind, Body, and Society*. Edited by Bessel Van der Kolk, Alexander Mc Farlane, and Lars Weisaeth. London: The Guilford Press, 1996. 398-414.

Diamond, Elin. *Unmaking Mimesis: Essays on Feminism and Theater*. New York: Routledge, 1997.

DiCenzo, Maria. "Charabanc Theatre Company: Placing Women Center-Stage in Northern Ireland." *Theatre Journal* 45 (1993): 175-84.

Eco, Umberto. "The Frames of Comic Freedom." *Carnival*. Edited by Thomas Sebeok.

New York: Mouton, 1984. 8-9.

Eliade, Micrea. *Myths, Dreams, and Mysteries*. London: Fontana, 1968.

Ellen, Roy. "Rates of Change: Weasel Words and the Indispensable in Anthropological Analysis." *When History Accelerates: Essays of Rapid Social Change, Complexity and Creativity*. Edited by C.M. Hann. London: Athlone, 1994. 54-74.

Elliott, Marianne. *Watchmen in Sion: the Protestant Idea of Liberty*. Derry: Field Day Theatre Company, 1985.

Etherton, Michael. *Contemporary Irish Dramatists*. London: Macmillan Publishers Limited, 1989.

Fairweather, Eileen. *Only the Rivers Run Free: Northern Ireland, the Woman's War*. London: Pluto Press, 1984.

Fanon, Frantz. *Black Skin, White Masks*. Translated by Charles Lam Markmann. New York: Grove Press, 1967.

Feldman, Allen. *Formations of Violence: The Narrative of the Body and Political Terror in Northern Ireland*. Chicago: University of Chicago Press, 1991.

The Fifth Province--Some Contemporary Art from Ireland. Toronto: The Ireland Fund of Canada, 1991.

Fitzgerald, Garrett. "Steps towards Reconciliation." *Troubled Times:* Fortnight *Magazine and the Troubles in Northern Ireland, 1970-91*. Edited by Robert Bell, Robert Johnstone, and Robin Wilson. Belfast: Blackstaff Press, 1991. 20-23.

Flackes, W.D. and Sydney Elliott. *Northern Ireland: A Political Directory, 1968-1993*. Belfast: Blackstaff Press, 1994.

Foster, John Wilson. *Forces and Themes in Ulster Fiction*. Totowa, New Jersey: Rowman and Littlefield, 1974.

---. "Imagining the Titanic." *Returning to Ourselves: Second Violume of Papers from the John Hewitt International Summer School*. Edited by Eve Patten. Belfast: Lagan Press, 1995. 325-343.

---. "Richard Kearney - A Reply," *The Honest Ulsterman*. 82 (Winter1986): 43-46.

Foucault, Michel. *Power/Knowledge: Selected Interviews and Other Writings, 1972-1977*. Edited by Colin Gordon. Translated by Colin Gordon, Leo Marshall, John Mepham, and Kate Soper. New York Pantheon Books, 1980.

Fowler, Joan. "Another Country: Differences and Identifications." *The Fifth Province--Some Contemporary Art from Ireland*. Toronto: The Ireland Fund of Canada, 1991. 30-35.

Freud, Sigmund. *General Psychological Theory*. Translated by Joan Riviere. New York: Collier, 1972.

---. *The Standard Edition of the Complete Psychological Works of Sigmund Freud. Vol. I-XXII*. London: Hogarth Press, 1953-1974.

Friel, Brian. *Freedom of the City*. London: Faber and Faber, 1974.

---. *Volunteers*. Boston: Faber and Faber, 1979.

Gallagher, A.M. "Civil Liberties and the State." *Social Attitudes in Northern Ireland: The Second Report, 1991-1992*. Edited by Peter Stringer and Gillian Robinson. Belfast: The Blackstaff Press, 1992. 81-101.

Gibbons, Luke. *Transformations in Irish Culture*. Cork: Cork University Press, 1996.

Grant, David. *Playing the Wild Card*. Belfast: Community Relations Council, 1993.

Gray, Fances and Janet Brady. "Radio Drama and the Politics of Northern Ireland: A Study of Two Plays and Their Relationship to the Depiction of Northern Ireland and the Media." *Text and Context* 1.1 (1986): 46-58.

Greacen, Robert. *Collected Poems, 1944-1994*. Belfast: Lagan Press, 1995.

Haire, John Wilson. *Within Two Shadows*. London: David-Poynter, 1973.

Hall, Stuart. "Cultural Identity and Diaspora." *Identity: Community, Culture, Difference.* Edited by Jonathan Rutherford. London: Lawrence and Wishart, 1990. 222-237.

Hann, C. M. "Fast Forward: The Great Transformation Globalised." *When History Accelerates: Essays of Rapid Social Change, Complexity and Creativity.* Edited by C.M. Hann. London: Athlone, 1994. 1-22.

Harbison, Joan. *Children of the Troubles.* Belfast: Stranmillis College, 1993.

---*Growing Up in Northern Ireland.* Belfast: Stranmillis College, 1989.

Harris, Claudia. *At the End of the Day: Theatre as Politics and Politics as Theatre in Northern Ireland.* (Unpublished Doctoral Dissertation)

---. "A Living Mythology: Stewart Parker." *Theatre Ireland.* 13 (Fall 1987): 15-17.

---. "Stewart Parker." *Irish Playwrights, 1880-1995,* Edited by Bernice Schrank and William De Mastes. Westport, Conn.:Greenwood Press, 1997. 279-299.

Hartman, Geoffrey. "On Traumatic Knowledge and Literary Studies." *New Literary History.* 26 (1995): 537-563.

Heaney, Seamus. *Crediting Poetry.* Loughcrew, Co Meath: Gallery Press, 1995.

---. *The Cure at Troy.* London: Faber and Faber, 1990.

---. "Forked Tongues." *Troubled Times:* Fortnight *Magazine and the Troubles in Northern Ireland, 1970-91.* Edited by Robert Bell, Robert Johnstone, and Robin Wilson. Belfast: Blackstaff Press, 1991. 114-116.

Heidegger, Martin. *Being and Time.* Translated by John Macquarrie and Edward Robinson. New York: Harper and Row, 1962.

Hill, Ian. "Staging the Troubles." *Theatre Ireland* 31 (1993): 42-46.

Hillyard, Paddy. "Law and Order." *Northern Ireland: Background to the Conflict.* Edited by John Darby. Belfast: Appletree Press, 1983.

Hogan, Robert. *Dictionary of Irish Literature.* Westport, Conn.: Greenwood Press, 1996.

Hoge, Warren. "The Troubles." *New York Times Book Review.* 15 March 1998. National Edition:18.

Jameson, Fredric. *Modernism and Imperialism.* Derry: Field Day Theatre Company, 1988.

---. *The Political Unconscious: Narrative as a Socially Symbolic Act.* New York: Cornell University Press, 1981.

Joyce, James. *Finnegans Wake.* London: Faber and Faber, 1943.

Julien, Isaac, and Kobena Mercer. "De Margin and De Centre." *Staurt Hall: Critical Dialogues in Cultural Studies.* Edited by Davis Morley and Kuan-Hsing Chen. (New York: Routledge, 1996). 450-64.

Jung, Carl. *Analytical Psychology.* New York: Vintage Books, 1968.

---. *Memories, Dreams, Reflections.* New York: Vintage Books, 1989.

---. *Symbols of Transformation.* Translated by R.F.C. Hull. Princeton: Princeton University Press, 1990.

Kardiner, Abram. *The Traumatic Neuroses of War.* New York: Hoeber, 1941.

Kearney, Richard. *Myth and Motherland.* Derry: Field Day, 1984.

---. *Poetics of Modernity.* Atlantic Highlands: Humanities Press, 1995.

---. "The Transitional Crisis in Irish Culture." *The Honest Ulsterman* 92 (Winter 1986): 30-42.

Kelley, Kevin. *The Longest War: Northern Ireland and the IRA.* Dingle, Co Kerry, Brandon Press, 1982.

Kiberd, Declan. "Anglo-Irish Attitudes," *Ireland's Field Day.* (Derry: Field Day Theatre Company, 1985): 83-105.

---*Inventing Ireland.* London: Jonathan Cape, 1995.

Kristeva, Julia. *Powers of Horror.* Translated by Leon Roudiez. New York: Columbia

University Press, 1982.

Lacan, Jacques. *The Four Fundamental Concepts of Psycho-Analysis*. Translated by Alan Sheridan. New York: Norton, 1981.

Leerssen, Joep. *Mere Irish and Fíor Ghael*. Cork: Cork University Press, 1996.

Lloyd, David. *Anomalous States: Irish Writing and the Post-Colonial Moment*. Durham: Duke University Press, 1993.

Longley, Edna. "Opening Up: a New Pluralism." *Troubled Times:* Fortnight *Magazine and the Troubles in Northern Ireland, 1970-91*. Edited by Robert Bell, Robert Johnstone, and Robin Wilson. Belfast: Blackstaff Press, 1991. 141-44.

---."What Do Protestants Want?" *The Irish Review*. 20 (Winter/Spring 1997): 104-120.

Longley, Michael. "Letter." *Irish Times*. 2 March 1985. 23.

Lynch, Martin. *The Interrogation of Ambrose Fogarty*. Dondonald: Blackstaff Press, 1982.

MacNeice, Louis. *Collected Poems of Louis Mac Neice*. Edited by E.R. Dodds. London: Faber and Faber, 1966.

Maxwell, D.E.S. *A Critical History of Modern Irish Drama, 1891-1980*. Cambridge: Cambridge University, 1984.

---."Northern Ireland's Political Drama." *Modern Drama* 33 (1990): 1-14.

Mbembe, Achille, and Janet Roitman. "Figures of the Subject in Times of Crisis." *The Geography of Identity*. Edited by Patricia Yaeger. (Ann Arbor: University of Michigan Press, 1996): 153-186.

McCartney, R.L. *Liberty and Authority in Ireland*. Derry: Field Day, 1985.

McFarlane, Alexander and Giovanni de Girolamo. "The Nature of Traumatic Stressors and the Epidemiology of Posttraumatic Reactions." *Traumatic Stress: The Effects of Overwhelming Experience on Mind, Body, and Society*. Edited by Bessel Van der Kolk, Alexander Mc Farlane, and Lars Weisaeth. London: The Guilford Press, 1996. 129-154.

McGuinness, Frank. *Carthaginians*. (with *Bag Lady*). London: Faber and Faber, 1988.

---. *Observe the Sons of Ulster Marching Toward the Somme*. London:Faber and Faber, 1986.

McMaster, Johnston. *The Churches and Cross Community Work with Young People*. Belfast: Youth Link, 1993.

Montague, John. "Heroics." *A Rage for Order: Poetry of the Northern Ireland Troubles*. Edited by Frank Ormsby. Belfast: Blackstaff Press, 1992. 40.

Monte, Christopher. *Beneath the Mask* Philadelphia: Harcourt Brace Publishers, 1995.

Moxon-Browne, Edward. "National Identity in Northern Ireland." *Social Attitudes in Northern Ireland*. Edited by Peter Stringer and Gillian Robinson. Belfast: The Blackstaff Press, 1991. 23-30.

Murray, Christopher. "Drama, 1690-1800." *The Field Day Anthology of Irish Writing*. Vol. I. Edited by Seamus Deane. Derry: Field Day Theatre Company, 1991. 500-507.

---."Brian Friel's *Making History* and the Problem with Historical Accuracy." *Crows Behind the Plough: History and Violence in Anglo-Irish Poetry and Drama*. Amsterdam: Rodolphi, 1991. 61-78.

---. *Twentieth Century Irish Drama*. Manchester: Manchester University Press, 1997.

"New Book on Ulster Theatre." *The Linen Hall Library Newsletter*. (Autumn/Winter 1997): 4.

Ó Connor, Fionnuala. *In Search of a State: Catholics in Northern Ireland*. Belfast: Blackstaff Press, 1993.

O'Connor, Mairead. "Armagh." *Cuirt Journal*. 4 (1996):40-50.

Ó Hehir, Brendan. *A Gaelic Lexicon for Finnegans Wake*.Berkeley: University of California

Press, 1967.

Olasov-Rothbaum, Barbara and Edna Foa. "Cognitive-Behavioral Therepy for Posttraumatic Stress Disorder." *Traumatic Stress: The Effects of Overwhelming Experience on Mind, Body, and Society.* Edited by Bessel Van der Kolk, Alexander Mc Farlane, and Lars Weisaeth. London: The Guilford Press, 1996. 491-509.

O'Malley, Conor. *A Poet's Theatre.* Dublin: Eco Press Ltd., 1988.

O'Toole, Fintan. *Strongholds: New Art from Ireland.* Liverpool: Tate Gallery, 1991.

Parker, Stewart. *Catchpenny Twist.* Dublin: Gallery Press, 1980.

Patterson, Glenn. "29/12." *Troubled Times:* Fortnight *Magazine and the Troubles in Northern Ireland, 1970-91.* Edited by Robert Bell, Robert Johnstone, and Robin Wilson. Belfast: Blackstaff Press, 1991. 145-46.

Pegg, William. *Prejudice Reduction: A Workshop Approach.* Coleraine: Centre for the Study of Conflict at the University of Ulster, 1992.

Pilkington, Lionel. *Representation of the Northern Ireland Crisis in Contemporary Drama: 1968-80.* (Unpublished Doctoral Dissertation).

---. "Violence and Identity in Northern Ireland: Graham Reid's *The Death of Humpty-Dumpty.*" *Modern Drama* 33 1 (1990). 15-29.

Powell, T.G.E. *The Celts.* London: Thames and Hudson, 1989.

Reid, Christina. *Did You Hear the One about the Irishman?* and *The Belle of Belfast City.* London: Methuen, 1989.

---. "Letter to Bernard McKenna." 19 September 1995.

---. *Plays 1.* London" Mehteun, 1997.

Reid, J. Graham. *The Closed Door.* Dublin: Co-op Books, 1980.

---. *The Death of Humpty Dumpty.* Dublin: Co-op Books, 1980.

Richtarik, Marilynn. *Acting between the Lines: Field Day Theatre Company and Irish Cultural Politics, 1980-1984.* Oxford: Oxford University Press, 1994.

Ricoeur, Paul. "The Symbol as Bearer of Possible Worlds." *The Crane Bag of Irish Studies* (1982).

Roach, Joseph. "Culture and Performance in the Circum-Atlantic World." *Performitivity and Performance.* Edited by Andrew Parker and Eve Kosofsky Sedgewick. New York: Routledge, 1995.

Roche, Anthony. *Contemporary Irish Drama: From Beckett to Mc Guinness.* Dublin: Gill and Macmillan, 1994.

Rolston, Bill. *Drawing Support 2: Murals of War and Peace.* Belfast: Beyond the Pale, 1995.

Rumens, Carol. *Selected Poems.* London: Chatto and Windus, 1987.

Said, Edward. *Orientalism.* New York: Random House, 1978.

Schrank, Bernice and William De Mastes. *Irish Playwrights, 1880-1995.* Westport, Conn.: Greenwood Press, 1997.

Second Commission on the Status of Women. Dublin: Stationary Office, 1993.

Seton-Watson, Hugh. *Nations and States. An Inquiry Into the Origins of Nations and the Politics of Nationalism.* Boulder: Westview Press, 1977.

Shaftesbury, Anthony Ashley Cooper, Earl of. *Characteristics of Men, Manners, Opinions, Times.* Edited by John Robertson. Indianapolis: Bobbs-Merrill, 1964.

Solomon, Zahava, Nathaniel Laror, and Alexander Mc Farlane. "Acute Posttraumatic Reactions in Soldiers and Civilians." *Traumatic Stress: The Effects of Overwhelming Experience on Mind, Body, and Society.* Edited by Bessel Van der Kolk, Alexander Mc Farlane, and Lars Weisaeth. London: The Guilford Press, 1996. 102-114.

Teilhard de Chardin, Pierre. *The Phenomenon of Man.* New York: Harper Colophon

Books, 1975.

Turner, Stuart, Alexander Mc Farlane, and Bessel Van der Kolk. "The Therapeutic Environment and New Explorations in the Treatment of Posttraumatic Stress Disorder." *Traumatic Stress: The Effects of Overwhelming Experience on Mind, Body, and Society.* Edited by Bessel Van der Kolk, Alexander Mc Farlane, and Lars Weisaeth. London: The Guilford Press, 1996. 537-558.

Tyrrell, Jerry, and Seamus Farewell. *Peer Mediation in Primary Schools.* Coleraine: Centre for the Study of Conflict at the University of Ulster, 1995.

Van der Kolk, Bessel and Alexander Mc Farlane. "The Black Hole of Trauma." *Traumatic Stress: The Effects of Overwhelming Experience on Mind, Body, and Society.* Edited by Bessel Van der Kolk, Alexander Mc Farlane, and Lars Weisaeth. London: The Guilford Press, 1996. 3-23.

Van der kolk, Bessel. "The Complexity of Adaptation to Trauma." *Traumatic Stress: The Effects of Overwhelming Experience on Mind, Body, and Society.* Edited by Bessel Van der Kolk, Alexander Mc Farlane, and Lars Weisaeth. London: The Guilford Press, 1996. 182-213.

Van der Kolk, Bessel, Alexander Mc Farlane, and Onto Van der Hart. "A General Approach to the Treatment of Posttraumatic Stress Disorder." *Traumatic Stress: The Effects of Overwhelming Experience on Mind, Body, and Society.* Edited by Bessel Van der Kolk, Alexander Mc Farlane, and Lars Weisaeth. London: The Guilford Press, 1996. 417-440.

Welch, Robert. *The Oxford Companion to Irish Literature.* Oxford: Oxford University Press, 1996.

White, Patrick. *The Needs of Young People in Northern Ireland.* Belfast: Youth Link,1993.

Woods, Vincent. *At the Black Pig's Dyke.* unpublished typescript, 1994.

Young, Dudley. *Origins of the Sacred.* edited by New York: St. Martin's Press, 1991.

Index

ABOUT THE AUTHOR

Bernard McKenna is Assistant Professor at Drew University. His previous books include *James Joyce's Ulysses: A Reference Guide* (Greenwood, 2002).